THE
MURDOCH
METHOD

Irwin Stelzer is a consultant on market strategy for US and UK industries. He worked closely with Rupert Murdoch for thirty-five years. He has a regular column in the *Sunday Times* and is an occasional contributor to *The Guardian*, *The Daily Telegraph* and the *New Statesman*. He has received the ICAP Comment Award for Economics Commentator of the Year and has a doctorate in Economics from Cornell University. He has held positions at Harvard University's John F. Kennedy School of Government, Cornell University and New York University, and been a visiting fellow at Nuffield College, Oxford University.

THE MURDOCH METHOD

NOTES ON RUNNING A MEDIA EMPIRE

IRWIN STELZER

Atlantic Books

London

Published in hardback and trade paperback in Great Britain in 2018
by Atlantic Books, an imprint of Atlantic Books Ltd.

10 9 8 7 6 5 4 3 2 1

A CIP catalogue record for this book is available from the British Library.

Hardback ISBN: 978 1 78649 575 4
Trade paperback ISBN: 978 1 78649 400 9
E-book ISBN: 978 1 78649 402 3

Printed in Great Britain by Bell & Bain Ltd, Glasgow

Credits for photo insert: plates 1, 3, 6, 8, 10, 11, 14 © Getty Images;
plates 4, 7 © PA Images; plate 9 © Reuters; plates 2, 5, 12, 13 © Rex
Shutterstock/AP; plate 15 © EPA/EFE The Walt Disney Company.

Atlantic Books
An imprint of Atlantic Books Ltd
Ormond House
26–27 Boswell Street
London
WC1N 3JZ

www.atlantic-books.co.uk

For Cita
Who has made this book and much else possible

'I'm a strange mixture of my mother's curiosity; my father, who grew up the son of the manse in a Presbyterian family, who had a tremendous sense of duty and responsibility; and my mother's father, who was always in trouble with gambling debts'

Rupert Murdoch, 2008[1]

'I would hope they [my children] would lead useful, happy and concerned lives with a very responsible view of what they should and are able to do according to their circumstances'

Elisabeth Murdoch, circa 1989[2]

'I am a curious person who is interested in the great issues of the day and I am not good at holding my tongue'

Rupert Murdoch, 2012[3]

CONTENTS

TIMELINE

1931

March   Keith Rupert Murdoch born

1950

October   Goes up to Worcester College, Oxford

1952

October   Father, Keith Arthur Murdoch, passes away. Rupert
             inherits father's stake. The will is complicated, so the
             precise date of possession is difficult to pinpoint

1953

             Family approves of Rupert becoming managing director
             of Adelaide papers, *News* and *Sunday Mail*

1956

             Marries Patricia Booker

1958

             Daughter Prudence (now Prudence MacLeod) born

1964

July   Launches *The Australian*, a serious, nation-wide
             broadsheet in Australia, and his first new title

1967

             Divorces Patricia Booker
             Marries Anna Torv (now Anna Murdoch Mann)

1968

January   Acquires *News of the World*
August   Elisabeth Murdoch born

1969

September   Acquires *The Sun*, at the time a broadsheet

1970

November The first genuine Page Three girl appears in *The Sun*

1971

September Lachlan Keith Murdoch born

1972

December James Rupert Jacob Murdoch born

1973

December Acquires *San Antonio Express*, the *News*, and their combined Sunday paper. First US acquisition

1976

November Acquires *New York Post*

1978

August New York newspaper strike

October Author meets Murdoch for first time at birthday party for his wife Cita at Lutèce restaurant in New York

1981

February Acquires *The Times* and *The Sunday Times*

1983

November Acquires *Chicago Sun-Times*

1985

March Rupert acquires 50 per cent of 20th Century Fox and the balance in September of that year

September Rupert becomes an American citizen

1986

January *The Times* and *Sunday Times* move to Wapping and strike begins

1989

January Acquires William Collins Publishers and combines it with Harper & Row, acquired a year earlier

February Sky Television launched

1990

January   Purchases two Hungarian newspapers, *Mai Nap* and *Reform*

1992

June   Rupert fires Steve Chao over performance at company conference in Aspen

1993

September   Rupert claims satellites threaten dictatorships and is thrown out of China

December   Rupert (Fox) acquires TV rights to NFL for four years for $1.58 billion

1996

James Murdoch sells Rawkus Records to News Corp. in 1996 and joins the family firm

October   Rupert launches Fox News Channel

1998

May   Murdoch issues apology to Chris Patten for cancelling publication of and disparaging his book

1999

June   Divorces Anna Murdoch. Marries Wendi Deng the same month

2001

November   Daughter, Grace Helen Murdoch, born

2003

July   Daughter, Chloe Murdoch, born

November   *The Times* switches to tabloid format alongside broadsheet, which is abandoned in November 2004 in favour of tabloid format

2005

July   News Corp. buys Intermix which owns Myspace for $580 million, value grows to $12 billion, sold for $35 million June 2011

Lachlan Murdoch resigns from News Corp. after Rupert undermines his authority

2007

August   Acquires *The Wall Street Journal*

2008

January   Settles defamation suit with author Judith Regan

2011

February   Elisabeth Murdoch sells her company (Shine) to News Corp.

2012

February   James Murdoch resigns from News International and heads to Fox in Los Angeles

April   Rupert testifies at Leveson Inquiry

December   Dame Elisabeth Murdoch dies

2013

June   News Corp. split into News Corp (without the full point) and 21st Century Fox. Succession established as described in the book

November   Divorces Wendi Deng Murdoch

2014

August   Rupert drops out of bidding for Time Warner to preserve credit rating

2016

March   Marries Jerry Hall

July   Roger Ailes resigns as CEO of Fox News and Rupert becomes acting CEO

2017

December   Sells 21st Century Fox Entertainment assets to Disney

2018

January   Murdoch purchases 10 television stations, some in important sports markets.

Note: Dates cover and surround most events mentioned in the book.

RUPERT MURDOCH: THE MAN, HIS METHOD AND ME

'I count myself among the world's optimists. I believe that the opportunities we face are boundless, and the problems soluble' – Rupert Murdoch, 1999[1]

'His greatest asset is that he is contemporary. He's always got a new angle on something. He doesn't just bang on about some old thing' – John Howard, 2011[2]

'Murdoch has never made a dollar from his acquisitions of the tabloid *New York Post* or the well-regarded *Times* of London. He loves newspapers for the visceral connection to them he feels as the son of a newspaper executive … A chief executive with a stronger affinity for the bottom line would have jettisoned those newspapers long ago' – David Folkenflik, NPR media correspondent, 2013[3]

I have known Rupert Murdoch for more decades than either of us cares to count. These years were hectic, exciting times that Rupert kindly characterised in a handwritten note as being 'filled with 35 years of great memories'. I mention that not as a form of name-dropping, but as a warning to readers that I am not certain I have achieved sufficient distance from those years to be as dispassionate in my appraisal of Rupert's managerial techniques as perhaps I should be. But I have given it a good try.

I am unlikely to forget either the date or the doings at my first meeting with Rupert Murdoch – a small dinner given in honour of the birthday of one Cita Simian in October 1978, at that time an employee of my consulting firm. I told Cita, who later became my wife, that I wanted to give a dinner party in honour of her forthcoming birthday. She responded that two old friends, Anna and Rupert Murdoch, had already organised one. I had not heard much about Mr Murdoch other than that he had bought the *New York Post*, prompting *Time* magazine to produce a cover with Murdoch's superimposed head on a gorilla's body, the grotesque figure astride New York and a headline 'EXTRA!!! AUSSIE PRESS LORD TERRIFIES GOTHAM.' With Cita's permission I called Murdoch to ask if I might act as a joint host at the dinner. He agreed.

So it was that the Murdochs, Cita with her date, and I with mine, showed up at a fashionable New York eatery for one of the more unpleasant evenings any of us had ever experienced.

Our respective dates probably sensed early on that Cita's interests and mine were less with them and more with each other, and undoubtedly wanted the evening to come to a quick end. Rupert was in the midst of a battle not only with the print unions, but with the *Daily News* and *The New York Times*, competitors of his struggling *New York Post*. He had purchased the city's only surviving afternoon daily for $30 million two years earlier, and converted it from the voice of the New York left to a feisty tabloid that took a somewhat different view of events from that of its previous, ultra-liberal owner. And was bleeding red ink. Overmanning was rife in the industry; nepotism ruled on the shop floor and in the distribution network. The publishers, deciding they had had enough, posted new work rules that cut down on staff. Strikes by several unions followed, closing all the city's newspapers.[4] The proprietors were calling for solidarity in the hope of breaking the strike – and in the case of the then-financially-robust *New York Times*, of prolonging the strike to further weaken and perhaps destroy the *New York Post*, which it regarded less as a competitor than as an embarrassment to the industry because of its gossipy nature and its place on the right of the political spectrum. It is an old adage that *The New York Times* is read by people who think they should run the country, and the *New York Post* is read by people who don't care who is running the country so long as they do something truly scandalous, preferably while intoxicated. Unfortunately for the pretentions of *The New York Times*, *The Wall Street Journal*, now owned by Murdoch, is read by the people who actually do run the country.

Since solidarity with competitors is not Rupert's long suit, he broke with his fellow publishers and settled with the unions after bearing the losses of the strike for about six weeks. The *Post*, sniffed W. H. James, publisher of the *Daily News*, 'was seeking the temporary quick buck at the expense of its former allies'.[5] Indeed. Murdoch knew he could have the market to himself for at least long enough to acquaint potential readers with the *Post*, and to earn some advertising revenue from retailers starved of outlets in which to trumpet their wares – this was before multiple alternatives to print advertising became available. Rupert took personal charge of the *Post*'s labour negotiations – an early hint of how he reacts in a crisis – and settled with the unions, becoming for about a month the sole newspaper available on the streets of New York City. Murdoch agreed to a 'me too' deal: he would give the unions whatever they were able to wring from the *Daily News* and *The New York Times*.

That go-it-alone move took place only a few weeks before the dinner to celebrate Cita's birthday, with rather unfortunate consequences for the success of the party. Because he had a stake in the terms to which the other papers would finally agree, and because negotiations between the unions and the other publishers were reaching their climax, Rupert was repeatedly called from our table to take telephone calls from his staff, the union representatives and, I assume, Mayor Ed Koch, who owed his election to the *New York Post* and who was worried about the eighty-three-day strike's adverse effect on retail sales and employment in the city. Meanwhile, Anna presided graciously over the remains of the party, while the rest of us hoped dessert would be served quickly so that we might get the evening over with.

After that dinner party I was increasingly included in the overlapping social lives of the Murdochs and Cita. When Rupert and Anna first came to America they had a weekend place in upstate New York, where Cita, then a senior aide to Governor Hugh Carey, was living. They had been told by mutual friends to look up Cita, which they did. Rupert said she had been described as 'this interesting young woman', and he undoubtedly realised she might be a useful contact in New York politics, to provide introductions (this being the days before the purchase of the *New York Post* gave him automatic entrée into those circles) and enrich his understanding of the personalities, feuds and issues that dominate life in New York City and Albany.

Rupert and I quickly became interested in each other's news and views about the US and world economies, politics and mutual acquaintances, as well as the gossip that contributes to the vibrancy and vitality of life in New York. A friendship blossomed, with many private dinners and shared events. At one point the Murdochs – Rupert, Anna, Liz, Lachlan and James – spent Thanksgiving with us in our postage-stamp-size log cabin in Aspen, Colorado, the boys sleeping in an attic, the others in two tiny bedrooms.

A good time was had by all, if you count as a good time the robust arguments among the Murdoch clan about the meaning of current news events. Such discussions were, and long remained, part of Rupert's ongoing training programme for his children. When things got out of hand, as they frequently did, Anna would soothe wounded feelings, in this case by refocusing attention on the carving of the Thanksgiving turkey and changing the subject to which nearby house might be suitable for purchase by the

Murdochs. At that time, when the children were of an age at which they had a strong preference for vacationing with friends, Rupert and Anna wanted something that would enable them to do just that without sacrificing family time. The home they finally settled on, a stone's throw from our own, had an indoor pool and multiple bedrooms. And enough large public spaces to accommodate the inevitable parties for business associates, politicians and others for whom there was only one conceivable response to a Murdoch invitation.

I recall telling Rupert as I left for the five-mile drive into town one morning that I was going in to buy a newspaper (no iPads in those days), but didn't want to take him along since he might do just that and end up owning a small-town newspaper. Instead, I took James, aged nine, who educated me in an Australian's concept of space. Our house sits atop a hill on a small plot, most of which is too steep to be habitable. When we had driven about four miles from the end of our property, in the direction of downtown Aspen, James asked me to let him know when we reached the end of our property, which we had actually left some four miles back.

At one point in our developing relationship Rupert invited me to breakfast at his New York apartment and said that it would be unfair of him to continue picking my brains on economic matters without paying me a fee. Without some such arrangement, he wouldn't feel free to call, at least not as frequently as he had been doing. Since the Murdochs were Cita's friends initially, I was reluctant to accept a fee, but Cita advised me that if I did not I could count on far fewer interesting conversations with Rupert. So we agreed a consulting arrangement, terminable by either of us whenever we saw fit.

During the following decades I was a consultant to Rupert and to his company, advising him – although sharing views with him might be a more accurate description – on whatever topic he cared to raise, day or night, weekday or weekend: the trend in interest rates; the development of regulations in the UK and the US and, at times, in Australia; the prospects for the Chinese economy and the potential for investment; his expectations concerning his lifespan and the corporate succession that, deep down, he did not believe would ever be necessary. I had no illusions that I was the only person or even the most important person with whom he discussed whatever happened to pique his curiosity or interest: it was his practice not to share with anyone the information he had picked up from other experts, which meant that each of us was being tested against a huge database, the contents of which we could only guess.

My time as adviser and, I like to think, friend covered:

- the years of rapid expansion and multiple acquisitions;
- the financial crisis resulting from Sky's expensive challenge to the BBC, beneficiary of some £3.7 billion in guaranteed income from the licence fee,[6] which BBC supporters claim 'is not just another tax. It is a payment for a service',[7] although payment is due even if you never use the 'service' by watching BBC channels;
- the struggle to get Fox News onto the key New York City cable system to challenge the dominant liberal broadcast networks and cable news channel CNN;
- his twenty-year stalking of *The Wall Street Journal*;
- times when the US regulatory authorities were challenging an acquisition or sale of a company, or the UK authorities some of his business practices;
- financial problems threatened his hold on his company and his dynastic ambitions;
- a campaign in *The New York Times* aimed at upending his effort to purchase *The Wall Street Journal*;
- the day he had to tell his mother that he would seek American citizenship so that he would be eligible to meet

government regulations concerning ownership of television stations.

And more. I do not pretend to have been a key player in these and other events, or to have been the only person Rupert asked to organise his thoughts into important speeches such as his provocative MacTaggart Lecture in 1989 or his consequential 1993 address extolling the key role satellite broadcasting might play in bringing down dictators, of which more later. In the case of the regulatory issues I often had the lead role in preparing presentations for the American and British authorities. In others, I offered such advice as I could, and in still others provided a sounding board as Rupert considered his options. At other times, I contributed merely by being there. In no sense was I ever 'the chief adviser to Rupert on just about every matter', as Woodrow Wyatt, a long-time Murdoch friend with significant influence in the Thatcher government and a columnist for the *News of the World*, claimed,[8] or Rupert Murdoch's 'secret agent' or his 'representative on earth', as the left-wing press would have people believe,[9] or stand 'in the same kind of relationship to Murdoch as Suslov did to Stalin', as the right-leaning *Spectator* would have it.[10] Rupert needs no 'representative on earth'; his intelligence, political and financial shrewdness, and the power of his media empire are enough to provide him with any access he might need to the business and political communities. As he put it to the Leveson Inquiry, appointed in response to the hacking scandal, when asked whether I was his 'economic guru': 'No, a friend, someone I enjoy talking to.' I will settle for that. The addition of 'He's a fine economist' was frosting on the cake.[11]

We were both fortunate that I was financially independent, which allowed me to be incautious in situations in which company employees might reasonably feel more constrained. In the many years in which I ran my consulting firm, my partners and I held to the view that no client should be allowed to become a large enough portion of our business to make us fearful of losing him. That, I argued, was in the client's interest as it assured him of advice unencumbered by the financial needs of the firm. So we established an informal rule that no client would be allowed to become so large that it accounted for significantly more than 5 per cent of our total revenue. After my partners and I sold the firm, and I became a freelance, solo consultant, I could not take on and properly serve enough clients to observe a 5 per cent limit. I preserved the spirit of that rule by not allowing any client to be so important that I would fear antagonising him when called on to advise him. In Rupert's case, the practical application of the 'independence rule' was to retain other clients, the right to return to my position at Harvard's Kennedy School, and have an understanding that the engagement could be terminated by either party. Wyatt, a keen observer who included Cita, myself and Rupert at many wonderful dinner parties, writes in the diary he swore he was not keeping, 'Irwin still argues with Rupert and is always ready to pack his bags and go if Rupert doesn't like it. But he remains very fond of him, as I do.'[12]

All of this resulted in an unanticipated 'bonus': the complete freedom, with no confidentiality agreement, to write this book. As I reflect on the decades of consulting with Rupert, I have come to feel that the pace of events, the often urgent nature of the decisions to be made, prevented me from realising that what at the time had seemed to me successive applications of often-brilliant ad hoc solutions were in fact applications of a management method, one that might be of interest to the following: corporate leaders faced with the need to develop a trade-off between central control and the encouragement of entrepreneurship – intrapreneurship, to use the more fashionable term – and creativity, but suffer from overexposure to traditional management courses and texts; entrepreneurs and executives who must do computations before putting what Rupert often calls 'the odd billion' at risk, and who must balance the various interests of owners and stakeholders in these post-2008 financial crash years in which corporate behaviour is under a micro-scope; policymakers who must protect consumers without at the same time stifling innovation by protecting incumbents; and, of course, to Murdoch-watchers from New York to London to Beijing to Adelaide who have always followed Rupert's career with a mixture of curiosity, wonder, admiration and distaste.

What I have come to think of as the Murdoch Method, at times the stuff of the tabloids, at others of the financial press, has enabled Rupert to build his empire to a globe-girdling enterprise with 100,000 employees, a market cap (total value of all shares) of some $56 billion,[13] and annual revenues of more than $36 billion in its 2017 fiscal year.[14] But that very same style and approach to business has at times almost brought him down. The management techniques that allowed him to invade the turf of formid-able competitors such as the BBC and the American television networks also led him to fail to build Myspace and other acquisi-tions into the powers they had every possibility of becoming, and to risk ruin, or at the least embarrassment, by excessive reliance on short-term borrowing and by creating a culture that did not always respect the limits beyond which even tabloid journalists cannot stray with impunity. 'We have made some bad mistakes along the way,' Rupert told a group of his executives before he had scandals to add to his list. 'We have had our share of one-issue magazines, odd blunders by some of our editors and managers, and financial overreaching by me. But we're still here.'[15]

The Murdoch Method is the sum total of the management techniques that grew out of his attitudes and conceptions, many of them conscious, many not. Rupert did not sit down and make a how-to-manage list, which makes the idea of a Murdoch Method mine, not his. Nor did he come to management without a set of guiding stars – most important, his parents. To them we should add a list of fundamental beliefs: in competition as a system of providing choice and rewarding the able; in a mission to discomfit an exclusionary establishment; in keeping his word; in the need for him to be directly engaged at all levels of his companies; in taking risks others would not take, relying on his own estimate of the risk–reward ratios; and, above all else, in a plan to pass control of his empire to his children. Rupert lives on what he described to biographer William Shawcross as 'the risk frontier', and relies much more on his own informed intuition than on formal risk-management techniques – intuitive, but an intuition informed by an ability to separate the relevant from the irrelevant in the information he gathers from a global network of contacts tapped as he searches for the latest news and gossip from business, political and other informants. He knows as well as anyone else that risk-takers don't always win, but is convinced that safety first does not build great companies, and that failure can provide valuable lessons to future behaviour. Those of us who have watched him blow out a knee skiing, or lose part of a finger crewing with far younger men in a dangerous yacht race, or been with him when he drives from office to home when late for a dinner party, will attest to the fact that he finds it exhilarating to take chances, even if some have less-than-happy endings.

The Method also includes a willingness to take a long view denied executives who must, or believe they must, respond more immediately to the desires of shareholders for short-term gains. I remember helping prepare notes for a speech for Rupert in which I referred to a company operation becoming profitable after seven years, and Rupert inserting the word 'only' before 'seven years'. There is an ongoing battle between executives who feel pressured to wax triumphant on quarterly calls with Wall Street analysts, and critics of what they see as capitalism's excessive emphasis on so-called short-termism. Never mind that these very critics often also object to a corporate structure based on two classes of stock, voting and non-voting, an arrangement that gives Rupert and other executives who do not own a majority of their company's shares freedom from the need to elevate short-term earnings results to a primary goal.

Another ingredient of the Murdoch Method that might be worth studying for those who want to build or manage great companies is its view of traditional notions of proper corporate organisation, such as establishing what to most executives are essential: clear lines of authority. Rupert worries that overly rigid rules will impinge on creativity and the sheer joy of coming to work in the morning that can be such a key motivator of the best and brightest. A distinguishing characteristic of the original News Corp. and its successor companies, 21st Century Fox and News Corp (without the period), is a professed disdain for the sort of organisational structure on which other companies lavish so much time. Rupert puts it this way:

> Fortunately for our company all of us know that the structure can work well only when it is periodically subverted. This means that when someone jumps 'the chain of command', he or she is not disciplined for doing so, but instead rewarded for that initiative if the subversion of the system helps us to reach our goals ... We are greedy: we want to develop a management technique that gives us the best of entrepreneurial individualism AND the best of organisational teamwork.

As one executive put it, 'While our competitors are organizing and communicating, we are taking away their markets.'[16] I have often thought that anyone attempting to prepare an organisation chart of the old News Corp. or the new News Corp or 21st Century Fox would first have to study the art of Jackson Pollock.

But make no mistake: when attention to organisation is important – among other things to minimise tax burdens, as many multinationals do in performance of their fiduciary obligation to shareholders; to provide upward paths for talented employees; to make certain that informality does not morph into chaos; and to maximise interaction and creativity – attention is paid. Murdoch believes that 'structure alone can't take us very far', but knows that the day is past when fleeting conversations in hallways, or one-day drop-ins by him, will provide necessary coordination and interaction. So he introduced what he calls a 'more formal consultative structure', but done in a way that reflects his ambivalence about that action: 'Such a structure will be more formal than we have had in the past, but much more relaxed than is characteristic of the corpocracies with which we have to contend in the marketplace.'[17]

There is much to learn, too, from how Murdoch balances his desire for growth, profit and the construction of a dynastic empire against what he sees as his requirement to fulfil his father's interdiction 'to be useful in the world'.[18] There is a good deal of discussion these days, some of it useful, about corporate responsibility, and debates about whether corporate managers can best serve their constituents, and by extension society, by concentrating on maximising profits or by including in their remit responsibility to what are called 'stakeholders' – employees, consumers and the environment. This is an especially important question for media companies in general, and more particularly for News Corp and now 21st Century Fox, headed as they are by a man who is his parents' son and who has strong views on matters of social and political policy. Media companies are different: they are not ordinary manufacturing operations, or trophy properties like sports teams. They can shape opinion and tastes; they can degrade the culture or enrich it; they can help to solidify the status quo and the place of the dominant establishment, or remain outside the establishment and make their voices heard on behalf of members of society scorned by establishment elites. But media companies – electronic or print – can only be effective in the long run if they are profitable, as James Murdoch pointed out in his 2009 MacTaggart Lecture, to the consternation of his sister, who three years later used her own MacTaggart Lecture to challenge what she saw as his excessively narrow view of the role of media companies.

The special characteristics of media companies cannot change the fact that, like all private-sector enterprises, they can be profitable and operate in a socially beneficial manner only if they are well managed, especially at a time when good management must include developing responses to what in today's jargon are called 'the disrupters', or, as Joseph Schumpeter better put it, to 'a perennial wave of creative destruction'.[19] The so-called disrupters are challenging not only the market share of traditional media companies, but their very existence, by developing new sources of what is called 'content', new ways of delivering such news and entertainment to the multiple devices consumers now possess, and by offering advertisers precisely targeted audiences at reasonable prices.

My hope is that elucidation of the Murdoch Method, its successes and failures, its virtues and its limitations, will prove valuable to all those with corporate management responsibilities, and to those wishing to learn more about the public policy issues surrounding the media business.

My close association with Rupert ended when he appointed his son James to oversee the company's UK and other overseas interests. James (full disclosure here: Cita is his godmother) had his own cadre of loyalists and advisers, and quite sensibly preferred to have them around him as he moved up the News* ladder. The last thing he needed was to have his father's old friend and consultant hanging around, perhaps reporting back to Dad should he

---

* Throughout the book 'News' is used as a shorthand for the Murdoch companies.

stumble while transferring his talents from Sky to print and other areas of the Murdoch operation.

Looking back, I am not surprised that I found working with Rupert so exciting. For one thing, the immediacy of the media business is intrinsically intoxicating – get it quickly, get it right, move on. For another, as this book will make clear, the Murdoch Method differs from the calmer, less personal, more routine methods of many of my other clients: being around Murdoch and News is not the same thing as strolling the corridors of your local electricity company. Finally, and most important, the anti-establishment DNA that underlies the Murdoch Method had and has great appeal to this Jewish consultant, who initially found the doors to most 'white shoe' law firms (many now defunct), utilities and other businesses off-limits. My ethnically impaired consultancy eventually succeeded because of the hard work and intelligence of my partners and our staff, many of whom could not even obtain an interview from companies dominated by the WASP ascendency. One perfectly polite and sensible client, who hired my firm because we were able to communicate with regulators who respected facts rather than lineage, told me over dinner he was glad that the new Civil Rights Act did not make Jews a group that could benefit from its anti-discrimination provisions, because, unlike the groups that were protected, we would be upward-thrusting and after his job. Another congratulated me on starting the firm, and told me that if he ever hired Jews, we would be among the first. No surprise that I understood and was driven by the same motive as Rupert, to take on and win in a game rigged against us, although for different reasons.

A word about how this book has been written. I have never kept a diary, for two reasons. First, I was so busy doing that I had no hours to spare in which to record what I had done. Second, whenever I considered keeping such a record, I always rejected the idea lest the keeping of the diary end up dictating what I did, rather than the other way around. So this book may contain errors of detail. I decided that it would be better to live with such unfortunate mistakes than to ask Rupert and his staff to check some of my recollections against their records, for that would have meant notifying them of this book before its publication, which I did not want to do. So, advance apologies for slip-ups and mis-recollections of the incidents in which I was heavily or peripherally involved. I believe it fair to say that those recollections, when possible checked against public reports, provide a sufficient and solid basis for any conclusions I have drawn.

CHAPTER 1

THE CORPORATE CULTURE

'The psychological key to Murdoch is his capacity to continue to think of himself as an anti-establishment rebel despite his vast wealth and his capacity to make and unmake governments' – Robert Manne, in David McKnight's *Rupert Murdoch: An Investigation of Political Power*, 2012[1]

'I am suspicious of elites [and] the British Establishment, with its dislike of money-making and its notion that public service is the preserve of paternalists' – Rupert Murdoch, 1989[2]

'Throughout his [Murdoch's] long career, he has fixed his gaze on an established competitor and picked away at its dominance ... His ... is ... a broader grudge match against the toffs, the chattering classes, and the top drawer of society on whatever continent he happens to find himself' – Sarah Ellison, *Vanity Fair*, 2010[3]

Never mind the composition of the Murdoch companies' boards; never mind the organisation chart, if there is one; never mind any of the management tools that have been layered on the one thing that underpins the management of News Corp[4] – its culture. All companies have cultures – a definable ethos, a style of thought, informal means of communication, systems of rewards and punishments. It doesn't take a keen-eyed consultant to notice the difference in the cultures of, say, your local utilities and Google, or Facebook and General Motors. Or to notice that many of the companies in a particular industry have similar cultures; witness the distinctive dress styles and political outlook of many Silicon Valley executives, and the very different uniforms, even now, of most investment bankers and many lawyers.

Nowhere is a guiding culture as important a determinant of how a company is run as it is at News Corp. The managerial method that reflects that culture – the Murdoch Method as I have chosen to call it – has propelled the company from a single newspaper in an obscure corner of Australia into a multi-billion dollar media empire. That style, which has produced the good, the bad and sometimes the ugly, can best be described as arising from a rather unique view of the world: it is 'them vs us', we outsiders versus, well, just about everyone else, including 'the elite', any powerful incumbent that Murdoch selects as a competitive target, and most especially 'the establishment'.

No matter that Rupert benefited from what even he must admit is an elite education at one of the finest prep schools in the world, Geelong Grammar, the 'Eton of Australia', which in later years he claimed he did not enjoy, 'although I'm sure I had some happy times there – I was there for long enough',[5] and Oxford, which, judging from his later benefactions to Worcester College, he seems to have enjoyed.[6] No matter how successful he has been, no matter the lifestyle that such success permits, Rupert continues to identify himself as an outsider – outside conventional cultural norms, outside the models on which other media companies are built, outside the Australian, British and (later) American establishments.

Definitions of the 'establishments' vary, some using the rather vague 'its members know who they are'. Owen Jones is more specific: 'Powerful groups that need to protect their position ... [and] "manage" democracy to make sure that it does not threaten their own interest.'[7] Perhaps the most useful for our purposes is Matthew d'Ancona's definition of a member of this 'caste' as 'the privileged Englishman: such an individual grew up surrounded by Tories, took for granted the fact that he would have homes in the country and in London ... and inhabited a social milieu in which everybody knew everybody.'[8] Rupert, owner of *The Times*, which media commentator Stephen Glover is not alone in calling 'the newspaper of The Establishment', believes the establishment inhibits social mobility, and will fight fiercely to retain its privileges. Sitting atop the establishment pyramid is the Royal Family, many of the members of which Murdoch often characterises as 'useless', and supporting the structure from the bottom are the deferential cap-doffers. Here is the way Rupert, invited to address the 750th anniversary celebration of the founding of University College, Oxford, hardly a rally of radicals seeking to 'occupy' the Sheldonian Theatre, chose to describe the virtues of the technological revolution in the world of communications:

> You don't have to show your bank statement or distinguished pedigree to deal yourself into a chat group on the Internet. And you don't have to be wealthy to e-mail someone on the far side of the globe. And thanks to modern technology … you won't have to be a member of an elite to obtain higher education and all the benefits – pecuniary and non-pecuniary – that it confers.

In this regard, Rupert is rather like all my Jewish friends who rose in the professional and business worlds in New York City despite (I rather think because of) an effort by 'the establishment' to keep us in our place. No amount of success can change our view of ourselves as outsiders even though many of the previously restricted clubs and apartment buildings are now officially, and in some cases actually, no longer off-limits. In Rupert's case, it was first the Australian establishment that found him unacceptable because his father's attacks on the Gallipoli campaign had been unwelcome reading for the powers that be in the government and the armed forces. Then, the British establishment would not accept an Australian interloper, especially one who published the irreverent *Sun*. Add to the establishment charge sheet against Rupert the rumours that he is a republican at heart, stifling his anti-monarchy views in deference to his mother and her memory, and aiming his media products specifically at those outside of the establishment, at men and (according to Rupert) women who deemed it harmless fun to ogle semi-clad girls in *The Sun* until that feature was dropped, who prefer sport to opera on TV, families that prefer to watch a popular movie to listening to some elevating lecture, and people who enjoyed the first-rate political commentary featured in *The Sun*. I was occasionally called upon to contribute the typical 600-word commentary, and the standards of exposition required of such political commentary and reporting on America were exacting indeed.

No matter that Page Three girls are gone, and that they were not introduced into the paper by Rupert. That feature, which passed its sell-by date a few years ago, was the invention of Larry Lamb, the first editor of *The Sun*. Rupert was in Australia when the first such photo appeared, and professed himself 'just as shocked as anybody else', although he later called what became a national institution 'a statement of youthfulness and freshness'.[9] Rupert's mother undoubtedly disagreed, as she did with other features of the tabloid. In a widely watched television interview, she complained of his gossip columnists' invasion of the privacy of the royals, celebrities and others who made it onto the pages of the Murdoch tabloids. To critics confronting him with his mother's comments, a chuckle and 'She's not our sort of reader'.

No matter that Murdoch's Sky Television offers significantly more 'high culture' programming such as operas than the establishment's beloved BBC ever did: to the elites you are either 'in' or 'out', and Rupert, by his choice and theirs, most definitely is 'out', even though by ordinary metrics – wealth, power, influence – he most definitely is 'in'.

In America, the old establishment quite rightly sees in Murdoch's

Fox News Channel a threat to its ability to control the political agenda and consensus, and in his *New York Post* an assault on its notions of propriety. Homes in Sydney, London, New York and Los Angeles, among other places, flitted to and from by private jet, possession of a beautiful yacht and other trappings of great wealth cannot change Rupert's vision of himself as an outsider opposed to and at times reviled by a 'them' that he believes to be impeding economic growth with their sloth and aversion to innovation, and upward mobility by their snobbery and dislike of 'new money'. For a child of a child of the manse, imbued with a demanding work ethic, it is perfectly consistent with material success to retain the outlook of an outsider, especially for an Australian-born mogul, raised in 'an unofficial culture imbued with ... hostility towards the country's class society and snobbery. Above all, Australian culture ... celebrated the ordinary citizen, opposing the elite.'[10]

That the culture of the Murdoch enterprise has deep Australian roots there can be little doubt. Rupert puts it this way: 'Our Australian company ... will always be the cultural heart of what we are – adventurous, entrepreneurial, hard-working and with a special loyalty and collegiality in all that we do.'[11] His eldest son, Lachlan, echoed that sentiment years later: 'An Australian influence nourishes the family, even in the States ... I have got to say that I love both countries deeply, and they are both an essential part of my identity.'[12] To which his father added, 'I share my son's sentiment.'[13]

The Murdochs' pride in their Australian heritage exists despite Sir Keith Murdoch's constant battle with the establishment there over his decision to publicise the senseless slaughter of Australian soldiers at Gallipoli. Then a young reporter, Keith defied military censorship while reporting on the First World War Gallipoli campaign, the Allies' failed attempt to knock Turkey out of the war by seizing control of the Dardanelles and capturing Constantinople (modern Istanbul). Keith Murdoch drafted what is now the famous Gallipoli Letter, laying out in vivid prose and great detail the mismanagement of the campaign by British officers selected on the basis of their social standing, the poor morale of the troops and the unnecessary waste of young lives.[14] He delivered it to the Australian prime minister and to Britain's minister of munitions, David Lloyd George, who passed it on to Prime Minister Herbert Asquith, all in violation of Keith's signed agreement 'not to attempt to correspond by any other route or by any other means than that officially sanctioned … [by] the Chief Field Censor'. The result was the sacking of General Sir Ian Hamilton as commander of the Allied Mediterranean Expeditionary Force, the removal of Winston Churchill from the Admiralty and, soon after, the withdrawal from the Dardanelles of Australian and other Allied troops, but not before suffering 142,000 casualties, 28,000 of them Australian. Of the 44,000 killed, 8,700 were Australian,[15] this in a country of under five million at the time. The United Kingdom, with almost ten times the population of Australia, took fewer than three times as many casualties. That Aussie casualty rate, the result of poor leadership, proved to Rupert that his father had done the right thing, and that the criticism of him was unjust. Some sixty-six years after his father's letter was published, Rupert funded *Gallipoli*, a movie set on the Anzac battlefield, graphically illustrating the futility of the campaign. It won the award for 'best film' and numerous other 'bests' from the Australian Film Institute. Murdoch family ties run deep and long.

Rupert styles himself not only an outsider, but also a revolutionary. In his student days, he kept a bust of Lenin in his rooms at Oxford, rooms that were 'one of the best rooms in college – the De Quincey room'.[16] He dismisses such behaviour with 'I was young and even had other hare-brained ideas'.[17] My guess is that the episode was not due to the mere youthful innocence of a university student, but was aimed at upsetting the British establishment.

The list of establishment insiders includes a number of formidable enemies, whom I shall describe in terms that I believe capture Rupert's attitudes. First on the list are the trade unions and their resistance to technological progress and sensible staffing. He jousted with the unions early on in Australia, won them over to his side in Britain when they supported his acquisition of *The Sun* and the *News of the World* as a superior alternative to his rival, Robert Maxwell, and then more or less destroyed them on the battlefield of Wapping. If you are a union leader of printers and related crafts, or merely a trade unionist who watched as Murdoch took on and defeated the print unions in Britain, you see him as evil incarnate. Rupert probably won no friends in the UK when he compared the Australian and British work ethics in an interview with an American reporter: 'When I came to Britain in 1968, I found it was damn hard to get a day's work out of the people at the top of the social scale. As an Australian, I only had to work eight or ten hours a day, 48 weeks of the year, and everything came to you.'[18] His victory in the epic battle of Wapping, in which violence forced him to ring the Wapping print facility with barbed wire while Margaret Thatcher provided the necessary police protection, propelled the entire industry into the modern era of computers and other technology, to the silent applause of proprietors of competing newspapers who cowered in their boardrooms while Rupert did the hard lifting to get their industry into the modern age. Had it not been for Murdoch's willingness to take on the unions, the British newspaper industry would by now probably have been consigned to the ash heap of history, where many once-great British industries now reside, partly because of managements' failures to overcome union opposition to modern technology.

Second on Rupert's list comes the BBC, funded by what it calls a licence fee but its critics say is in effect a tax collected even from those who do not watch the BBC, and run by an elite for elites. Rupert argues that the 'Beeb' and its supporters believe that 'the people could not be trusted to watch what they wanted to watch',[19] and has 'always thought that its tastes are synonymous with quality – a view, incidentally, that is natural to all governing classes'.[20] Murdoch's Sky (later BSkyB) successfully promoted a technology that permitted multi-channel broadcasting of twenty-four-hour news, movies, sports and other programme genres not fully available on the BBC. And, not coincidentally, caused the BBC's market share to shrink, calling into question the justification for taxing 100 per cent of television owners to support programming that captures only one-third of the market. Murdoch's anti-BBC stance is the result of a combination of his view of himself as a protector of the masses who want access to a wide variety of programmes, and his frustration at having to compete with an organisation that has an assured revenue stream regardless of its audience ratings. And it is not shared by all conservatives or economists, many of whom point out that all members of society benefit from what we might call the elevation of the culture that the BBC is believed to provide, just as childless couples benefit from an education system that produces talented and well-developed adults and, not least, informed voters.

A more amorphous set of enemies are liberals who attempt to freeze out others by presenting their left-of-centre point of view as society's consensus, rather than as one of many competing political philosophies. Managers of the television news outlets that dominated mainstream news reporting in America until the successful launch of Fox News could not imagine that an overtly conservative news channel would attract millions of viewers and come to dominate cable news. Charles Krauthammer, a Pulitzer Prize-winning *Washington Post* columnist, observed shortly after

Rupert launched Fox cable news, 'Rupert found a niche market for television news – half of America.'* And so he had, driving media executives to follow the lead of Butch Cassidy, who at one point in the 1969 film asked of the persistent pursuers who were out to do him in, 'Who are those guys?' Those guys were the forgotten audience of Middle America. To serve them, Murdoch had to overcome Time Warner's attempt to protect its CNN twenty-four-hour news channel by denying Fox access to its key, monopoly New York City cable system, and therefore to the ad agencies that allocate their clients' 'spend'. That barrier to entry crumbled in the face of a successful antitrust challenge by Fox, in which I assisted News' lawyers. Fox News originally styled itself 'Fair & Balanced', although its founding genius, the late Roger Ailes, in moments of candour admitted that 'fair and *balancing*' was a more accurate description,[21] since he was not aiming for balanced programming within Fox News, but a balancing of the total news output of American newscasting. In the post-Ailes era 'Fair & Balanced' has been replaced with 'Most Watched. Most Trusted',[22] a claim not likely to win applause from liberal competitors consumed with regret at having failed to see that between the two coasts on which they live there is a vast American hinterland – they call it 'fly-over country' – that is patriotic, believes in God and the constitutional right to own guns, and is uncertain that the social agenda of the liberal establishment is in the national interest.

Then there are the media industry elitists – content providers, reviewers, executives of the three oligopoly networks and regulators who equate programme popularity with vulgarity, and who know what is best for television viewers. To them *The Simpsons*, an

---

* At a private luncheon to honour Dr Krauthammer, who Rupert much admires and who now is a commentator on Fox News while continuing his weekly column for *The Washington Post*, Rupert jokingly promised to forgive Krauthammer for winning the Pulitzer Prize for journalism, an award Rupert believes goes to journalists out of touch with the sort of news in which most people are interested.

adult cartoon programme, and *American Idol,* a reality programme featuring non-professional entertainers, were designed to appeal to the lowest common denominator. As television columnist Brian Lowry put it in *Variety,* the voice of the entertainment industry, 'Rupe' frequently 'led TV down a path of dubious standards and questionable taste … Its programmes coarsened the national debate … Fox clearly led the race to the bottom on several fronts …. Fox News has … been an especially divisive force.'[23] Worse still, Rupert and Barry Diller, then the CEO of Fox, overrode all advice and positioned *The Simpsons,* a cartoon and a genre then in its infancy, opposite the massively popular *Cosby Show* in a key prime-time slot, the first time in six years anyone had dared mount a serious challenge to Bill Cosby's family-oriented show, 'one of the most popular sitcoms in the history of television'.[24] *The Simpsons'* 'off-beat characters quickly became America's best-loved family',[25] and long outlived *The Cosby Show.* The replacement of an apple-pie-and-motherhood programme such as *The Cosby Show* with what some might consider the dysfunctional Simpsons and friends did not delight the establishment. One public health specialist pointed out that the Simpsons were depicted smoking cigarettes 795 times over the eighteen seasons during which the show was aired. Worse still, smoking was depicted in a 'negative context', as a health hazard, only 35 percent of the time.[26]

On this incomplete list of enemies we also have 'snobs', a subset of the establishment. They use the word 'downmarket' rather than 'popular' to describe many Murdoch offerings, and sneer at tabloid journalism, print and broadcast, most especially the *New York Post* and Fox News in the US, and in the UK *The Sun,* the now-defunct *News of the World,* and many offerings on Murdoch's various television holdings around the world. They find offensive the gossipy *New York Post* and its Page Six exposés of the foibles of American high society and the celebrities who crave its coverage – until they wish they hadn't. And are offended by *The Sun,* 'a stew of sexual titillation, moral outrage and political aggression'.[27] Rupert believes, or says he does, that many who sneer at *The Sun* secretly read it, but hidden behind the pages of *The Times*.

Wall Street analysts and investment bankers have a special spot on Rupert's list of enemies, or at least of people with whom one must sup with a long spoon, if supping with them becomes essential. These model-builder's and bean-counters' and investment bankers' 'siren songs'[28] lured him down a path that nearly brought the company to ruin when he financed Sky's incursion into the UK television market with short-term loans, as detailed in Chapter 6, and then forced him to sell some of his assets to meet his loan obligations. Moreover, the investment analysts among them do not understand that great businesses are built for the long run, that anyone buying News stock knows that he is putting his money into an enterprise controlled by Murdoch through the voting rights attached to his shares, and that Rupert's stated aim of having his children succeed him means he will take the very long view in assembling his media empire. If there is a risk that at times he will act in pursuit of that goal, rather than in the interest of all of the shareholders, that risk is a well-advertised one.

Finally, we have governments, or many of them. Overtaxing, overregulating governments that create entitlement states that have no way of honouring the promises they make, and that stifle economic growth, are special targets. Politicians such as Margaret Thatcher and Ronald Reagan who promise to roll back the state are on quite a different list – those few especially worthy of support.

All on this formidable list of enemies are among the 'other' against which Rupert defines himself and News Corp. There is no lack of 'them' for 'us' to attack, and the greater their outrage, the louder the satisfied chuckling in News' executive dining rooms. No entrenched interest loves a revolutionary, especially one with a proven record of successful creative destruction, as Uber, Amazon, Facebook, Google and others are discovering, with the European

Commission leading the way. To some of these disrupters, most notably Google, News is just another entrenched interest, living off an outdated technology that involves chopping down trees and spreading ink on them. In what some will call a touch of hypocrisy, Rupert and his associates have taken to calling for government constraints on Google, which has become a significant and successful competitor for advertising, in their view pirating the content created by News and other companies for use by its search engine. In both Britain and the US newspapers are seeking to work out agreements for joint efforts to cope with Google and Facebook, which News calls 'the digital duopoly'.[29] Whether the US papers can obtain the antitrust exemption they need is far from certain, especially since the Trump administration has no love for the print media, and the *New York Post*, thanks to Murdoch a Trump supporter until now, headlined its story on a meeting of the president's son with representatives of the Kremlin, 'Donald Trump Jr. is an Idiot'.[30]

Those general targets, those 'thems', include, of course, some more specific ones, among them *The New York Times*, a target Rupert hoped to destroy, using his *Wall Street Journal* as the weapon. The plan was to broaden the coverage of *The Wall Street Journal* so that it could replace America's leading national newspaper and the voice of the liberal establishment. In pursuit of his goal, Murdoch initially improved both the breadth and depth of *The Wall Street Journal*'s coverage of the world beyond finance, while maintaining its leading role as a chronicler of financial developments. According to the Pew Research Center, under Murdoch the front-page business coverage of *The Wall Street Journal*, which accounted for 29.8 per cent of the news hole before Rupert acquired it, fell to 19.5 per cent by 2011, while coverage of non-US and US foreign affairs increased from 26.3 to 29.1 per cent. Front-page coverage of government went from 2.9 to 8.1 per cent of the page one news hole. 'Overall … when it comes to the quantity of coverage of major topics, the evidence suggests that the *Times* and the *Journal* have indeed become more competitive since Murdoch bought the paper.'[31]

Unfortunately for his plans, even a vastly improved and broadened *Wall Street Journal* could not stem advertisers' continued flight to other media, forcing a significant reduction in the size and coverage of the *Journal*. It is not clear that the current version of the newspaper represents as great a threat to the still loss-making *New York Times* as *The Wall Street Journal* did shortly after Rupert acquired and expanded it, although the *Journal*'s lush magazine and increased arts, entertainment and sports coverage makes it a closer substitute for *The New York Times* than was the pre-Murdoch version.

There can be little doubt that Rupert will persist in his battle against *The New York Times*, for two reasons. The first is the long view he takes of matters such as this. Second, his goal of supplanting *The New York Times* is not a traditional newspaper circulation war: it is another battle by 'us' to unseat 'them', a 'them' that sneered when Murdoch bought the *New York Post* and again when he acquired *The Wall Street Journal*.

It is over forty years since that day in November 1976 when Murdoch strolled into the rather tacky offices of the newly acquired *New York Post*, close to the famously smelly Fulton Fish Market. That day his conviction that he was looked down upon by the establishment was confirmed, in part because of his launch in 1974 of the *National Star* and his purchase of the *National Enquirer*, supermarket tabloids (and both since sold), and his use of tabloid headlines to boost sales of his two small broadsheets in San Antonio, Texas. 'KILLER BEES HEAD NORTH' is the most famous, over a report that 'a species of bee with a potentially fatal sting ... had been spotted minding its own business somewhere in South America'.[32]

That sort of thing is more than *The New York Times* can tolerate.

One of its columns focused on *The Sun*: '*The Sun* is a newspaper, in the sense that it appears every morning but Sunday and is published on newsprint. But its news is rarely what the editors of other newspapers call news.'[33] A *New York Times* executive, asked if he was worried about the entry into the New York newspaper market of the *Post*, an aggressive new competitor, sniffed, 'We don't see the *Post* sale as a threat to us ... He doesn't really alarm us. It's like Carnegie Hall looking down the street at a dance hall that's been rebuilt, and wondering if it will lose its patrons.'[34] Fast-forward three decades. When Arthur Sulzberger's *New York Times* ran an editorial the day after Murdoch's purchase of *The Wall Street Journal* was closed, accusing Rupert of interfering in the (London) *Times* and kowtowing to the Chinese, Rupert responded with an immediately leaked 'Dear Arthur' letter: 'It was a pleasure to meet you last night ...' followed by a denial of the charges, and concluding, 'Let the battle begin.'[35]

If I ever had any doubts about the forces driving Rupert to acquire *The Wall Street Journal*, they were dispelled by several conversations with Rupert as the battle for the *Journal* reached its conclusion. He was clearly more than annoyed that he should be considered an unsuitable suitor for the paper that the posh, establishment Bancroft family's neglect had brought to the brink of financial disaster. That snobbery undoubtedly reminded him of that day long ago when he had to submit to a 'suitability' interview before he was allowed to acquire *The Times* titles in 1981, an experience that left him shaking with anger and undoubtedly confirmed what one interviewer describes as his 'evident loathing for elites, for cosy establishments, for cartels, for what he's called "strangulated English accents"'.[36]

Murdoch and his team also have sports channel ESPN, owned 80 per cent by the Walt Disney Company and 20 per cent by Hearst Corporation, and the twenty-four-hour business news channel CNBC in their sights. Both channels are the sort of targets at which I have watched Rupert take aim – long-unchallenged entities with dominant market shares. This makes them what Jamie Horowitz, president of Fox Sports National Networks (until he was recently removed as the result of yet another law firm investigation into sexual harassment charges, which Horowitz denies),[37] called 'big bets … against traditional news and information shows',[38] bets Rupert intends to win the same way Fox News bested CNN – with patience, by overbidding for programmes and by right-leaning counter-programming, in the case of sports by appealing to a more conservative audience than ESPN's liberal broadcasters who support gestures by sports stars who refuse to rise for the national anthem.

The challenge to ESPN – Fox's national sports networks remain with Murdoch – is proving more difficult than the challenge to CNBC. The latter is a twenty-four-hour business news specialist, as is Fox Business, and both are competing in a growth market. That is not true of the market for sports broadcasting. It is facing techno-logical changes that have viewers leaving cable networks in droves while the supply of sports programmes is increasing more rapidly than advertisers' budgets, putting pressure on ad rates.[39] Indeed, there is talk in the industry of 'oversaturation' of football broad-casts, one of the key attractions for sports fans.[40] Both Fox Sports and ESPN are bleeding subscribers[41] and redoing programming plans in hope of returning to a growth pattern.[42] ESPN remains the clear ratings leader, but Fox Sports has gained a foothold in this market, topping all cable networks on 13 June 2017 when its line-up of NASCAR, the USA vs Mexico FIFA World Cup quali-fier and drag racing attracted an average viewership of nearly 1.2 million.[43] And because of Fox's regional tilt, as compared to ESPN's national line-up of sporting events, 'Fox Sports [could be] better placed with TV rights moving forward: a regional channel such as FOX Sports Detroit can provide coverage of all of the city's baseball, hockey, basketball and most of its (American) football games at a far cheaper subscription rate than ESPN's national coverage.'[44]

Despite the technological and other challenges, sports remain a compelling entertainment product. Unlike much that appears on television screens, sporting events have uncertain outcomes, making it difficult to rely on recordings and the skipping of ads, since the results are immediately reported in news media of all sorts, and are difficult to avoid. It is fair to say that ESPN, which retains a ratings lead, now has a formidable competitor – FS1 led all networks with nine sports Emmys[45] – that sports fans' range of choices has markedly increased, and that, thanks to streamers, consumers with no interest in sports are gradually finding ways of avoiding bundles that require them to subsidise the high prices cable companies must pay for sports rights.

As for Murdoch's business channel, critics, this writer among them, thought that Fox did not understand that market well enough to succeed in wooing viewers from CNBC, much less displacing it, a view Rupert told me rather emphatically he did not share. He was going on air as the best way to find out just what the market was for business news, and whether he could successfully challenge CNBC's business model of appealing to elite, wealthy viewers.

It reminded me of the day in his office when he agreed to hire Bill Kristol to start *The Weekly Standard*, and to get the first edition of the magazine onto the newsstands without bothering with focus-group testing. And of the day in my London apartment when he said he planned to get Sky on the air only a few months after the satellite was due to go up. In both cases, he added, 'We'll fix it as we go along.' That maxim had worked when Rupert launched Australia's first national newspaper and rounded up bank financing and advertisers, set up distribution and arranged printing – all within four months. The early editions were a mess, but he fixed the paper as he went along, an experience that stood him in good stead in later years.[46] Big gambles that experience would prove the best teacher are an ever-present ingredient of the Murdoch Method, one that allows executives to learn by doing and surely keeps the adrenaline flowing.

In the case of Fox's Business Network (FBN) that tactic paid off. In March 2017 FBN finished ahead of CNBC for a record sixth consecutive month in business day viewers, according to Nielsen Media Research. It bested CNBC by 19 per cent in business day viewers and almost won the battle for the twenty-five- to fifty-four-year-old demographic cherished by advertisers, hitting its highest rated quarter while CNBC hit its second lowest rated quarter in that demographic.[47] 'FBN also emerged as the go-to network for financial breaking news,' topping CNBC when the Dow Jones average broke a record 20,000, again when it broke 21,000, and with its prime-time coverage of the Brexit vote. 'It's fair to wonder if CNBC's strategy of targeting affluent viewers during the banking hours of old can still be a successful model in the modern, changing landscape.'[48] Still, there is something to be said for CNBC's strategy. Some seventeen million viewers with incomes in excess of $100,000 watched CNBC over a seven-day period, roughly double the number of affluent viewers who watched Fox. Furthermore, CNBC's annual revenue of $735 million handily topped Fox's $260 million.[49] Murdoch, taking his usual long view (odd for a man impatient in so many other contexts), knows that CNBC has been around for twenty-eight years while FBN is only ten years old: there are still lots of dollars to play for.

Sports and business news are only two of the many areas in which Murdoch takes aim at an established competitor, or the limits of conventional culture. Because the culture of News is built on poking the establishment and the guardians of contemporary cultural standards in the eye, everyone I have met in the company views himself or herself as both a representative of the masses ignored by traditional media companies and as a buccaneer, an outrider, an accident waiting to happen to News' competitors. As Murdoch once told a group of journalists, 'If the market isn't growing, you have to eat someone else's lunch.'[50] At private meetings of top executives, I met no objection when I characterised the company as a pirate ship, one that can never comfortably sail in Her Majesty's navy.

At one of the corporate gatherings, Rupert and I were assigned adjoining trailers to use as offices during the meetings – a touch of Hollywood, along with Rupert's consideration that I needed a place to work if I were to fulfil other obligations during the meetings. I met with him during one break to discuss the items I proposed he might include in his talk, all of which he rejected. Instead, he said, he wanted the many executives and content creators who recently joined fast-growing News to understand its culture, its attitude towards elites and the establishment, how it had been successful because he had never accepted 'the King's shilling', or sought the approbation of those in power. He also wanted to convey the excitement of being in the business of news and entertainment, the need to take risks. I am reminded of Stephen Sondheim's lyrical urging, 'Tilt at the windmill, and if you fail, you fail', and later of Rupert's remark at a memorial service for his mother: 'She taught us that it was OK to stumble.'[51] Members of the audience should leave, he told me, with the feeling that they were indeed fortunate to be in their chosen careers, and even more fortunate to be at News Corp., where they could thrive in an atmosphere of service and excitement.

Multiple drafts later, Rupert shared this bit of history with his executives:

> After my father died, when I was still at college, the opposition newspaper, which enjoyed an 80 percent market share, went to my mother, and with a fake show of friendship, offered to buy us out at a discount. They said

their board had decided to put out a competing Sunday newspaper which would destroy our only profitable activity. My mother was given the wonderful opportunity of selling half the company for less than $300,000 – this, for control of a company now worth well in excess of $30 billion. Wise woman that she was ... she insisted on time to call me before giving her answer. I gave what can only be characterized as a rude response. *I then did something that I like to think set the tone for the behaviour of our company as it is today, and will be in years to come: I broke the rules of the establishment* and published our opponents' offer on the front page of the paper under a headline that screamed 'Bid for press monopoly.' And I included in the story a photograph of the confidential letter to my mother. That ruined any chance I might ever have had of being invited into the better clubs of Adelaide. Which set another precedent that still guides us: *ignore the elite who offer clubiness in return for acquiescence in the status quo.* [Italics added by the author reflect Rupert's emphasis in his oral presentation.][52]

It is this outsider's war against the establishment and his drive to disrupt the status quo that keeps Murdoch going when younger men are working on their golf handicaps, and accounts for his view of the world as 'a jungle ... danger lurks behind every tree; and predators are prepared to pounce', some with 'deceptively sweet names' such as Mickey Mouse and computer mouse, 'both capable of devouring us and eager to do so. But we have no intention of being devoured, least of all by mice.'[53] Rupert undoubtedly believes there is a difference between being 'devoured' and pocketing $66 billion.

It is important to remember that no corporate culture is without its faults. Neat, hierarchical cultures can avoid serious errors capable of bringing a company to its knees, but can also stifle innovations and miss opportunities, as Microsoft did when mobile devices became competitive with desktop computers. Relaxed management styles can produce cost-raising chaos, with everyone doing his or her 'own thing' to the detriment of the organisation as a whole, as seems to have been the case with Google until the recent introduction of financial discipline and a restructuring of the company.

The Murdoch Method cannot be classified as either 'rigid' or 'relaxed'. It leans heavily on the 'them vs us' culture that Rupert has created. Its advantages are reflected in the financial success and the cultural victories of News. The disadvantages can be seen when some company employees take 'them vs us' to mean that there are virtually no constraints on their assault on societal norms, and disrespect for the mores of the establishment morph into violations of the law.

Rupert is the only one who really knows in borderline cases just where the line between responsible and irresponsible, between acceptable and unacceptable, between what he characterises as 'the bawdy and the vulgar'[54] can be drawn. That does not mean that his executives are completely in the dark. They have precedent to guide them. They have their own knowledge of their markets. They have experience and in most cases common sense. But at times they fall back on trying to guess what Rupert would do in the circumstances in which they find themselves. They must guess just how applicable to a specific circumstance is the general interdiction to be aggressive, to assault the establishment, to push the envelope, but not to cross the often indistinct line between responsible and irresponsible. And to do so knowing that what only a few years earlier might have been unacceptable is now on the verge of becoming mainstream – or vice versa.

This requirement to play a guessing game is perhaps the greatest weakness generated by Murdoch's approach to management.

Although Rupert succeeds in making his wishes known to many more of his executives, high and low, than one would imagine possible in an organisation of News' size and geographic reach, there are inevitably times when decisions have to be made without specific sanction by The Boss. No less a force in the company than Peter Chernin, president and CEO of News Corp from 1996 to 2009, told his colleagues that the secret of success is to be more like Rupert: 'We have to remember what got us here: We have to be nimble and bold. You know those "be like Mike" [Michael Jordan] commercials? We have to be like Rupert. We have to institutionalise the imagination, nerve and vision he represents.'[55] It is no surprise that News' executives want to behave 'more like Rupert', and often, when wondering 'What would Rupert do?', do not always come up with the correct answer. Kelvin MacKenzie, irrepressible former editor of *The Sun*, later an executive at Sky and until May 2017 a *Sun* columnist, survived when his 'It's The Sun Wot Won It' headline violated Rupert's sense of the degree of political power a newspaper should claim. MacKenzie once joked that the only decision executives at Wapping ever made was to toss a coin to determine who would call Rupert in New York to find out what they should do.[56] A Murdoch favourite, MacKenzie did not survive a second misreading of the acceptable limits of envelope-pushing: he was fired for a statement that, although not so intended, was deemed to be racist.[57]

Nor should it come as a surprise that, having been chosen for their no-holds-barred competitive spirit, having then embraced the adversarial culture that is so much the stuff of which News is made, there is a tendency for Murdoch's lieutenants to opt for the more aggressive course, a reputation for timidity not being perceived as career-enhancing.

I remember one meeting to discuss the most efficient allocation of territories to distributors of News' British newspapers. The system of dividing the profitable distributorships by postal codes seemed to me suboptimal, both from an economic and a regulatory point of view. The assembled group disposed of my objection with, 'That's the way Rupert wants it.' That seemed implausible to me, so I asked Rupert about it when next we met. The response: 'I was sitting in a meeting about this, got terribly bored, and said "Use postcodes" to give me an excuse to get out of the meeting.' The result of this decision was the creation of local distribution monopolies that eventually prompted the Office of Fair Trading to initiate a long inquiry, forcing News to spend millions answering the regulators' requests for data and other information, a cost to weigh against the Murdoch Method's benefits. As I described it at a regulatory proceeding dealing with cross-promotion, chaired by the very capable John Sadler, 'it does not take an instruction from some central authority figure in an organisation where people are trying to divine what will please the central authority figure'.[58]

Finally, there is the not small matter of the effect of some of Fox's television and movie fare on the culture of the nation. As any student of Adam Smith knows, the effective functioning of the free-market system that Murdoch so admires depends on an underlying culture of respect for the law, of civility, of understanding that there is a difference between preventing a minority from imposing its value system on society so as to maintain its own dominant position, and what historian Gertrude Himmelfarb calls 'coarsening' the nation's culture and 'trivialization of morality itself'.[59] A management system built around the notion that we outsiders have to count it a plus if we offend establishment elites risks excess. It is one thing to attack elites for assuming that they should be the taste-makers, determining what lesser persons can read in their newspapers and see on their screens. It is quite another to assume that it is good policy for a media company to offer anything people want to see or hear and are willing to pay for. In economists' terms, the media industry creates externalities, a subject to which I will return in the Epilogue. The effects of its products go far beyond those on the readers or viewers who choose to watch or read what it produces. This industry sets a tone that affects even those who do not directly purchase its offerings, and has a responsibility to think hard about the attitudes its products generate. When Rupert announced, 'My own view is that anybody who, within the law of the land, provides a service that the public wants at a price it can afford is providing a public service',[60] he was careful to include the notion of respect for the law, but ignored what he at other times referred to as the special responsibility of a media company to truth and decency.

In America, the First Amendment to the Constitution limits the legal restraints that can be put on what is shown and published. Media companies can see that as allowing them to produce almost anything that will sell, or placing an even greater burden on them to operate within bounds that do not produce an ugly culture that Irving Kristol argued at a gathering of News executives is inconsistent with the maintenance of a polity capable of operating a democracy.[61] The question of whether violent films, television programmes and video games produce real-word violence is an open one: credible studies arrive at different answers, some finding a causative relation between media violence and crime,[62] some finding no such causation, some pointing out that those who commit most violence in films and on television get their just deserts, driving home a 'don't do it' message. David Gauntlett, a researcher at the Institute of Communications Studies at Leeds University, says that most television violence shows the aggressor being punished, reassuring viewers that good triumphs over evil.[63] One interesting fact is that the television fare in Windsor, Ontario, Canada, is about the same as that in Detroit, Michigan, just across the border, yet the crime rate in Windsor is far below that of Detroit.[64] But Canada has stricter gun control laws than the United States, so we simply cannot be certain that the culture projected in the media does not have its impact on behaviour, as at least one study claims to have proved.[65] The safest conclusion is that 'we just do not know the relationship between viewing or playing and aggression in the real world. Research to date does not inform us. But we should be concerned and wary of risks.'[66] Some media products, although protected from censorship by the First Amendment, might nevertheless be considered inappropriate for distribution by responsible executives, at least not without prior consideration of their impact on behaviour of some segments of society. True, media industries have established rating systems that do a reasonably good job of warning concerned consumers what is in store for them and their children. And true, too, that Murdoch's free-market and libertarian tendencies compete with a certain sense of propriety, or prudery as he would put it. I recall a corporate gathering that included families, at which a somewhat vulgar Fox movie was being released. An embarrassed Rupert stammered through an apology-cum-warning to potential attendees. This was not the only time he has found it difficult to walk the line between his desire to *épater le bourgeois* and the sense of propriety preached by his mother, with its heavy emphasis on responsibility to family, friends and society. For her, the path to profits was not the only road to be taken. She told one interviewer, 'Making money is not greatness'; disapproved of his purchase of the British tabloids; and was reluctant to endorse his decision to divorce Anna, telling a reporter, 'When you take a vow to be loyal to someone for all your life, you don't hurt other people for your own happiness. I'm still so fond of Anna that I find it hard to accept Wendi, but I must, of course.'[67] She expanded on that view when I had the good fortune to sit next to her at the party following James's wedding, in the process gripping my arm so forcefully – she was then ninety years old – that I later examined it for fingerprints.

Murdoch might not have followed his mother's teachings in every aspect of his life, but I have lost count of the number of times that, after making a decision such as becoming an American citizen, therefore eligible to acquire television networks under US law, or spending lavishly on something, Rupert would muse, 'I wonder what my mother will say.' Her passing has not reduced her ability to make Rupert pause and reflect before acting. At times such reflection results in a decision to apologise for some News product, as was the case with Judith Regan's planned book on the O. J. Simpson case, and a *Sunday Times* cartoon depicting an Israeli prime minister building a wall with blood-soaked mortar, published on Holocaust Memorial Day. The cartoonist, Gerald Scarfe, Rupert said in a tweeted apology, has never reflected the opinions of *The Sunday Times*. 'Nevertheless, we owe [a] major apology for [the] grotesque, offensive cartoon.'[68]

It would be unreasonable to argue that Murdoch draws the line where his mother would, but correct to argue that she is ever on his shoulder, whispering her sensibilities in his ear. What she would have advised when Disney came calling with buckets of cash we can only guess.

CHAPTER 2

POWER, POLITICS AND THE MURDOCH METHOD

'What the proprietorship of these [opposition] newspapers is aiming at is power, and power without responsibility – the prerogative of the harlot throughout the ages' – Stanley Baldwin, 1931[1]

'We are really only minor facilitators in the game of shaping society' – Rupert Murdoch, 1999[2]

'Go ask Ed Koch if I ever asked him for anything. Go ask Margaret Thatcher. Go ask Tony Blair. Ask anyone if I ever asked for anything' – Rupert Murdoch, 2006[3]

'Power is the great aphrodisiac' – Henry Kissinger, 1971[4]

'I love competition. And I want to win … Ours is a company that has prospered by injecting competition into industries and countries which for a long time favoured monopoly suppliers' – Rupert Murdoch, 1999[5]

There are two major differences between Rupert Murdoch and his fellow businessmen. The first it that his views on policy issues are better informed, more nuanced – not because he is more clever than other big-time executives, although in my experience he is cleverer than most, but because he is in a business that requires him to keep pace with trends in political thought, or at least in politics; to be in contact with politicians; and to read and hear what the pundits he employs are saying and thinking about the issues confronting most countries. This gives him access to a range of views on policies towards economic growth, labour markets, allies and enemies, free trade, trade union activities and more. This is the stuff of his every working day, which is not the case with most busy executives, who have neither the time nor the inclination to be the policy wonk that Murdoch's vocation requires him to be. This is perhaps the main reason why he loves what he does. 'Murdoch loves to talk politics, and he is a news junkie. He spends a good part of each day calling his editors around the world,' notes John Cassidy after a long interview with his former boss.[6] Andrew Neil, former editor of *The Sunday Times* and chairman of Sky, whose relationship with Murdoch was often fraught, puts it more strongly: 'Rupert is a highly political animal: even meetings about some technical matter to do with colour or pagination will invariably begin with an exchange of views on the current political scene in America or Britain ... He is fascinated by politics for its own sake – but also because politics affects the business environment in which he operates.'[7]

My own experience is very much like that of Neil and others. Conversations with my other clients are typically confined to the business matter at hand, after the obligatory nod to the results of recent sporting events; with Rupert, they always, or almost always, ended up in long discussions about subjects ranging from the state of this or that economy to some politician's recent success or failure in pursuing some goal or other. And I recall a conversation with a frustrated potential Murdoch biographer, who complained to me that he could never keep Rupert on the subject this writer needed to have discussed: the life and times of this media baron. Rupert always consumed most of the allotted time questioning him about breaking news and political issues. The would-be biographer finally gave up the project.

Second, Murdoch is a media mogul – not a steel mogul, not a high-tech entrepreneurial mogul, not an oil mogul. His newspapers and television properties provide him with a megaphone. Successful executives in other industries can influence events and policies by making bundles of cash available to campaigning politicians, which provides them with access to the winners. But that access permits a word in the ear, the presentation of some special pleading to a favoured official who might or might not act on it, and that's the end of it. If Murdoch has a view he wants heard, he, too, can have access to those in power, but not because he is a source of contributions, although he sometimes backs favoured candidates with hard cash. Rupert can offer two things the ordinary executive cannot: information he has routinely gathered on subjects of interest to the politician, and a megaphone. If a politician can persuade Murdoch, he is likely to have gained an ally who will manage to have those arguments repeated in newspapers in which Murdoch has a say in editorial policy, and on air to millions of Fox News Channel viewers. And if that politician has somehow made an enemy of Murdoch by taking a policy position with which Rupert disagrees, or by failing to perform in office as Rupert feels the public interest demands, or has committed an indiscretion, he might well find his election campaign more difficult. Hence Tony Blair's statement at a corporate gathering at Pebble Beach: 'When I first met you, I wasn't sure I liked you, but I feared you. Now that my days of fighting elections are over, I don't actually fear you, but I do like you.'[8] This was, of course, before Rupert accused Blair of having an affair with his then wife Wendi Deng, which Blair denies. The acknowledgement of fear of Rupert's power by a phenomenally popular politician about to launch one of the most successful electoral careers in British history tells a great deal about the perceived power of the Murdoch press. In its heyday, roughly through the Thatcher and Blair years, support of *The Sun* was deemed to be so consequential that everyone was eager to find out which candidate or party it would support. In a sign of both its arrogance and its love of fun, the paper erected a large furnace, planning to send up billows of blue, yellow or red smoke to indicate it had decided in favour of the Tories, Lib Dems or Labour. In 1997, red smoke came billowing out of the chimney, signalling the end of twelve years of *Sun* support for the Tories and a switch to Labour. Like the Pope, *The Sun* had no divisions, to borrow from Stalin's characterisation of the Pontiff's power. But it thought enough of its electoral clout to mimic the Vatican's method of advertising that a new man, in this case Tony Blair, had been chosen. This expression of belief in the tabloid's power to sway elections has never been supported by unambiguous data on voter behaviour, or shared by Murdoch. But to the extent that politicians believe what self-important editors tell them, they fear newspaper proprietors – witness Donald Trump's obsession with an almost uniformly hostile media.

Other corporate chieftains also have the wherewithal to hire lobbyists, that flock of fallen or retired politicians and lawyers who make their homes in the capitals of nations of the world and of the European Union. In America, they populate Washington's K Street, where, along with law firms that often specialise less in caring about the effect of legislation on the public interest than in influencing it, they perform the useful function of providing information to legislators and the less useful one of putting a concealing gloss on the actions of companies and countries that have done things they shouldn't have done.

The rise of the lobbying industry from Washington to Brussels testifies to the fact that all industries can exert some political power. Insurance companies in America importantly shaped President Obama's most transformative legislation, the Affordable Care Act, or Obamacare as it is widely known. Investment banks pour millions into political campaigns and in return obtain access to the politicians whose successful campaigns they have supported, and some special benefit tucked into a thousand-page bill that Congress passes without so much as reading it. In Brussels, lobbyists for powerful European incumbents are waging war on American 'disrupters' who threaten their clients' economic viability, and the Americans are responding by beefing up their own lobbying efforts: Google, Facebook, Amazon and Microsoft have launched 'a charm offensive'[9] in Brussels, with Google increasing its annual spending-in-search-of-understanding – or influence, if you prefer – from €600,000 in 2011 to between €4.25 and €4.5 million today,[10] some of it to offset charges hurled at it by News Corp, with Murdoch personally accusing it of stealing his company's 'content'.[11] Microsoft, a Google competitor in some markets, matches Google's spending euro for euro.

We must, however, be careful not to overstate the power of lobbyists, who are always on the hunt for clients who confuse access – a drink with a legislator, often of minor influence – with real influence, or to understate the power of media companies, despite doubts about their ability to swing specific elections. Their power takes other forms. No other industry has the media's power to affect the lives of politicians, to set the political agenda by deciding which stories to report in print and on television, and which to ignore; whom to interview and whose request for airtime to refuse; which tales will adorn the front pages of a newspaper, above the fold, and which will go unreported or languish at the bottom of page seventeen.[12] To which historian David Nasaw adds, 'An event becomes news only when journalists and editors decide to record it.'[13]

Economic competition among media companies can be sufficiently vigorous to deny any one of them significant *economic* power. Newspapers compete not only with each other, but with newer sources of news and entertainment such as Facebook. But the absence of economic clout does not mean that newspapers lack *political* power, perhaps not equal to those of the media barons of the eighteenth and early nineteenth centuries, but power nevertheless. Even as their economic power is diluted, even as they scramble for readers and advertisers, the political and cultural power of newspapers remains potent. *The New York Times* faces competition for readers and advertisers in its New York and national markets from *The Wall Street Journal*, local newspapers, electronic news, and others – and it is struggling to construct a newly profitable model. But that does not dilute the political power of the Sulzberger family, power disproportionate to their profits or wealth: they are media moguls. If proof is needed, consider the willingness of politicians to submit to grilling by the editorial boards of those and other newspapers in an effort to win the backing of proprietors, editors and reporters.

Still, Franklin Roosevelt was elected and re-elected despite the opposition of most of the nation's newspaper proprietors, who regarded him as a traitor to his class. His tool: direct communication with voters through his radio broadcasts, the 'fireside chats'.[14] More recently, Donald Trump, wielding a new media weapon of direct communication with the voters, Twitter, used its 140 characters to offset the hostile editorials and news coverage of the leading newspapers, in part by forcing them to report each tweet. But the old print products still possess enough clout to control much of the agenda of national discussion.

Newspapers face a new generation, members of which have never bought and will never buy a newspaper, and who regard Twitter and Facebook as their primary news sources. The print industry's ability to survive that competition in anything like its present form is uncertain, but in my view likely, for two reasons. The first is that the world is moving at a pace that is creating a hunger for news presented in a way that explains the images popping up on television sets and all sorts of other devices. Second, the disappearance of more and more newspapers leaves survivors with a larger share of the shrinking market – the Murdoch 'last-man-standing' scenario.

Unlike the Sulzbergers, whose dominance of the news agenda in America has been weakened but remains formidable, Murdoch's power in America comes in large part from his Fox News Channel (FNC), supplemented by the opinion pages of *The Wall Street Journal*.[15] That power, of course, is not overwhelming. FNC competes for viewers and ads with powerful broadcast networks and more liberal cable channels such as CNN and MSNBC. And with such as Facebook, increasingly the primary source of news for millions. The presence of those alternatives to Fox News as a source of information and a platform for advertisers can diminish but not wholly extinguish Fox's ability to wield political power. Politicians scramble for guest slots, even liberals who know that Fox News' interviewers do not find their views congenial. True or not, the perception that FNC was crucial to the election of Donald Trump has further enhanced its power, and as a by-product the animosity of James Murdoch. Although scandals have brought down Roger Ailes, FNC's creator, and star presenter Bill O'Reilly, among others, 'Fox News has remained No. 1 for the year [2017] to date in every key TV news rating measure'.[16] An audience that loyal surely conveys more than a dollop of political power.

The views of your average CEO and a folksy billionaire such as Warren Buffett, the fabulously successful liberal 'Sage of Omaha', matter, but those of a media mogul such as Rupert Murdoch matter more; witness the stir he created by merely tweeting that a presidential run by former New York Mayor Mike Bloomberg might be good for the country.

This is not to argue that the power of any single media outlet is what it once was. It isn't. In colonial America a wildly partisan press dominated political discussion, and a pamphleteer such as Tom Paine could importantly influence the course of events by rallying opinion in favour of the American Revolution when 'the summer soldier and the sunshine patriot' were abandoning the cause.[17] In Abraham Lincoln's day 'The press and politics often functioned in tandem as a single, tightly organised entity in the furious competition to win power and to promote – or, alternatively, resist – political and social change', writes Lincoln scholar and prize-winning author Harold Holzer.[18] Lincoln himself noted, 'He who moulds public sentiment, goes deeper than he who enacts statutes or pronounces decisions.'[19]

In the late nineteenth and early-to-mid twentieth centuries it was the press barons who wielded political power. Lords Northcliffe and Beaverbrook 'exercised detailed control over their favourite papers through a constant barrage of instructions ... Northcliffe and Beaverbrook shaped the entire content of their favourite papers, including their layout',[20] something Murdoch is said to have done from time to time with the *New York Post*, including changing the front page when Lachlan was supposed to be in complete charge of that tabloid. In the early days of the First World War, Northcliffe's *Daily Mail* is credited with playing a major role in bringing down Asquith's Liberal government.[21] In America, the famously self-promoting William Randolph Hearst, proprietor of the *New York Journal*, claimed paternity of the Spanish–American War, running a headline, 'How Do You Like the Journal's War?'[22] He never went so far, however, as to claim that 'It's The Journal Wot Won It'. Reports that Hearst cabled a photographer asking leave to come home from Cuba because there was no war cannot be verified: 'You furnish the pictures and I'll furnish the war.'[23] But if he did not 'furnish' the war, Hearst did give war fever a boost. His influence also extended to national and, especially, New York City elections.

Hearst, viewed by many of his contemporary British counterparts as 'the notorious anti-English American newspaper magnate',[24] might have had more influence in the long run on British than on American politics. In 1929, before his US lecture tour, Churchill wrote to Hearst, 'We must discuss the future of the world, even if we cannot decide it',[25] from which it is reasonable to conclude that Churchill, in addition to wanting to flatter Hearst, considered him a man of significant influence, for several reasons. Hearst's newspapers had a circulation of fifteen million, wide exposure for Churchill's political views. They might in addition provide lucrative writing assignments in the future. And, as Churchill wrote to his wife Clementine, Hearst introduced him to a circle of 'leading people' in America. Some provided private railroad cars and other luxuries that Churchill enjoyed. Some would later prove helpful when the Churchill finances were in disrepair, and when a wartime prime minister needed support from people of influence in America for his policies. But that was for another day: the trip during which Hearst had proved a generous host, wrote Churchill to Clementine, had enabled him to earn so much money that they would be 'comfortable and well-mounted in London this autumn'.[26]

Alfred Harmsworth, later Lord Northcliffe, went into the newspaper business because his successful magazine empire 'could not satisfy a growing appetite for influence'.[27] Later, in America, Henry Luce, dubbed 'the most influential private citizen in the America of his day',[28] felt no such need to branch out from the magazine business. He used revenue from his enormously successful magazines – *Time, Fortune* – to fund a large number of lucrative assignments for Churchill, and his influence to make life difficult for Franklin Roosevelt and his New Deal, and for any politicians who called for normal relations with communist China.

It is fair to say, then, that since around the turn of the twentieth century, when public opinion became a rising force in political life, media have mattered. But never as much as newspaper proprietors believed, or said they did. In 1931, Lords Beaverbrook and Rothermere, powerful press barons of their day, opposed Duff Cooper, Baldwin's candidate in a by-election for the parliamentary seat of Westminster St George's, a seat that would determine control of the House. Cooper nevertheless won.[29] As noted earlier, almost all newspaper proprietors opposed the election and re-election of Franklin Roosevelt, a 'traitor' to his and their class, but they failed to prevent him from handily winning four elections, defying not only the proprietors, but the two-term tradition established by George Washington, and despite obviously failing health that killed him only three months into his last four-year term. The millions who tuned in to FDR's fireside chats heard his deep, calm voice tell them where he planned to take the nation during the economic troubles of the early 1930s and in the run-up to war later that decade. Judging by the election returns, voters found those fireside chats more persuasive than the hostile print press, but not so overwhelmingly persuasive to develop support for the president when he overreached himself, as when he attempted to pack the Supreme Court with men (no women in those days) more likely to uphold the constitutionality of his New Deal legislation than the men already on the bench, or intervened in local congressional elections, to the annoyance of local politicians and the electorate.

The fireside chats were an early sign that a new technology – actually an old technology redeployed – could make print media less influential by enabling politicians to communicate directly with the electorate, and commentators to have their views heard without needing print media as an outlet. In FDR's day it was radio, also effectively employed by Churchill to become the 'roar' of the British lion. But despite his ability to take on and defeat newspaper proprietors, Roosevelt was keenly aware that print media were important transmission routes for his ideas and policies.

So he further reduced press proprietors' influence by going below their heads to charm their employees – columnists and reporters – among them Joe Alsop, whose columns ran three times a week in 300 newspapers from 1937 to 1974. Alsop intended his reportage and columns 'not to enlighten but to *effect*, to move the principal players on decisions'.[30] Roosevelt struck a bargain with reporters: he held frequent, informal chats with them in his office, providing them with news and scoops. In return they provided him with news and gossip from Washington and around the country. If they responded with favourable treatment of the president, they were ensured an invitation to the next news-making chat. That symbiotic relationship between reporters who need news and scoops, and who value the appearance of being 'insiders' who travel with presidents and prime ministers, and politicians who need favourable coverage, exists to this day, although the multiplicity of outlets provided by the internet much dilutes the importance of newspapers that few young voters read, and of proprietors. Indeed, even before media outlets began to proliferate, no less an influence in his day than Joe Alsop, by then retired, told an interviewer, 'No columnist has any power at all … The idea that anyone in the United States is foolish enough to think the way they do because some damn columnist thinks that way in the morning paper is an idea that only a columnist could believe.'[31] In 1979 over half *The Sun*'s readers 'voted contrary to its advice' to vote Conservative, and voted Labour.[32] Later, in 1987, only 40 per cent of *Sun* readers followed the paper's editorial call to vote Conservative.[33] More recently, Martin Kettle, associate editor of the left-leaning *Guardian*, argued that 'The big error politicians make is to believe that newspapers change the way that people vote',[34] a view that Stephen Glover, a British journalist who often comments on matters related to the press, shares. He put it succinctly in one of his columns: 'Newspapers cannot simply instruct their readers how to vote.'[35] That, of course, leaves open the possibility that newspapers can influence how their readers vote.

John F. Kennedy's mastery of television, including his decision to televise press conferences, substantially diminished newspapers' influence,[36] and his unflappability helped him overcome the opposition of a one-party press.[37] His effective use of that relatively new medium was decisive in his defeat of Richard Nixon, who at the time regarded television as a 'gimmick', changing his mind only when a young media consultant named Roger Ailes persuaded him to take the medium seriously.[38]

Which, of course, brings us to Rupert Murdoch, perhaps the last in the great line of media moguls and newspaper proprietors whose interest in influencing policy matches and in some cases exceeds his desire for profits. Rupert's view of the power of the press, including his own, is not easy to determine with complete confidence. For one thing, he knows that the perception that such power exists cuts two ways. It can increase his political influence, but it can also lead to calls for regulation of that power if it is seen as being so great as to enable him to subvert the democratic process. About a dozen years ago I told an interviewer from *The Observer*: 'I know that the editor's claim that "It's *The Sun* wot won it" ... is great stuff – but I don't believe it.'[39] Rupert did not disagree. He thought that *Sun* editor Kelvin MacKenzie's boast after John Major's surprise defeat of Neil Kinnock in the 1992 general election was simply incorrect, and that it would have been much more accurate to have headlined it, 'It's Kinnock Wot Lost It'. After all, the Labour leader ran what is generally regarded as a disastrous campaign, capped by a show of premature triumphalism.

Murdoch also objected because he knew that MacKenzie's boast was dangerous – it laid claim to more power than would prove to be politically acceptable in the long run. Some twenty years later he told the Leveson Inquiry that he found the headline 'tasteless and wrong' and that his son James recalled that MacKenzie received 'quite a bollocking' from his father at the time.[40]

Of course, Glover is right that newspapers cannot simply instruct voters how to vote. Just as it was not *The Sun*'s opposition but Kinnock's inept campaign wot lost it for Labour, it was not the *New York Post*'s opposition that brought Mario Cuomo's New York City mayoral bid to a sad end, but Cuomo's early and later-corrected failings as a campaigning politician. But even if Kettle, Glover and, if we take his denial of power at face value, Rupert are right to argue that the power of the press is more limited than its critics believe, so long as politicians believe that newspapers change votes, even if they are mistaken in that belief, they will act as if their belief is correct. That confers power on the press, deserved or not.

In addition to the direct effects on elections that newspapers and cable television have – not decisive, but not trivial – they affect the agenda in which the vote-seeker must operate. It is not only at election time that the views expressed in the editorial page of *The New York Times*, or in the op ed columns of *The Wall Street Journal*, or in Britain's *Sun*, or on Fox News Channel, matter, but in the intervening years when the agenda is being set for the campaigns. The media, points out Johan Norberg, a senior fellow at the European Centre for International Political Economy, 'reinforces a particular way of looking at the world'. Or, as the *Financial Times*' John Gapper puts it, 'Fleet Street's residual skill is agenda-setting. Television has wider news reach: ... But the stories that newspapers select and the opinions they express resonate.'[41] During the last great newspaper strike in New York City, television channels hired out-of-work reporters and editors to set the agenda for their news programmes, there being no print media from which to take guidance.

Print media also paint images of candidates and events that affect voters' interpretations of what they say and do. Remember: in addition to editors there are those often pesky investigative reporters who wield not insignificant power – the power to expose activities that politicians and governments prefer to keep secret. *The Guardian*'s Glenn Greenwald was instrumental in publicising

Edward Snowden's leaks of National Security Agency documents. *The Daily Telegraph* exposed MPs' use of public funds for private purposes. The *New York Post*'s Fred Dicker keeps New York State's political class on tenterhooks as its members do things they would prefer remain unnoticed, especially by government prosecutors. Former Supreme Court Justice Louis Brandeis had it right when he wrote, 'Sunlight is said to be the best of disinfectants',[42] and it is sunlight that investigative reporters provide.

In addition to editors and investigative journalists, the media industry includes the commentariat which can, as one member of that group put it to me, 'alter the atmosphere' in which political discussion occurs – witness politicians' concern with the views and writings of columnists such as *The Sun*'s Trevor Kavanagh and *The Guardian*'s Polly Toynbee in the UK and, in the US, *The Washington Post*'s conservative Charles Krauthammer and George Will, and *The New York Times*' liberal Tom Friedman and more moderate David Brooks. My guess is that in close elections the background music created by columnists far in advance and up to polling day does matter. Not as much as the punditry likes to believe, not as much as newspapers once did, but not as little as Alsop claimed.

It is enough to give key proprietors, including Rupert Murdoch, access to national leaders, often at their invitation. Rupert once complained to me that every time he came to Britain he felt obligated to say 'yes' to the incumbent prime minister's invitation to tea, or dinner, rather than devote all his time meeting with his executives. Not every business executive who finds himself in London, New York City or Canberra is implored to come to tea or dinner at No. 10 Downing Street, or City Hall, or The Lodge. And not every prime minister or mayor needs to be reminded, other than by Rupert's very presence and his history, that he is taking tea or dining with a man with strong policy views, who can be a useful ally or a dangerous enemy, albeit a charming dinner companion.

When Murdoch and Tony Blair, then leader of the opposition, met at a corporate gathering in Hayman Island, Australia, in July 1995, I watched with interest as they sized each other up, Blair trying to figure out whether he could possibly win the support of the Murdoch press, most particularly *The Sun*, Murdoch trying to determine whether this attractive, glib politician was more than that. Andrew Neil, who was also present at the conference, says Blair 'indicated that media ownership rules would not be onerous under Labour'.[43] Blair has since denied that any such conversation occurred, as has Murdoch, although New Labour did abandon the party's previous opposition to newspaper groups' purchase of ITV or Channel 5. I was with Murdoch and Blair during much but not all of the time they were together on Hayman Island – Blair left almost immediately after his speech – and never heard a specific discussion of media ownership policy. This does not mean it did not occur, but I am certain of three things: Murdoch was impressed with the willingness of Blair to beard the big bad media baron in his den; he was convinced that Blair's political strategy was not to reverse the Thatcher revolution but to seek the 'aspirational' vote by assigning Old Labour's high-tax, interventionist policies to the ash can of history (from which Gordon Brown later extracted them); and it is highly unlikely that Rupert put a direct question related to his commercial interests to the wannabe prime minister, or threatened to keep *The Sun* in the Tory camp if the answer were unsatisfactory. For one thing, Rupert always has had *The Sun* respond to his views on policy issues rather than to his commercial interests, and a threat to support John Major, whom Rupert and the key members of the *Sun* staff deemed somewhere between hapless and hopeless, would have been seen as an empty threat indeed. Equally important, someone with real power never has to resort to 'or else'. It is a key part of the Murdoch Method never to use those words in the presence of a politician. And I have never seen Murdoch in a situation in which he had to. Still, I hesitate to discount a factual assertion made by Neil.

My conversations with Rupert suggest four reasons for his switch to New Labour. First, he saw in Blair an opportunity to support a rising politician without jettisoning any of the policies he held dear: lower taxes, a more sensible welfare state, a vigorous pro-American, pro-Israel foreign policy. Second, it would be several years before Rupert forgave the Tories their knifing of Margaret Thatcher, one of his two favourite politicians – Ronald Reagan was the other. Rupert believed that Lady Thatcher, as she later became, saved Britain from imminent disaster by privatising the 'commanding heights of the economy' and taming the trade unions. Indeed, Rupert followed his idol's reining in of the coal miners' union by breaking the print unions. That, he believes, would have proved more difficult than it had been, or perhaps impossible, had Thatcher not insisted that her obligation to uphold the rule of law compelled her to provide police protection at Murdoch's new print facility in order to restrain rioting printers and the rent-a-mob that showed up in huge numbers, some, I was told, with new £50 notes in their pockets. The benefit to Murdoch was ancillary to her main purpose. I once asked Rupert why he did not make a similar effort to break the unions that so hampered the efficient operation of his *New York Post*; he said that was because Margaret Thatcher was not mayor of the city.

Third, Murdoch did not believe the incumbent Tory PM, John Major, capable of effectively leading the scandal-ridden party, divided over Europe and much else. Finally, after eighteen years of Tory governments, Rupert believed the nation would benefit from the restoration of two-party government, with Blair working to free Labour from the control of the trade unions, while the Tories repented their defenestration of Thatcher and developed policies appropriate to the coming twenty-first century. James Curran and Jean Seaton, by no means fans of Murdoch, summarised the situation reasonably well: 'Forced to choose between a failing government that had betrayed the Thatcher legacy, and a market-friendly opposition politician, he [Murdoch] was ready to do business',[44] even though, according to Murdoch, the switch to Labour led to 'the direct loss of 200,000 circulation'.[45]

Once Blair was in office, his and Rupert's views did not always coincide. Blair was an enthusiast of the European Union, Murdoch was not. Blair was eager to trade the pound sterling for the euro, not so much for economic reasons – economics was not his strength – but in order to have a seat at the top table of Europe and eventually realise his ambition to become president of the EU; Murdoch was opposed to the surrender of control over economic policy that such a scuppering of the pound would inevitably involve: he had even expressed concern about the loss of policy control that would result from Gordon Brown's decision to grant independence to the Bank of England.

The prime minister never did attempt to push through adoption of the euro, which might have been at least in part due to an unwillingness to lose the support of the Murdoch press. But it also might have been due in greater part to his inability to cope with his anti-euro chancellor of the exchequer, Gordon Brown, whose knowledge of economics he respected and whose ability as a relentless political infighter he feared.

Surveying the scene in Britain, it is fair to say that Murdoch held, and still holds, not inconsequential political power, constrained in part by the emotions he arouses among powerful elites that resent his assaults on the nation's cultural norms, and politicians opposed to his free-market, anti-union, free-trade, EU-sceptic views. In an effort to determine just how consequential a force Murdoch and his media holdings are in Britain, William Shew, a colleague with considerable empirical skills, and I attempted to measure that influence by determining how much time media users spent with

Murdoch products. That study, which survived critical review by most economists and even many Murdoch critics, found that readers and viewers spent 3.4 per cent of the time they devote to all media on Murdoch products. The dominant force in setting the national agenda when this study was done was the BBC, which captured some 44 per cent of time spent by consumers with all media products.[46]

In America, the situation is somewhat different, the constraints less binding. In part this is because Murdoch's political views do not arouse the intense hostility that they do in Britain, even following his support for Donald Trump and the emergence of Fox News as a political force to be reckoned with. In part it is because the First Amendment to the Constitution, guaranteeing the right of free speech, makes the libel laws less of a constraint on the operation of media properties in the US than in the UK, although those statutes cannot be completely ignored by proprietors such as Murdoch.

In New York City, the *New York Post*, a freewheeling tabloid similar but not identical to Britain's *Sun* – no nudity, tests having shown that such photos discouraged working-class readers from buying the then-afternoon newspaper on the way home from work – Rupert was able to rescue the seemingly doomed political career of Ed Koch, propelling the self-styled 'liberal with sanity'[47] into the mayor's chair with unrelenting pro-Koch stories and editorials. In the words of a vitriolic anti-Murdoch piece in the left-leaning *New Republic*, 'The [*New York*] *Post* practically invented the Koch candidacy.'[48] I well remember sharing an impromptu, no-servants-present fried chicken dinner in my New York apartment with Ed during the campaign. He told me that without the *New York Post* he didn't have a chance of winning the primary against the formidable Mario Cuomo, who later became governor of the state.

Once again we must be careful not to exaggerate Rupert's power. For one thing, Cuomo ran a disastrous campaign,[49] in part because he was either too principled or too doctrinaire to make the compromises necessary to get elected and then to manage the faction-ridden, diverse electorate in a city that was near bankruptcy, and in the throes of a blackout-induced bout of rioting and looting that made New Yorkers sympathetic to Koch's call for the restoration of the death penalty, something Cuomo would not support. Equally important, Cuomo displayed the ambivalence that was to become characteristic of his later political life – 'My frame of mind throughout was reluctance,' he later noted in his diary.[50] Which is why Cita and I were not entirely surprised in 1991 by another Hamlet-like performance by Cuomo. He was considering a run for the White House the following year, and party officials asked Cita, who had worked successfully with Mario when he served as lieutenant governor to Hugh Carey, if she would help manage his Washington office. We waited word in our Aspen office while the plane to take Mario to New Hampshire to file candidate's papers idled on a runway. Mario did not show up for the flight, for reasons never explained. I must confess to some relief, partly because I didn't fancy moving to Washington, and partly because I felt the anti-Murdoch press would be less than kind to Cita as the wife of a business associate of Murdoch at the time.

But the tabloid that was powerful enough to play a key role in turning City Hall over to Koch proved unable to win him the governorship of the state. When Koch and Cuomo re-engaged to battle for the Democratic nomination to state-wide office, Murdoch again supported Koch. To no avail. For one thing, the *Post*'s largely city-wide readership counts for less in state-wide than in city-wide elections. For another, Cuomo was a much-improved candidate, less uncertain that he wanted to win. And then there was Ed Koch's interview with *Playboy*, the soft-porn magazine that was somehow able to get politicians to talk too much – it was *Playboy* that got Jimmy Carter to admit, 'I've looked on a lot of women with lust. I've committed adultery in my heart many times.'[51]

And it was *Playboy* that probably cost Koch the nomination. In an interview with the magazine Koch shared his contempt for anyone living outside the limits of his beloved New York City. He told the interviewer that suburban life is 'sterile ... It's wasting your life', and rural life a 'joke ... wasting time in a pickup truck ... [and] a gingham dress'.[52] Even Murdoch's *New York Post* could not help Koch overcome the effect on suburban and rural voters of such an unsympathetic view of their lifestyles.

Rupert also lost a battle to hand the 1980 New York State Democratic primary to President Jimmy Carter, who was opposed for his party's presidential nomination by Senator Edward Kennedy. Kennedy won the state's primary over the opposition of Rupert's *New York Post*, but could not carry enough other states to overcome Carter. He returned to the Senate a dangerous enemy of Murdoch, pushing through legislation to prevent him from owning both a newspaper and a television station in the same city – a cross-ownership rule. 'Don't get mad, get even. Teddy Kennedy and Rupert Murdoch are a perfect match, just pure gladiators,' commented Sir William Rees-Mogg,[53] the man whose approval enabled Rupert to acquire the *Times* newspapers.

In Boston, Rupert held on to the *Boston Herald*,[54] but with considerable reluctance disposed of the *New York Post* in order to retain control of the city's profitable television station. Kennedy had, at least temporarily, got his own back: I recall the pain Rupert felt at the forced sale of the *Post*.

But the saga did not end with a *Post*-less Murdoch. After several twists and turns, the new owners found they could not make a profit and threatened bankruptcy and closure. The governor of New York, the same Mario Cuomo who had been savaged by the *Post* in more than one campaign, pleaded with Murdoch to resume ownership lest hundreds of workers be laid off. He was joined by Cardinal John Joseph O'Connor, Catholic Archbishop of New York, who was aware that many of the employees who would lose their jobs were Catholic. Murdoch was offered a temporary waiver from the cross-ownership rules but turned it down. The governor, the Archbishop, the trade unions and others pressured the FCC to grant Murdoch the permanent waiver he was demanding. He got it. And with it the ability once again to publish the loss-making tabloid.

This took place amid the joy of all save *The New York Times*. 'There should be no illusion that he is a healthy influence on American journalism ... his newspaper journalism has often been, at bottom, politically and professionally dishonest ... Mr Murdoch brought to New York second-tier tabloid journalism built on the flawed model of Australia and Britain ... Will print anything to make a penny ... counter to ethical standards crafted by American journalists since World War II,' claimed its editorial.[55] More was to follow over a decade later when Rupert made a bid for *The Wall Street Journal*.

Rupert's losses in local and state-wide elections do not mean that his newspaper is of no consequence. If it were, he might not be willing to bear the losses involved in ownership of the *New York Post*, especially now that the print company, News Corp, must stand on its own two feet. Conservative pundits find it a useful outlet for their views. Politicians want to have the *New York Post* on their side rather than have it trolling for stories that might damage them. Celebrities want it to cover their latest wanderings around the city in the latest fashions or in the relaxed garb they favour on off-days. Movie-makers using New York City locations want publicity while their films are being made. All those 'wants' represent favours that are Rupert's to grant – or not.

Rupert's successful re-acquisition of the *New York Post* after several twists and turns of the application of cross-ownership rules to his paper is still another example of his patience when stalking some prize and his ability to take the long view in matters of acquiring and owning assets.

Although the power of the *New York Post* decreases as the political battlefield widens geographically, that of another Murdoch asset increases. On the national level, Fox News Channel is a force, powerful enough to be given credit for turning the candidacy of Donald Trump from a joke into a victory over primary opponents left, right and centre, and then into a triumph over odds-on favourite Democrat Hillary Clinton.

There is no better testimonial to the power of FNC than the attitude of two of America's most important liberal politicians: Hillary Clinton and Barack Obama. Hillary Clinton did not woo Murdoch during her last Senate run because she agreed with his views, or admired the *New York Post*'s coverage of her husband's dalliances – 'horndog-in-chief' was one of the *Post*'s favourite titles for the commander-in-chief.[56] She sought the *Post*'s endorsement, which she received, to ensure that her victory would be by a margin so impressive that it laid the basis for future campaigns, as indeed it did, although those were waged without Murdoch support and ended badly for Clinton.

As the New York senatorial campaign got under way in 2006, and Rupert surveyed the field, forgiven were Hillary's attempts to restructure the healthcare system into a government-run enterprise; the rather arrogant manner in which she once had Murdoch tracked down on a boat on which we were sailing on Chesapeake Bay on a Sunday. In the rather bossy manner that still plagues her, she summoned him to a breakfast at the White House the following day, although he had previously refused that invitation to dine privately with her because he felt it would diminish the role of his reporters and editors. Rupert's preferred venue was the office of the *New York Post*, and a meeting that included his editors. He prevailed.

Mrs Clinton reciprocated a Murdoch-sponsored fundraiser at News' New York offices that added $60,000 to her already overflowing Senate campaign chest by appearing with him at the posh Café Milano in Georgetown at a party for Fox News Sunday, the network's flagship programme, an event staged with the glamour that only a Hollywood studio such as Fox can conjure (as we had come to appreciate while on the boat on the Hudson River on which the Murdoch–Deng wedding was held – to the accompaniment of a fireworks display that lit up the Manhattan skyline). Mrs Clinton's act of metaphorically sleeping with the enemy is one reason that to this day the left wing of her Democratic Party does not trust her. At the time, she defended her relationship with Murdoch: 'He's my constituent and I'm very grateful that he thinks I'm doing a good job.'[57] One constituent, one vote – except that this one owns the *New York Post* and Fox News.

President Barack Obama's willingness to appear on the channel for interviews with star Fox commentators and reporters is another proof of Fox News' clout. The president was regularly dragged over the coals by Fox News for his position on everything from healthcare and tax policy to foreign policy and his use of executive orders, and made his hatred of Fox News known at every opportunity. He surely would have continued his boycott of the channel had he not felt the need to gain access to an audience otherwise unavailable to him. Of course, it took a Murdoch-brokered peace between Obama and FNC boss Roger Ailes to make these interviews happen, but that merely emphasises the national power Murdoch created when he overcame losses and barriers to entry erected by cable companies to make FNC the power it now is.

Again, the power conferred by the news channel does not mean that Rupert wins all of the policy battles near and dear to his heart. He is a committed free-trader and for relatively open immigration, neither of which positions President Trump has adopted. Murdoch has also been unsuccessful in getting the US government to move against Google and other companies that he contends regularly steal his companies' intellectual product. They have tapped into 'a river of gold … They take [news content] for nothing',[58] he told a National Press Club audience. 'A platform for piracy',[59] echoed Robert Thomson, then chief executive of News Corp, in a letter to Joaquín Almunia, at the time European Commissioner for Competition.

And even though he now has an exemption, he would very much like the cross-ownership rules relaxed. Those rules might be one reason Murdoch did not make a bid for the *Los Angeles Times* – he owns a television station in LA – even though Anna Murdoch was quoted as saying that it felt odd to live in a city in which they did not own a newspaper.

All this begs for consideration of a much-asked question – does Murdoch exercise his power out of conviction or to further his commercial interests? I have had enough conversations with him about this to feel competent to offer an answer, but one sufficiently nuanced to leave neither Rupert's critics nor his defenders completely satisfied.

In the case of Rupert's support of Donald Trump's presidential bid, we should weigh up some conflicting evidence. As already noted, Trump's views on immigration and trade, restricting the former and sharply limiting the latter, are wildly at odds with Rupert's. Yet, despite that, Murdoch supported him. 'A plain-talking entrepreneur with outer borough, common-sense sensibilities … He's not one of "them".' For that read: an anti-elitist populist. It is undeniable that Murdoch, whose self-effacing personality is in sharp contrast with Trump's, would personally benefit from lower corporate taxes, the promised elimination of the inheritance tax and the repeal of a raft of regulations that the Trump team wants gone. But Rupert also feels, and believed before Trump came on the scene, that those policies are in the national interest as well as his own.

I rather lean towards the view that the Trump endorsement was less due to self-interest than to Rupert's desire to see the political establishment humiliated, and to a hope that the 'rookie mistakes' of this 'New Yorker, born and bred' would give way to a more presidential demeanour over time.[60] But there is more to guide us than this surmise: there also is history. I have seen instances in the UK when policy trumped self-interest. Rupert continued to suggest to his team that News support Gordon Brown, a high-taxing interventionist whose anti-free-market proclivities would hardly serve Rupert well were Brown to move into Downing Street, and whose Middle Eastern policy was inconsistent with Rupert's views on how to handle Iraq. Rupert's support for Brown, which had columnists and attack dogs at *The Sun* straining at the leash to back David Cameron, could hardly have been based on a cold-blooded consideration of News' commercial interests, which are hardly coincident with the views of the left wing of the Labour Party. In my conversations with Rupert I came away with the impression that his support for Brown stemmed from admiration for the Scot's work ethic, his personality and the fact that Brown's background was not dissimilar to that of his father, who grew up a son of the manse in a Presbyterian family. He also rather admired the ferocity of the guerrilla war waged against Blair from the Treasury. In the end, *The Sun* supported David Cameron's Tories, but by that time the decision was less Rupert's and more James Murdoch's – in fact, Rupert regretted the decision, or at least the decision to announce it on the very day that the Labour Party was conferring the keys to No. 10 on Gordon Brown. But in this instance, as in others, family solidarity was given top priority.

And it surely was not only a crass commercial motive that accounts for the intensity of Murdoch's support for Margaret Thatcher. Certainly her free-market policies, and intentions of shrinking the state and reining in the trade unions, were in line with his commercial interests. All to the good. But, in the end, the crucial factor was that she was no defender of the great and good that eventually became the so-called 'wets' that made her life miserable, the fact that she wasn't a toff. No force on earth could have shaken his decision to have *The Sun* back Margaret Thatcher, even though it risked antagonising the paper's Labour-leaning readership, masses of whom ignored its recommendation.

During these goings-on in British politics, nothing in any conversation I had with Rupert remotely suggested that his decisions turned on the question of what would be commercially advantageous. Whether that was a subject he preferred to keep to himself, I will never know, but I doubt it.

My view of the matter is not shared by everyone. His critics claim that he either backs likely winners or those who will add to his income and wealth, and cite his support of Hillary Clinton in her run for the Senate. They point out that Clinton's relatively unknown opponent for the New York Senate seat had no chance of winning, no matter how many editorials the *Post* carried on his behalf, and that Murdoch chose to ride a sure winner. One media lobbyist commented on the fundraising event sponsored for Senator Clinton by News Corp: 'Murdoch will be for the Republicans but he is also smart enough to know that the Republicans might not win. At some level, whether nationally or in New York, Hillary is the future and what savvy businessman would not want to put a line of interest in someone who will be the future?'[61] As it turned out, of course, Hillary Clinton proved not to be the future at all. The lobbyist was not alone. Several News Corp executives, reflecting the cynicism that is the hallmark of all good newsmen, also believe that Rupert first and foremost tries to pick and then back winners, especially those likely to protect his financial interests.

I think they are wrong. Mrs Clinton received that endorsement because she faced weak opponents, because she supported the Iraq

War and the state of Israel, causes dear to Rupert's heart, and because Rupert thought she was a good, hard-working senator, as *New York Post* editorials pointed out.

That support for a liberal Democrat was not extended to others of that ilk. Nothing, not even the many Democrats in key positions in the News organisation who were supporting Jimmy Carter and then Walter Mondale in their races against Ronald Reagan, could have persuaded him not to have the *New York Post* support the conservative Republican, an ageing actor and no sure winner at the start of the 1980 campaign: even with Murdoch's support, Reagan could garner only 37 per cent of the vote in the city's five boroughs. And the almost certain prospect of a second coming of the Clintons in 2016 could not persuade Rupert to back Hillary, the almost certain winner, in a city in which his chosen candidate, Donald Trump, did no better than Reagan in Manhattan, the *New York Post*'s major market. Murdoch's support could not persuade more than about 10 per cent of voters to opt for Trump.

None of this is to say that Murdoch is unaware of the value of political contacts and of the relation of his media outlets' positions to his business interests. Those who argue that he expects and receives a commercial quid pro quo for the support of his media properties can cite several examples of what on the surface appears to be political back-scratching. Ed Koch, who became mayor primarily because of Murdoch's support, during a newspaper strike allowed trucks of distributors of the *New York Post* (and all other newspapers) to use city highways usually barred to trucks to minimise the possibility of union attacks. Rudi Giuliani, whom the *Post* supported for mayor of New York, worked hard but unsuccessfully to persuade Ted Turner to allow Fox Cable News onto Time Warner's cable system in New York, which Turner refused to do on the prescient ground that Fox News would prove a formidable rival for Time Warner's CNN. Murdoch's support for conservative politicians was rewarded when key members of the Bush administration readily agreed to interviews by Fox News, boosting its ratings in the important war of the Sunday news shows for audiences.

But in the complicated world of the relation of media to politics, nothing is simple. Many instances of what seem to be political favours were also what the politicians providing them firmly believed to be in the national interest, or at least in the interest of their constituents. Margaret Thatcher provided police protection from rioters who attempted to bar access to News International's new plant at Wapping because, as she said, there is a national interest in preserving law and order. Blair's widely publicised[62] attempt to help Murdoch challenge former Italian prime minister Silvio Berlusconi's tight grip on the Italian television market by calling his counterpart, Romano Prodi, was no more than British prime ministers have always done for important UK companies by, for example, dragging key exporters along on foreign visits. The Koch and Giuliani moves were in the interests of the New York City economy, with perhaps some peripheral benefit to News Corp from having a friend at City Hall. Appearances by politicians such as those serving under President George W. Bush, and by President Obama, were as important to the politicians as they were to Fox News. And Blair did not take Britain to war in Iraq because Murdoch is some latter-day William Randolph Hearst, the newspaper mogul of yore who claimed credit for starting the Spanish–American War. Blair, like Churchill long before him, believed it was in Britain's long-term interests to stand with America, and would have done so regardless of Rupert's position on intervention, as he continues to maintain in the face of enormous pressure to recant.

But it would be naïve not to recognise that Murdoch knows that even though he does not seek quid pro quo deals with politicians who court his favour, his easy access provides him with an aura of power that gives him opportunities for commercial advantage that his rivals often do not have, especially in international markets. But he also finds access to politicians, their gossip, their views, exhilarating. Economists call this psychic income: non-financial rewards that come with a job. But from my conversations with Rupert I sense that there is even more to it than that. Rupert feels real pressure to carry out his father's command to affect events in a way that will improve the world, an instruction and example he takes extremely seriously. In 1908 Keith Murdoch, at the tender age of twenty-two, the same age at which Rupert was named managing director of the Adelaide paper after his father's death, went off to London and was willing to risk every cent he had to become 'qualified for good journalistic work … I'm sure I'm following the call of duty.'[63] Rupert feels he is also following the call of duty when he supports some candidate, or exposes the foibles of another, or tilts at the establishment.

All that said, what matters most to Rupert are issues, issues that transcend both his commercial interests – there are exceptions, as will be revealed – and his support for individual politicians. Blair won kudos from the Murdoch press for supporting the invasion of Iraq and the unseating of Saddam Hussein, and brickbats for his relaxed attitude towards rising crime and his support for multiculturalism. Brown won support for rejecting the euro, and was blistered for raising taxes. In my experience, when it comes to Murdoch, policy trumps commerce more often than the other way around. I am inclined to believe Rupert's statement, 'I take particular pride in the fact that we have never pushed our commercial interests in our newspapers.'[64] 'Never' might not be entirely accurate, but the basic observation is, in my view, correct. But thoughts of Rupert's commercial interests cannot be far from the minds of politicians who seek his support. And he knows it.

It is easy to infer from this book that Murdoch, an interventionist proprietor in the style of an old-fashioned press baron, operates without constraints on his power. That is not true. Constraints include libel laws, regulations on mergers and cross-media ownership;[65] the fairness doctrine applied to over-the-air networks in the US and regulatory restraints in the UK; reader and advertiser preferences; the views of his editors and columnists; the presence in all markets of competitors; the need to behave as a responsible corporate citizen and an overwhelming desire to discharge the heavy burden of responsibility placed upon him by his father.

There is no doubt that the fragmentation of the media markets makes Northcliffe, Hearst and Luce figures of a past that will not return. But neither is there any doubt that the effect of the changes in media markets on Murdoch's power is offset in part by several factors. The first is the sheer scale and scope of the Murdoch enterprises, even after the Disney sale. With 120 newspapers and HarperCollins Publishers, the print group is, according to Murdoch, the largest publishing operation in the English-speaking world.[66] That alone would attract courteous treatment from politicians and celebrities. Throw in the fact that Rupert presides over a media company that has an important presence not only in the news business but, still, in the very visible and popular worlds of sports and entertainment, and you have an operation that cannot go unnoticed in any country in which it operates. Politicians cannot but be aware of that power, especially those who will someday want one of his book publishing houses to publish and distribute their inevitable diaries or memoirs – such as Margaret Thatcher's memoirs and, despite Rupert's less than full admiration for him, John Major's. Or invite them to mingle with Tony Blair, Bill Clinton, Mikhail Gorbachev, Richard Nixon and other regulars at one of News' posh and intellectually rich corporate gatherings.

That, of course, is a blessing when News needs something from government and a curse when government decides News is too powerful to be allowed to operate without regulation or scrutiny or, in the case of China, to operate at all.

A second reason Rupert's influence has not been diluted quite as much as that of some of his competitors by the fragmentation of the sources of news and entertainment is his decision to diversify into some of those new areas, and take a huge risk in developing Fox News Channel into a conservative bulwark against the complete domination of such liberal influentials as the proprietor of *The New York Times* and the owners of competing cable channels. US cable channels such as Fox News are not bound by regulatory rules that require over-the-air networks to present what regulators deem to be unbiased reporting. Any politician dealing with Rupert knows that not only does the loss-making *New York Post* take its orders from Murdoch, but so, too, Fox News Channel, more so now than ever as the powerful Ailes is gone and Rupert occupies his seat, spending some 80 per cent of his time on maintaining that channel's lead during its time of troubles. Conservatives flock to its news and comment, and politicians angle for live interviews, as do celebrities who want to continue being famous for being famous. Meanwhile, celebrities who importantly influence the national culture and its fashion and other industries are aware that Fox Sports and the movie studio are best kept onside if at all possible.

Although fragmentation of the sources of news, entertainment, sports and commentary has reduced the power of many traditional players, and seen the emergence of Facebook, Google and a host of important bloggers, Murdoch still matters. Flush with cash, and operating in a regulatory environment more favourable to expansion, Murdoch has decided to 'pivot at a pivotal moment', as he puts it. For those counted among 'them' in his 'them vs us' equation, that is bad news. For those who aimed to upset the existing order, like Margaret Thatcher, Ronald Reagan and, it must be said, Donald Trump, it is good news.

CHAPTER 3

DEALS

'Bargain tough, but keep your promises' – Rupert Murdoch, 1998[1]

'If Rupert owes you one, you can bank on it you'll collect it somewhere in the future, in some way, undefined' – John Malone, *Financial Times*, 2009[2]

'Murdoch's great skill has – again, and again – been in deploying profits from one business to invest in growth elsewhere, creating *The Sun*, the Fox television network, and Sky' – Dan Sabbagh, *Guardian*, 2011[3]

'Rupert … is at his best as a consummate deal-maker, maybe the most formidable in the world for spotting an asset with potential and then acquiring it with the most imaginative financing methods' – Andrew Neil in *Full Disclosure*, 1996[4]

Rupert is seen by some as more of a deal-maker than a journalist, more of a financial engineer than an operating executive. That's an exaggeration, but there is little question that, in addition to what is called organic growth, Rupert has built his empire by shrewd deal-making, with significant failures along the way, rather like the dry holes successful oil companies drill to find the one-in-nine gusher that more than pays for the failures. He might rely on lawyers and bankers to close, or even seek their suggestions along the way, but the concepts, the vision as to where the pieces fit, is pure Murdoch. He is in charge, and any colleagues involved are supporting players. Rupert is an effective deal-maker because he brings to the table, in addition to cash or the ability to obtain credit, and effective methods of deal-making, a reputation that has been constructed ever since he first inherited his father's tiny newspaper, a reputation for integrity and for meaning what he says. No matter what anyone thinks of his politics, no matter whether the negotiators believe he has coarsened the culture, no matter whether regulators find some aspects of the transaction troubling, they agree on one thing: Murdoch will keep his word.

This is disputed by employees he has dismissed, including Harold Evans, a distinguished editor of *The Sunday Times* from 1967 until 1981, and then of *The Times*, until fired by Murdoch for reasons on which the two men disagree;[5] competitors he has bested; and some dispassionate observers of the media scene. In weighing the claims of the pro- and anti-Murdoch forces all I can do is rely on my personal experience over more than three decades, and what I was told by people on the other side of Murdoch deals, all of whom assure me that they found it safe to accept Rupert's word.

Against this valuable asset must be placed the liability side of the reputational balance sheet. For one thing, Rupert's reputation for overpaying or, more precisely, what failed bidders and some observers see as overpaying, encourages sellers to ask for higher prices than they might otherwise demand. For another, his association with racy tabloids, his unabashed enjoyment of them and the discomfort they cause the establishment, makes some sellers worry that if they allow Murdoch to buy the property he seeks, especially a newspaper, he will debase that product. That was a liability he carried with him into his negotiations to acquire *The Wall Street Journal*. Finally, there are Rupert's politics, and his refusal to conceal them from the liberal players that dominate the media industries. His political positions gave Hollywood a reason to oppose his entry into their liberal preserve, in which conservative actors complain of having difficulty finding work; New York elites a reason to bemoan his acquisition of the *New York Post*; and several cable systems a reason to deny access to the Fox News Channel, challenger to the liberal network oligopoly.

There can be little question that, viewed as a whole, Rupert's deal-making has been phenomenally successful. He didn't get from inherited ownership of a single struggling newspaper to control of a highly profitable media empire by relying on the cash flow from that tiny newspaper, or from persuading investors to make available the capital needed for that transition, at least not at first. He relied in important part on acquisitions: acquisitions of newspapers, a movie studio, television stations and a plethora of other pieces of what are now the twin spinoffs of News Corp. – News Corp, one of the world's largest print companies that includes all the newspapers and HarperCollins, and 21st Century Fox, an entertainment and news company that includes cable and broadcast television networks, and film studios along with related enterprises, some of which have been sold off.

But there is something different from the ordinary about these deals. Their success, at least from Murdoch's point of view, cannot be determined merely by counting beans, or studying profit-and-loss statements, or examining individual transactions. They must be viewed in the context of the long-run viability and growth of the enterprise. And weight must be given to non-economic factors, the psychic income mentioned in the previous chapter. The *New York Post*, finally reacquired after Rupert was forced to sell it to comply with rules against cross-media ownership, has never been profitable. But by any measure other than the conventional one it is a success – it conveys power and, for Rupert, is a very good reason to show up at the office every day. I remember one night, rather later than was our usual habit, coming out of '21' with Rupert after a quiet dinner. '21' was then one of New York's restaurants that catered to successful politicians (New York Governor Hugh Carey, Ted Kennedy, Richard Nixon), celebrities (Laurence Harvey, Lauren Bacall) and businessmen (Aristotle Onassis), the sort of place that prided itself, as the greeter once told me when in my younger day I asked where I might check my coat, on the fact that it didn't need a coat-check room because all its patrons had chauffeurs.

As Rupert and I walked up the few steps from the restaurant into the street, and were about to head up Fifth Avenue on foot to our respective apartments, a stranger stopped Rupert and said, 'God bless you, Mr Murdoch, for saving the *New York Post*.' That meant as much to Rupert as a similar blessing he had received from John Cardinal O'Connor for saving the jobs of so many of New York's Catholic pressmen.

So, too, with *The Wall Street Journal* (technically Dow Jones), for which Murdoch paid $5.7 billion, of which he had to write off $2.8 billion a few years later. Despite that loss, the acquisition was at the time, and remains to this day, the realisation of a long-held dream; *il ne regrette rien*. Like Murdoch's creation of *The Australian*, a serious broadsheet, and the purchase in Britain of *The Times* and *The Sunday Times*, the acquisition of *The Wall Street Journal* conferred the sort of respectability, not to mention clout, that does not come with owning a loss-making New York tabloid, or even profitable British ones. The addition of these three news outlets – *The Australian*, Times Newspapers, *The Wall Street Journal* – did little to enhance the company's bottom line, and indeed often hurt it, as conventionally computed. Yet, Rupert believes that each of these, especially when considered as part of the construction of the company as it now is, made good sense, that the red ink that accompanies the printer's ink was and is more than tolerable, especially when seen in the context of his dynastic ambitions.

Not that Rupert is fond of red ink. When acquiring newspapers in the UK he was initially able to stem the flow of red ink; more recently he has taken steps to do that at *The Wall Street Journal*. But he is not always successful in cutting costs – witness his experience with the perennially loss-making *New York Post*. Nevertheless, when it comes to newspapers he is reluctant to surrender to his accountants and some of his executives, and quit the field. He believes – this might well be an *ex post* rationalisation – that newspapers have an intangible value that can be made tangible in the context of a global media conglomerate with the scope of News Corp.

There is no doubt that his newspaper holdings in the US, Australia and the UK give him the power to influence events, and not only in the countries in which the papers are published. That power, in turn, gives the organisation a drive, a zest, an ability to attract executives and journalists who like to wake up every morning to go to a job that matters as much as or more than the bottom line. It provides an ingredient missing from many modern-day jobs – relevance, a form of compensation that the company can offer talented editors, artists and executives craving the excitement of immediacy, of having tales to tell and pulse-pounding experiences to share, not the least of which is contact with what Andrew Neil calls 'one of the smartest men in business with a restless, ruthless brain',[6] a description that my own experience verifies is as apt as it is colourful. Buy a newspaper and he gets more than presses and titles. He acquires intellectual capital on which he can call – savvy reporters with scores of contacts; columnists who are among journalism's best thinkers; archives and data that might be monetised; important pieces he can move around his international chessboard as needs not yet foreseeable emerge. Rupert summed it up after a closed meeting of his executives and editors: 'I can't imagine any life as interesting, exciting and rewarding as one spent in the centre of the media revolution.'

Finally, ownership of these assets, conveying the ability to affect public policy, enables him to fulfil his obligation to his parents to use his chosen profession for the good of mankind. As a young man, struggling to make his way in London, Rupert's father wrote to his own father, the Reverend Patrick Murdoch, 'My whole desire I think is to be useful in the world, really useful to the highest causes.'[7] Rupert's critics tend to view his references to Keith's influence as cynical, concocted to justify his ongoing quest for more and more power. I think they are mistaken – unless when Rupert discusses in private the effect of his parents' teaching he is the consummate actor, or at least good enough to fool me.

Always lurking in the background, whether of deals or of editorial positions, is a desire to discomfit the establishment. Clearly, this played a part in his persistent pursuit of *The Wall Street Journal*. Unless, of course, Rupert saw owning that property as providing the respectability that would make him a member of the establishment he professes to scorn, as some have suggested. Either way, that battle is worth examining as it involved the employment of many of the characteristics of what I term the Murdoch Method.

The first ingredient is Rupert's patience, a virtue not often attributed to this seemingly impetuous mogul. Over more than two decades Rupert occasionally mentioned to me his desire to acquire *The Wall Street Journal*, and I never doubted that if he succeeded it would be for him an acquisition as satisfying – perhaps more so – than his purchase of *The Times* and *Sunday Times*. (He once mentioned that he would trade his entire company for *The New York Times* and the power that would convey, but I put that down to idle chatter at a time before Fox News Channel provided national influence more than equal to that of *The New York Times*.)

Rupert had carefully followed the doings of each of the members of the Bancroft family, the controlling shareholders, for years, in a sense stalking them from a distance. The Bancrofts had owned *The Wall Street Journal* since 1902, an asset said to account for a little less than half of the family's current net worth of roughly $2.5 billion.[8] As a result of changes in the media industries and the family's policy of not interfering in the operation of the *Journal* – in essence, giving staff a blank cheque – the flow of dividends steadily declined, and with it several members' desire to hold on to what was becoming a trophy, a model of serious journalism, but also a financial drain. Rupert patiently waited for the strain of a declining asset to make itself felt on at least some family members.

In addition to his patience in stalking *The Wall Street Journal*, Rupert relied on another important feature of the Murdoch Method, the familiar driving force of 'us vs them'. Make no mistake: both parties were very much aware of this dimension of the fight for control. I know that to be the case not only from the Bancrofts' public statements, but from comments Rupert shared with me at the time. It was the practice of the UK company to arrange large invitation-only receptions on the occasion of many of Rupert's visits to London to provide him with an opportunity to meet and greet politicians, or, more precisely, for them to pay court to him. One such was held at the Serpentine Galleries. At one point, Rupert and I broke away from the crowd for a few minutes during which time he expressed his anger and frustration at the personal attacks the leaky Bancrofts were making, and *The New York Times* was featuring, disguising its desire to head off some real competition from a Murdoch-owned *Wall Street Journal* as mere reporting.

I couldn't help being reminded of reports of his anger at being forced to prove he was a fit and proper person to take the loss-making Times Newspapers Limited off the hands of the 2nd Lord Thomson of Fleet. In fact, Rupert was the only person the owners of Times Newspapers Limited trusted to honour his word to continue publishing the loss-making daily as well as the profit-able *Sunday Times*.[9] Still, Murdoch had to agree to being inter-viewed to determine his suitability as a future owner of Britain's newspapers of record. The very wise and universally regarded pre-Murdoch editor of and later columnist for *The Times*, William Rees-Mogg, helped Rupert clear that final hurdle to his acquisition of Times Newspapers by observing that the legalisms provided no real protection from a proprietor determined to ignore his guarantees. 'I thought therefore a judgment of character had to be made', and Rees-Mogg's judgement was that Murdoch would keep his word,[10] which he has.

But the process rankled. Indeed, when Russian oligarch and former KGB agent Alexander Lebedev bought *The Independent* with no such required showing of his proprietor's fitness (the print edition has since been discontinued), Rupert grumbled to me, 'A KGB agent is fit and proper to buy a newspaper, but when I bought *The Times* some said I wasn't.' This, three decades after he had to satisfy the establishment and the government of his fitness to own *The Times* – a long time for a perceived insult to rankle.

'They' made no secret of their disapproval of Murdoch's well-known love of sensationalist tabloid journalism, something the Bancrofts, some of whom felt they held the newspaper in some sort of trust for society, could not be expected to appreciate. Their view of their role as trustees is not dissimilar from Rupert's notion of his obligation to his father's injunctions, with this exception: Rupert has always known that to perform such a role profits are necessary, and to make money requires hands-on management of a newspaper. Many Bancroft family members, removed from the daily operation of *The Wall Street Journal*, neglected that imperative. Moreover, they believed that the tabloid style, if not the format, would be transferred by Murdoch, famously a hands-on proprietor, to the *Journal*, repelling readers and advertisers. My guess is that the Bancrofts believed the apocryphal story that the head of Bloomingdale's had once told Rupert that his store would not advertise in the *Post* because it is so downmarket that 'Your readers are our shoplifters'.

The Bancrofts were part of the very elitist, snobbish class that Rupert had always disliked. Their lifestyle did not appeal to the left-leaning *Guardian*, any more than did their agreement to sell to Rupert: 'They live a genteel life. They breed show horses. They sail. They farm … There was standing for principle and then there was $60 a share.'[11] One reason Rupert came to America was to escape a society in which members of England's self-styled upper classes regarded Australians as more like unlettered Americans than true-born English folk, a slight to which Anna was particularly sensitive. Leslie Hill, a Bancroft family member, resigned from the Dow Jones board by a letter in which she said that the good financial terms offered by Murdoch failed to outweigh 'the loss of an independent global news organisation with unmatched credibility and integrity',[12] the clear implication being that Rupert's 'integrity' was in question. Hill and other Bancroft family members and their advisers who agreed with her were undoubtedly thinking of the *New York Post* and perhaps even *The Sun*, without considering that *The Australian* and *The Times* and *Sunday Times* of London were far different, properly sober in their handling of news and opinion. After all, Murdoch understands the differences in the reader and advertising markets in which different newspapers must compete, and knows how to distinguish what is required to be successful in what he half-jokingly calls the 'unpopular press' market that he contrasts with the 'popular press' – his beloved tabloids. So the broadsheets remained unsensational. Murdoch was not about to spend billions on *The Wall Street Journal* and then destroy it.

The third feature of the Murdoch Method that was deployed in the battle for *The Wall Street Journal*, in addition to patience and reliance on the adrenaline produced by 'us vs them', was the development of an innovative structure to overcome objections by the sellers and regulators. The Bancrofts were worried not only about Murdoch's style of presenting news, but about the possibility that he would distort reporting of hard news to suit his political convictions, and reserve his opinion pages for right-wing columnists. When a similar issue emerged during Rupert's hunt for Times Newspapers he agreed to what in Britain are called 'undertakings'. To satisfy the objections of government regulators that his acquisition, added to his already formidable holdings, would give him excessive power over the nation's views and opinions, Rupert undertook to give an independent board the power to review his choice of editors.[13] In one election cycle, this arrangement resulted in sufficient independence to allow the editor of *The Times* to abstain from supporting the candidate favoured by the editor of *The Sunday Times*. And, in 2016, the editor of *The Times* supported the campaign to Remain in the European Union, while the editor of *The Sunday Times* backed the Leave campaign.

The only significant changes driven by Rupert were to convert *The Sunday Times* into a truly multi-section paper, and to change *The Times* from a broadsheet into a tabloid format in November 2003, neither of which contravened his undertakings. The multi-section *Sunday Times* was the brainchild of Andrew Neil, its then editor. He was convinced that the day of the one-section newspaper had passed. Neil rehearsed one of his several presentations with me in his London office, and off we went to beard Rupert at News Corp. headquarters. Neil explained that his goal was to allow the paper to be divided up in accordance with the separate interests of each family member. Rupert listened with mounting enthusiasm, made a few suggestions and turned Neil loose to revolutionise the weekend newspaper market. If recollection serves, my suggestion for a separate book review section, along the lines of the one in Sunday's *New York Times*, was rejected on the quite sensible ground that British publishers are too mean to spend significant sums on the advertisements needed to support such a section.

When Rupert decided to test-run a tabloid edition of *The Times*, alongside the broadsheet format, there was considerable discussion of whether the world was coming to an end. '*The Times* is overturning 218 years of tradition by going tabloid from next

Wednesday,' reported *The Guardian*.[14] Fear not, replied Robert Thomson, its editor at the time, the move was being made not to change the paper's 'values and content' but only its 'shape'.[15] The historic change was aimed at responding to the demand of commuters on the crowded Tube for a physically more manageable format. A former editor of *The Sun*, approving the change, told me at the time that it was necessary because not every commuter has a forty-inch wingspan. Rupert took a gamble. He knew that some advertisers who buy big, full-page display ads would be displeased,[16] but balanced that against the need to attract young readers who prefer the tabloid format, and to meet the competition from free sheets being distributed at Tube and railway stations. After an experimental period in which the paper was produced in both the broadsheet and tabloid formats, the larger size was abandoned.

But throughout all these changes, editorial policy remained in the editors' control. Under the terms of Rupert's undertaking at the time he acquired the titles, an editor has the right to appeal to an independent board of directors if 'he felt himself in conflict with the proprietor ... This board alone ... [has] the power to appoint or remove an editor.'[17] Therein lay a way to satisfy the Bancrofts. Rupert agreed that Paul Gigot, the *Journal's* editorial page editor, would have the authority to choose editorial board members and columnists, as well as the editors of the book review and other sections, and have final say over op ed pieces and editorial positions. If Murdoch interfered, Gigot could appeal to a special independent committee, which could publish its report on the *Journal's* editorial page, and have recourse to the courts should Murdoch breach the 'firewall' between the editorial page and its new owner.[18] The respected then publisher of the *Journal*, L. Gordon Crovitz, advised readers in an open letter, 'The same standards of accuracy, fairness and authority will apply to this publication, regardless of ownership.' In my view, the credibility of this feature of the deal hinged less on bits of paper than on Rupert's reputation for keeping his word, which he had demonstrated in other deals; most notably after acquiring Times Newspapers, and after bankers had rolled over the loans taken on by Rupert to finance Sky in exchange for promises of tighter financial control.

A fourth aspect of the Murdoch Method became apparent after the deal was closed. Rupert's decision to break the strike of Britain's technophobic print unions that followed the opening of a modern print plant at Wapping was a legend in the industry. It naturally unsettled the staff of the *Journal*, which wanted to hear from him his plans for the paper.

I had seen the show Rupert put on to reassure the *Journal's* staff before. In 1990 I accompanied him to Budapest in Peter Abeles' jet – cigar smoking blessedly permitted. Abeles was brought up in Budapest and made his fortune in Australia, where he started peddling books and clothing, and ended up controlling TNT, one of the world's largest transportation and shipping companies at the time. He and Rupert had done business before – when the railways refused to distribute Murdoch newspapers during the Wapping strike, Abeles' TNT took over that violence-threatened job. Rupert had invited me to accompany him to Budapest, where he was to close a deal for the purchase of a 50 per cent interest in two Hungarian newspapers, a tabloid, *Mai Nap* (Today's Day), and a weekly, *Reform*, for $4 million. Small change, but part of a plan to expand into Eastern Europe – Poland was next on the list – where democratic reforms were spawning new, independent publications. After a trip from the airport led by a police motor-cycle escort, sirens screaming, if I remember it right, intersections closed to prevent delays in our passage to the print plant, we were given a tour of the print works by a ministry guide whose assignment was to see the deal done and the state-owned bank that financed the publications taken out of the picture. As we were leaving the plant one of the employees, a reporter if I recall correctly, called out to Rupert that he would like to ask a few questions. The guide quickly responded with a loud 'No', and urged us on. Rupert ignored him, pulled up a chair and answered questions – in the same way as he did more than a decade later when he visited the offices of *The Wall Street Journal*. The deal was closed, but profits proved hard to come by as the independent papers found little market for their anti-communism after the collapse of those governments. Besides, Rupert doesn't really enjoy owning newspapers he cannot read.[19]

The Wall Street Journal's staff, employees who had operated for decades with no need to pay any attention to the paper's financial state, were not looking forward to submitting their careers, their expense sheets and the continuation of their pay cheques to the market forces they had always championed in their columns. It was far more restful to extoll the virtues of capitalism nestling in the arms of an organisation that functioned more as a welfare state than a profit-making enterprise. These staffers made panicked calls to the Bancrofts and to any influential opinion-makers who might matter, urging the Bancrofts not to sell and the influentials to use any power they had to prevent the sale. Those efforts failed.

As in Budapest, Rupert took to the newsroom to assure the staff that those who chose to stay with the paper and proved themselves competent had nothing to fear. He portrayed himself as the saviour of a paper doomed to fail if he had not stepped in, and told the staff that he was prepared to make a major investment in the paper, which he did, expanding the number of sections. Since that initial burst of investment, falling ad revenues have forced a degree of retrenchment in staff and size of the paper. But a new, sumptuously produced Lifestyle section survived the cuts and accompanies some weekend editions. A Review section features book reviews and coverage of the arts, to which a few pages of the daily editions are devoted. There is more coverage of sports, but not the extensive sports section once discussed. The weight given to various subjects has also changed. Murdoch moved the paper's page one from purely business coverage to that of 'a more general interest publication', part of his plan to compete more directly with *The New York Times*. 'The coverage of international events that directly affect the United States' has increased, at the expense of environment, education and the media.[20] Some critics say that stories are shorter in order to please readers (and upset writers).

Sarah Ellison, a former *Journal* reporter, details the changes Murdoch has made in the paper, commenting favourably on some, less favourably on others, in her *War at The Wall Street Journal*.[21] In an interview in 2015, five years after the publication of her book, she concludes that the paper has 'tilted rightward politic-ally' but 'the editorial page has stayed true to itself this entire time [since the acquisition]. There was always a real wall between the news section and the editorial page of *The Wall Street Journal*, and that continues to exist.' She sums up the seven years since Murdoch prised the *Journal* from the control of the Bancrofts:

> It's still a great paper, and you can't ignore the fact that it has maintained a newsroom at a time when many, many newspapers have hollowed out. One of Murdoch's great legacies will be that he is someone who believed in the newspaper business. That was something that defined him back in 2007 when the deal happened, but it makes him almost unique today. And for that, I think the people who are still at *The Wall Street Journal* today are very grateful.[22]

In the end, Rupert persuaded the Bancrofts that their choice was to sell to him, or watch the paper fade from the scene, just as he persuaded the owners of Times Newspapers and the regula-tors who would have barred him from reacquiring the *New York*

Post that it was him or closure. He didn't directly copy Margaret Thatcher's famous TINA slogan – there is no alternative – but he got his point across anyway. Murdoch was offering a large premium over the market price of the shares, so large that there were no other bidders, which the Bancrofts discovered when potential white knights, including Warren Buffett, groups put together by General Electric, another involving Barry Diller, and several others rebuffed pleas to persuade them to bid. When, at the last minute, Rupert agreed to pick up some of the legal costs reluctant family members had incurred while trying to derail his bid, the deal was done. The Bancroft family member who called Rupert's bid 'a reality check' understood that News Corp.'s resources would enable the *Journal* to survive the gale-force winds of change that were blowing through the newspaper industry. 'On the one hand it is quite sad, but on the other it was the only reasonable thing to do,' said family member Elisabeth Goth Chelberg. 'Now I look forward to a better Dow Jones. It's going to have more money and a world presence and all of the things that it could have and should have had but didn't.'[23]

How does it work in practice, this odd arrangement in which the entrepreneur who is risking large sums on a bet that he can turn around a declining enterprise cedes control of an important part of the operation of his newspaper to an independent board with huge power over his selection of the editor, perhaps his most important employee? Rather well, is the answer.

No less a fiercely independent soul than Andrew Neil, the brilliant editor of *The Sunday Times* from 1983 until 1994, and no toadying courtier in what he calls 'the Court of the Sun King', concludes in his autobiographical sketch of his days with Murdoch: 'He kept to the letter of his promises to Parliament of editorial independence when he bought Times Newspapers in 1981.'[24] The proprietor made clear what 'he liked and what he did not, where he stood on an issue of the time and what he thought of a politician in the news', but, true to his undertaking to maintain the authority of the editors, he never ordered Neil to spike a story or editorial. Not that Neil would take such an instruction, or that Rupert would issue one. Rupert knew a good editor when he saw one. I recall being told of the Saturday evening when Rupert and Anna wandered into Neil's office as he was putting the final touches on the Sunday paper. A shouting match arose between Neil, a Scot who opposed Scottish independence, and Murdoch, a Scot once-removed who was leaning in favour (his grandfather was a minister of the Free Church of Scotland). Anna, sensible as always, suggested to Rupert that they move on to their next appointment. *The Sunday Times* remained staunchly in favour of preserving the Union, and Neil remained in the editor's chair.

As is his habit, Rupert undoubtedly grumbled inaudibly as he retreated. And probably more loudly when Neil supported Michael Heseltine's effort to depose Margaret Thatcher as prime minister and leader of the Conservative Party. However, he made no move to do to Neil what Neil tried to do to Thatcher. And both Robert Thomson and John Witherow, then editors respectively of *The Times* and *The Sunday Times*, and both still in News' employ, say Murdoch 'has never tried to influence coverage or interfere in their running of the newspapers'.[25]

For this strange arrangement to work – a proprietor limited in his choice of editors – common sense must prevail. The independent directors know it would be unwise to impose on the proprietor (and source of funds) an editor he thought unsuitable, and the proprietor knows that he cannot ram a candidate, whose major qualification is a willingness to do as the proprietor asks, down the throats of the independent directors. Rupert tried to explain his view of the arrangement in an interview with *The Wall Street Journal*'s Andrew Higgins shortly before the Bancrofts agreed to sell:

In an interview in his New York office ... the Australian-born magnate spoke openly about his hands-on style.

'When a paper starts to go bad and go down the drain, the buck stops with me,' he said. Shareholders 'never ring the editor, they ring me,' he said, adding that has 'once or twice' led to 'very unhappy but necessary decisions' to replace editors.'[26]

As with Andrew Neil, so with Paul Gigot: the likelihood of a battle is small. Gigot and Murdoch agree on most things, and Murdoch has no desire to damage the reputation of the paper, into which he has poured millions to broaden its coverage, and make it a real general-purpose newspaper that includes extensive foreign coverage and now outsells *The New York Times* handily on weekdays, and runs about neck and neck with it on weekends – this as far as I can tell from circulation data now complicated by non-comparable data on digital circulation.

How this circulation battle will end may depend more on broad trends in the media industry than on the abilities of the owners and editors of *The Wall Street Journal* and *The New York Times*. The drift of eyeballs to internet products, the appearance of new, instant sources of news, advertisers' need to follow eyeballs, all are combining to force cutbacks in newspapers as print advertising declines, and at an accelerating rate.[27] Increases in digital subscriptions cannot seem to offset the revenue effects of declines in print advertising. In the case of the *Journal*, the cost cuts are designed 'to make the print newspaper more sustainable for the long haul and help accelerate the newsroom's digital transformation'.[28] *The New York Times* is following the same path as the *Journal*, cutting staff, including in its case the position of public editor, which had been established to receive and consider readers' complaints of bias and errors in coverage.[29]

One Murdoch-instituted change remains: the paper's coverage is still broader, especially of international news. Despite the temptation that straitened financial circumstances puts on Rupert to take control of the editorial content of the paper, the deal that left control of the op ed pages to editors and a board independent of Murdoch survives. This, even though the editors of the *Journal* persistently attacked Donald Trump during the 2016 presidential campaign, while the *New York Post*, a paper Murdoch does control, supported him.

None of this should be taken to mean that Murdoch is indifferent to who edits his newspapers. He has strong opinions on political and social matters and would not, for example, offer the outside directors for their approval a candidate with decidedly left-wing views. And he does need someone willing to stand with him when a major overhaul of a paper is needed, to do the bloody work of cost reduction, replacing dead wood, introducing new technology, all of which Andrew Neil did at *The Sunday Times* and Murdoch's managerial appointments have done at *The Wall Street Journal*.

Murdoch's penchant for deals that do not satisfy conventional standards of success does not stop with newspapers. Just as oil wildcatters know they must bear the cost of dry holes to come up with an eventual bonanza, so any deal-maker knows that he will regret some of his gambles. But Rupert's failed deals border on the spectacular. The history of his involvement with Gemstar, developer of an interactive television programme guide system, is too convoluted to detail here.[30] Suffice it to say that Murdoch wanted to acquire the patents of Gemstar, which he merged with his *TV Guide*, and after a round of deals with John Malone, who over the years has assembled a portfolio of cable and related companies, ended up with 41 per cent of Gemstar-TV Guide just as its shares started to slide. At one point the market capitalisation fell from $20 billion to $1 billion (before recovering somewhat) as new technologies took over the television listing business, and fraud by the company's former CEO was uncovered. Estimates of News Corp.'s eventual loss after disposing of what was left of the company are difficult to come by, but a reasonable estimate is upwards of $6 billion.[31]

Nor was Murdoch able to achieve the results he sought in another much-touted bit of deal-making. When he bought Myspace for $580 million in 2005, he outbid, among others, Viacom, whose chairman, Sumner Redstone, promptly fired his CEO, Tom Freston, for failing to outbid Murdoch; losing the bid was 'a humiliating experience',[32] Redstone told interviewer Charlie Rose. In 2006 Myspace surpassed Google as the most visited website in the United States, and until 2008 it was the most visited social networking site in the world – value, $12 billion. Enter Facebook and exit News Corp. from Myspace, which it sold in 2011 for $35 million.[33]

A partial summary of what went wrong is contained in an interesting article by tech reporter Ross Pruden:

> For anyone who used both of those social networks, the grievances against Myspace are easy to list: too many ads, irrelevant ads, poor programming leading to browser crashes and typographic eyesores ... Myspace users saw Facebook as a better run and cleaner social network. That's why we all migrated ...
>
> What went wrong? ... A very simple management mistake News Corp. made. News Corp tried to guide Myspace, to add planning, and to use professional management to determine the business's future. That was fatally flawed when competing with Facebook which was ... letting the marketplace decide where the business should go.[34]

The young, freewheeling staff at Myspace simply did not fit into the Murdoch culture, which had until then successfully accommodated a variety of talents and personalities, but which by the standards of the new generation of entrepreneurs was more than a bit buttoned up, never mind Murdoch's brief flirtation with black T-shirts and turtlenecks before compromising with the suit-but-no-tie he sported when last we met in his office. Besides, it is one thing to integrate a seemingly odd intellect or talent, another to do it with an entire firm from a very different industry.

It is also clear that News did not think through the implications for a major news corporation of retaining the relaxed attitude of Myspace towards questions of privacy and safety of young users. Most important, Rupert couldn't keep his hands off his new acquisition. He appointed one of his executives, Ross Levinsohn, to look after Myspace. Levinsohn, 'used to more disciplined execution',[35] decided to 'professionalise' the operation. 'Every time we tried to professionalise the place they resisted.' 'Professionalising' included raising prices at the Myspace cafeteria and lowering the per diem meal allowance, and, in the words of Chris DeWolfe, one of Myspace's founders, 'more meetings ... three different levels of finance ... you sort of end up taking your eye off the ball'.[36]

Throw in a bit of News Corp. greed that led to an increase in ads, many showing rotting teeth and stomachs bulging over trousers, ads that users resented both because of their number and their character, ads the founders could not get 'the various levels at News Corp to drop', and failure was assured.[37] 'We just messed up,' Rupert recently told an interviewer. 'The buck stops with me ... It was growing like crazy, and the chief executive of Fox and myself said, "well, we don't know enough. We've got to get advice." We took bad advice and put in a layer of bureaucracy from our own company that didn't know any more than we did ... We either should've had faith in that management, and let it run, or changed it and found someone.' Then, in what can be taken either as a lame attempt to justify failure or a statement of Murdoch's honest opinion of his failed deals: 'But we learned from it. You've got to learn from these experiences.'[38] Defeat, in short, has its value, not as great as winning, but greater than avoiding risk at all costs. I would add another lesson from the Myspace fiasco: Rupert is better at challenging an entrenched incumbent – newspaper barons in Australia, the BBC, the newspaper unions, the US television oligopoly – than in holding on to a market-leading position such as Myspace had, and lost to a feisty newcomer, Facebook.

I have always worried about Rupert's lack of familiarity with the digital/internet world. As early into the digital age as 1998, James Murdoch, then a tender twenty-six-year-old, told a meeting of company executives at Sun Valley, including his father, 'We are woefully unprepared for this digital tidal wave that is now only minutes from shore. And there is no one to blame but ourselves.' James was talking tough to proud veterans of the newspaper industry and victors in its wars, even advising one prominent *Times* journalist that unless the company embraced the digital age he might as well write his columns on the back of a paper napkin and toss it away. When I reviewed a draft of the speech, I told James that it might not bode well for his future to insult people with whom he would have to work. He persisted and, in the end, was right and I was wrong: News needed a wake-up call. Indeed, even as late as seven years after James tried to shake the organisation awake, Rupert told the American Society of Newspaper Editors, 'I'm a digital immigrant. I wasn't weaned on the web, nor coddled on a computer … The peculiar challenge, then, is for us digital immigrants – many of whom are in positions to determine how news is assembled and disseminated – to apply a digital mindset to a set of challenges that we unfortunately have limited to no first-hand experience dealing with … We've been slow to react.'[39]

James's display of stubborn courage, and knowledge of a world foreign to many of the company executives in the audience, is one reason I have always felt that under certain circumstances James Murdoch could combine his knowledge of that 'digital tidal wave' with a more modern sensibility – think Rawkus Records – to make an important contribution to the companies' success in the twenty-first century.

All this creates a dilemma for anyone trying to step back and take a long look at Murdoch's Method of deal-making. He bought the *New York Post* as his most significant entry into the world of New York politics and gossip. It has consistently lost money, which Rupert rather suspected it would – witness his statement to Alex Cockburn in an interview in 1976: 'You get to a paper that is not making money ... Then you make allowances that it's in New York and allowances for the fact that you're bloody keen to get it and a certain amount of sense goes out the window, and you do the deal. You've got a gut feeling about it.'[40] Murdoch felt then, and feels now, that the losses are worth taking 'for the thrill of owning a paper in New York – a city of enormous power and patronage and one of his principal homes. He could not contemplate living in a city in which he did not publish a newspaper,' writes his biographer, William Shawcross.[41]

His UK broadsheets occasionally eke out a small profit, but that's about all. News Corp recently had to write down the value of its Australian and UK print properties by US$785 million.[42] Rupert was forced to take a large, $2.8 billion write-down on the $5.6 billion he paid for *The Wall Street Journal*,[43] although the final verdict will not be in until we see what he can make of the *Journal*'s extensive database and other products. But move away from print, where the payoff is in power and where Rupert sees value in the intellectual capital and the opportunity to discharge his perceived obligation to his father, and the record of Murdoch's acquisitions becomes a happier one. Except for a few deals such as Myspace and Gemstar, his other acquisitions, such as those of television properties, sports rights and what is now 21st Century Fox, have paid off handsomely.

As have his big gambles on generic growth, each of which involved financial commitments every bit as large as any of his acquisitions. The billions he risked on Sky and on Fox News, both of which I watched bleed cash in their early days, are being repaid many times over. It was on 18 December 1988 that Cita invited Rupert, in London without his family, to come to our flat in Cadogan Square for Sunday lunch, just the three of us, as that was the absolute capacity of our flat. During lunch Rupert asked if I might get Harvard's Kennedy School to extend my leave so that I could stay in London and help Andrew Neil, who was to add to his chore as editor of *The Sunday Times* the job of getting a new enterprise, then called Sky Television, off the ground. I thought I could arrange it, which I subsequently did, and asked Rupert when he planned to be on air. February of next year was the response – only a few months away. And the satellite had not yet been launched. Not to worry, he assured me: the satellite is to be launched from French territory in Africa in December, and the French workers want to be home for Christmas.

My decision to forego time at Harvard, which I was thoroughly enjoying, in order to help Andrew with his new assignment proved to be one of the best I have ever made. The obstacles to the success of Sky were formidable. Labour town councils tried to make it impossible to install dishes in council flats; British Telecom initially could not provide us with the number of telephone lines we needed to solicit and serve customers; British Satellite Broadcasting's five-channel system had the backing of deep-pocketed companies, early regulatory blessing and what Neil calls 'the backing of the British Establishment',[44] and a two-year head start; equipment manufacturers were reluctant to produce the boxes and dishes we needed for fear that, if Sky failed, they would be lumbered with useless inventory; British consumers could not understand why the existing four channels did not provide more than enough choice; we had no marketing plan. It was a typical Murdoch venture: get it started and fix it as we go along.

That Andrew Neil was the man to tackle these and other problems I had little doubt, and so took on the role of his backstop – doing whatever was needed, day to day, to get Sky on air by Rupert's target date. That was not always easy. I would pick Andrew up at his flat in Onslow Square in the morning, en route to Sky headquarters at Isleworth, in an effort to get him to our first meeting on time. I sometimes succeeded. It now seems ironic that keeping our Disney partner onside was not easy, as the Disney hierarchy was not designed to function at Murdoch–Neil warp speed when it came to decision-making, requiring me to pour oil on waters troubled by Andrew's impatience and less than emollient approach to the Disney representative. As Neil puts it in his memoir, 'A merger between Disney's cautious corporate culture and the buccaneering Murdoch was not likely to be a marriage made in heaven … Disney was not used to doing business in this cavalier way. Its caution became an impediment in our rush to air.'[45] Neil is not famous for tolerating impediments.

But, in the end, it was worth the struggle, my reward coming in more than adequate financial compensation, excitement stemming in part from our ability to take on so many establishment opponents, and the success in meeting Rupert's target date for initiating the service. On Sunday 5 February at beautiful Syon House, Rupert pushed the appropriate button and scores of monitors displayed the Sky channels for an assemblage of notables. It was a close-run thing. Final construction was completed the previous day, and when we discovered that the lovely old pile at Syon had too few electrical outlets, a generator was flown in from France by Thomson to provide additional outlets for our monitors.

This venture reflected almost all the features of the Murdoch Method. It was aimed squarely at a competitor, BSB, which had as its model another competitor, the BBC.[46] It was a spine-tingling bet-your-company gamble, so innovative that no traditional cost–revenue projections, even if developed, could be credible. Instead, we had Rupert's judgement that he had an opportunity to do what he loves to do and does best: unseat the government's chosen entry into the satellite business and provide competition for the BBC. As Rupert saw it, there was considerable demand for programming not sufficiently provided to the BBC's massive audiences by the elites that controlled BBC programming. Sky would fill that gap, expanding coverage of sports such as football and many of the tennis tournaments not shown in full by the BBC, tapping into the film libraries of Fox and other studios, providing then unheard-of, rolling twenty-four-hour news, as well as plenty of high culture. And there were two revenue streams to be had: one from viewers who would subscribe to the service, another from advertisers eager for access to a mass audience, especially one that included large numbers of sport-watching males who buy beer, cars and other products.

As we geared up to offer the satellite service, I had a front-row seat from which to study the Murdoch Method. First, the political. It came as no surprise that the politicians did not relish a major Murdoch entry into television broadcasting. Some had been savaged in his tabloids; others genuinely feared concentration of media ownership; others disagreed with his political positions. Rupert decided to win over the politicians by funding a service they would deem essential – a twenty-four-hour, unbiased, rolling news channel that the political elite just had to have, even if that meant renting a Sky dish and subscribing to the service. I don't recall whether that was Rupert's idea, Neil's or one of Neil's lieutenants'. No matter: Rupert approved the budget for a costly service which had uncertain financial prospects. Margaret Thatcher made known her delight at having available an alternative to the BBC.

Second: the financial. I watched with mounting concern as every week £2 million disappeared down a hole that seemed bottomless, and growing deeper.[47] To say that even with Neil's confident and dynamic leadership we ran into problems of breathtaking magnitude would be to understate the situation very substantially. In each instance, Rupert intervened, and came up with a solution that raised the risk level even higher – and worked. For example, potential customers were faced with long waits between their decision to buy and the completion of credit checks. Demand was initially concentrated in socioeconomic groups that were dissatisfied with the BBC's elitist offerings, meaning those groups that most companies subjected to strenuous credit checks. But credit checks take time, and the decision to subscribe to Sky's service was often an impulse purchase, with that impulse gone by the time a credit check could be completed. Rupert decided that it would be less risky to forego credit checks and take bad-debt losses than to set stringent credit-check standards that prevented too many people who would prove creditworthy from paying for dishes and programmes. Our desire to get dishes installed before the rival BSB service could get on air also contributed to the decision to waive stringent credit checks. Murdoch, ever the populist, believed that lower-income groups, which in the Britain of recent memory could not persuade banks to allow them chequing accounts, were better risks than the establishment believed. So we waived credit checks, adding an element of risk not included in initial calculations of costs. The credit losses proved manageable and sales increased.

No manufacturer wanted to assume the risk of being burdened with unsold kit, so Rupert transferred that risk to Sky. Alan Sugar's Amstrad, understandably fearful that the satellite launch would be delayed or unsuccessful, declined to gear up production of the receiving equipment needed to enable subscribers to receive programmes, among them the all-important encrypted

Hollywood films, for which encryption technology was still in the development stage at a Murdoch subsidiary in Israel. At a meeting in Rupert's London office, he decided to order the necessary kit and assume the risk that it would lie forever in some warehouse if the satellite launch failed, or if demand for dishes and other kit did not materialise.[48] My joke that we might end up in the business of selling woks was not appreciated. In the event, and despite Rupert's willingness to assume some of the risk, the introduction of Sky was slowed by a shortage of Astra dishes, as production runs were kept too low to enable Sky to meet demand for the new service.[49]

Then came a large, costly decision to blast our way into the market – a big bet on sport. Rupert had long believed that sport drives viewership and attracts advertisers eager to get their messages to young males. As early as 1976, when acquiring the *New York Post*, Rupert told an interviewer, 'One must never take one's eye off sports.'[50] So he lined up rights to a February 1989 championship heavyweight prize fight between Mike Tyson and Britain's Frank Bruno. The fight was billed as an American-vs-British affair and, despite being shown from the Las Vegas Hilton, at an odd hour in the UK for viewing such an event, caused a rush of demand for dishes. Rupert also planned to lock up association football rights at what seemed exorbitant prices, and have David Hill, imported from Australia, develop ways of making cricket, horse racing and other sports more exciting on what were then the small television screens in most homes.

With sports rights lined up to appeal to men, Rupert turned his attention to women, and offered a babysitting service known as Disney. When we learned from house-to-house interviews in parts of London that a Disney channel would provide the babysitting function that many harassed mothers craved, Rupert hastened to strike a deal for a Disney channel, eventually leading to an amusing confrontation between the *Snow White* culture of Disney and the less staid culture of News. A Disney team flew to London for a review session. We convened in News' boardroom. The executives wore identikit blue suits, Disney ties and Mickey Mouse watches. If memory serves, and, given the mutual contempt of the parties to the deal, this might be a 'memory' too good to surrender, the quality of each timepiece, from stainless steel to diamond-encrusted, was geared to the status of the wrist it adorned.

It was the custom of News to have the day's papers laid out in the company boardroom, and some of the Disney people began thumbing through them, to find the ad for their channel on the page facing the Page Three girl of the day. Not exactly in the Mouse channel's image. It took a rather large dollop of the too-rarely-displayed Neil charm to soothe the ruffled feathers of the Hollywood contingent. The fragile peace did not survive Neil's decision to push forward with the construction of a customer service facility in Livingston, Scotland, without advising the Disney representative. Speed was of the essence, and we knew the Disney rep would have to return to Hollywood headquarters to obtain approval from our then partners. I had the difficult task of showing the poor fellow the press release announcing the opening of the facility. The relationship with Disney continued to have its ups and downs, the latter resulting in its termination because Disney felt it was not on an equal basis in the 50:50 partnership. Litigation followed, but in the end the Disney film library was made available to viewers for five years as part of a package offered by the merged Sky and BSB, renamed BSkyB.

Somehow, the individual deals and start-ups fail to capture the aggregate effect of Murdoch's risk-taking. Rupert knows that there is value in forward motion, in sheer momentum, that stops an organisation as threatened as a newspaper-based empire from becoming defensive, gloomy. He knows, too, that deals and gambles are energising, that the whole of the Murdoch enterprise is greater than the sum of its parts. Not an easy thing to explain to the green-eyeshade crowd, and not necessarily appropriate to other enterprises, but certainly an aspect of the Murdoch Method worth consideration by executives in whatever industry they find themselves, always keeping in mind the risks associated with this corporate style.

Of course, all the deals, the write-offs, the treatment of failure as a learning experience, the vision that is not bound by short-term considerations or immediately by an income statement, the value placed on psychic income, are made possible by Murdoch's position as dominant shareholder. Because his voting power is far greater than his share of the companies' equity, and is backed by a poison pill to deter a hostile takeover, Rupert can take the very long view. His controlling shareholdings free him from the pressure for quarterly results that bedevil so many leaders of public companies that depend on the approbation of investors concerned with the next quarter rather than the next decade. Murdoch's voting control not only allows him to take a very long view, it ensures him that a failed deal will not lead to a shareholder revolt and early involuntary retirement, or disrupt his plans to have his children succeed him. In the case of Myspace, he could consider the loss of billions of dollars a learning fee, and, as errant politicians like to say, 'move on'. There is something to be said for freedom to be in constant motion, leaving mistakes in your wake, soon to be forgotten.

This freedom from conventional constraints is not without its dangers. Without the normal constraint of a one-share, one-vote ownership structure, without the need to pay some attention to accountants' reckonings, with a management team that might move imperceptibly from admiration to sycophancy, destructive overreaching becomes a possibility. As was demonstrated when Murdoch almost lost control of his company to creditors when he relied too heavily on short-term borrowing to finance Sky's attack on the British and European television markets while at the same time pouring billions into new plant and equipment for the newspaper businesses. Rupert could have raised the cash for the investment in Sky by selling bonds, but preferred to gamble that the lower interest rates available from the banks on short-term loans would prove the more economical alternative. 'In the 1980s, if I had taken better advice, I'd have borrowed money on the bond markets instead of from the banks,' he later reflected. 'Now I seldom borrow from the banks.'[51]

But even executives not blessed with control of their own companies by two-tier shareholding have much to learn from the Murdoch Method of deal-making and enterprise building. First, do not ignore the importance of psychic income, or a feeling of relevance, whether from community involvement, devotion to a cause, or involvement in events that prove to be the stuff of cocktail-party conversations. Second, value any deal in terms of your long-term vision of the enterprise as a whole, rather than in terms of its stand-alone market value, going beyond a conventionally computed buyers' premium if necessary and, more recently, being a willing seller when the outlook for existing assets turns gloomy. When, in 1993, Rupert outbid CBS for the rights to air National Football League games, everyone said he had overpaid. His $1.6 billion four-year bid snatched the rights from CBS, which had owned those rights for thirty-eight years and which reportedly bid $100 million less per year than Murdoch's annual $400 million.[52] Those of us who gasped when Murdoch entered his bid overlooked the fact that the rights were merely one step in a plan to challenge the big three networks. Almost immediately after winning the rights Murdoch made a deal with Ron Perelman, another consummate deal-maker, giving him control of New World Communications' twelve television stations – eight affiliates from CBS, three from ABC and one from NBC. Popular football programmes plus powerful new affiliates increased Fox Networks' ratings and advertising revenues; secured a valuable tool on which it could showcase its other programmes in most of the nation's major television markets; and obtained what Murdoch calls 'the battering ram' that would get him into pay-television markets around the world, just as rights to association football later converted Sky into a force to be reckoned with in the British and European television markets. In fairness to CBS, which lost the NFL rights, the value of those rights to Fox, seeking to establish itself as a sports broadcaster and its network as a real force, probably exceeded their value to the incumbent, CBS, which had a great deal of other programming strength.[53]

In fact, in many of the deals in which Murdoch is said to have overpaid, he was in fact paying the cost of surmounting the barriers to entry erected by the powerful incumbents he was preparing to challenge for readers, viewers and advertisers. And earning that great intangible, psychic income. I remember having dinner with Rupert, alone, one evening shortly after he won the NFL bidding. He chuckled, 'For the first time the busboys as well as the maître d' know who I am.'

Rupert had long before pointed out that shortly after his father died he paid $200,000 for a small loss-making paper in Perth:

> As I recall, I paid $200,000 for the *Sunday Times*. And just to prove that the past is prologue, I was criticised for overpaying. Lesson: Don't listen to people who say you are overpaying if you are convinced that you see opportunities that more conventional thinkers don't. Since then we have 'overpaid' for soccer rights for Sky, we have 'overpaid' for American football for Fox, we have overpaid for 'Titanic', and for a host of other properties. And it's a good thing that we did![54]

The Wall Street Journal, when enough time has passed, might, but only might, prove to be another property for which Murdoch has not overpaid. So might Times Newspapers in Britain, although we must reserve final judgement until we see whether Rupert's 'last-man-standing' theory works: he believes *The Times* and *The Sunday Times* will become profitable and their value increase when some or all of several competing newspapers are no longer on the scene. So far, it seems as if he might be onto something. Circulation of *The Times* and *The Sunday Times* increased when *The Independent* abandoned its print edition, suggesting that some of its readers migrated to the Murdoch paper.[55] Earlier this year Mediatel reported, 'Amid a sea of declines, *The Times* is continuing to do something right, with both its daily and Sunday editions managing to increase their circulations over the year.'[56] If indeed readers of *The Independent* have transferred in some numbers to the Murdoch titles, it would mark a shift from a paper that originally styled itself 'free from proprietorial influence', the non-Murdoch newspaper.

In any event, the Murdoch Method is not to make every deal a winner, just enough to more than offset the effects of the losers. That means tolerating instances of genuine overpayment rather than establishing a culture in which such overpayment is to be avoided at all costs. That would require creating a risk-averse environment, the last thing in the world that Rupert would have his management style reflect.

The third lesson is do not confuse accounting and economics. In one of my frequent conversations with Rupert while I was watching millions of pounds disappear into what looked to me to be a bottomless hole called Sky, he told me not to call the disappearing sums 'losses'. 'You're an economist, not an accountant, so use your terminology rather than that of bean-counters – these are investments, no matter that they are booked as losses' was the gist of his admonition, one that I kept in mind when Rupert took on the liberal broadcasting monolith in America by starting Fox News.

The fourth lesson is that any manager attempting to emulate the Murdoch Method of deal-making – being willing to take losses and move on to the next deal, and pursuing a vision that ignores conventional standards of appraising the success or failure of an individual acquisition – must be willing to endure the criticism that such a strategy will adversely affect the price of the company's shares. It is widely believed that there is a 'Murdoch discount' of some 20 per cent off the price at which News shares historically have sold compared with other media stocks because investors are spooked by the prospect of Rupert's next big deal. 'The cold reality is that investing with Murdoch has been a losing move as long as Murdoch is in deal mode,' according to Doug Creutz, an analyst at Cowen and Company.[57] Perhaps.

But purchasers of stock in Murdoch companies know what they are getting into – an investment in a company in which voting rights are concentrated in Murdoch, a man given to making deals, and one with dynastic longings. Those who believe there is such a discount also believe that they are buying at a price reflecting that discount, and hope to benefit from share-price appreciation from that lower base.

The final lesson here is best summarised in the words of country and western singer Kenny Rogers: 'Know when to hold 'em, know when to fold 'em, know when to walk away, know when to run.' In the case of Myspace, Murdoch failed to take Rogers' advice, and paid a high price both in cash and in prestige for waiting too long to run, a mistake he did not intend to repeat by holding his entertainment assets in the face of possible declines in their value. But in the case of Fox News, Murdoch knew when to hold 'em, while others were advising him to walk away, or, better still, to run Fox News lost money for seven years: it now earns over $1 billion per year.

Whether the Murdoch of deals past is the Murdoch of today is uncertain. In 2014, after Time Warner refused to be wooed, much less wed, because Murdoch was unwilling to risk his investment-grade credit rating by increasing his offer,[58] he told analysts on a 21st Century Fox earnings call, 'We built ourselves.

If you look at all our best businesses, we've started them ourselves and we're very happy with that.'[59] A useful reminder that a substantial part of News' success has been due to organic growth. Equally important, he was signalling to shareholders, who had pounded Fox's share price – it dropped by 11 per cent during the period before the offer for Time Warner was withdrawn[60] – that the days of the 20 per cent 'Murdoch discount' should come to an end: no more major deals at prices out of line with tradition-ally reckoned values, in this case despite a loan commitment of $25 billion from Goldman Sachs and JPMorgan to fund the $73 billion bid.[61] Looking back, Murdoch concluded that he could have put together a financeable deal by raising his offer by some $10–12 per share. But Moody's, the rating agency, had warned that the price necessary to satisfy Time Warner would involve so much borrowing as to threaten Fox's investment-grade credit rating.[62] 'The fact is,' said Rupert, 'we would have had over $90 billion debt in the combined company. There will be other times. There will be other opportunities.'[63]

And one did come along. Tribune Media put on the market its string of forty-two television stations and WGN America, a Chicago-based network with nationwide reach. Add that to the Sinclair Broadcast Group's 173 stations and Sinclair would reach 70 per cent of American households. Ominously for Rupert, Sinclair appeals to the same conservative audience as does Fox News Channel. Early bidders for the Tribune properties included Sinclair and Nexstar, but late in the game 21st Century Fox tried to put together a joint venture with the Blackstone Group, a private equity firm. For reasons that are not entirely clear, that arrangement could not be cobbled together, and Rupert did not make a bid. The Tribune stations went to Sinclair for $3.9 billion, and a potential competitor to Fox is now in place,[64] at a time when displaced Fox stars are looking for a home. But Sinclair will have to take account of the political leanings of its local audiences: fare that finds favour in, say, conservative Salt Lake City, Utah, would likely cause audience defections in liberal Portland, Oregon, damaging the Sinclair station there.

The Murdoch of the pre-Sky financial crisis, who had less regard than many analysts felt he should have for his balance sheet and bond ratings, would, I suspect, at least have entered the bidding, especially since the Federal Communications Commission, now controlled by Trump appointees, would likely not have opposed such a merger.

In short, the scars of the Sky-induced financial crisis remain. Now flush with cash, Murdoch may still be in the big acquisition game, but he is not willing to risk the financial solidity of his company. Indeed, Murdoch's refusal to 'overpay' for Time Warner might mark the end of an era, the era of the media mogul intent on size. By one estimate moguls like Murdoch, Ted Turner and Sumner Redstone took write-downs of $200,000,000,000 – that's $200 billion – on overpriced acquisitions between 2000 and 2009.[65] Even by their standards, and allowing for benefits that cannot be captured by standard accounting, this is not petty cash.

But that does not mean that Murdoch will not leap at an opportunity if it presents itself. And one such opportunity did when in 2017 Brexit drove the value of the British pound so low that the outstanding shares of Sky became a bargain in dollar terms. Fox's £10.75 billion all-cash offer for the approximately 60 per cent of Sky that it does not own has been described by a person close to the deal: 'If the pound was still worth $1.50, they could not have made this move.'[66] Bankers at Macquarie Group estimate that the purchase price is only about 5 per cent more than the offer made some five years ago, before the hacking scandal forced its withdrawal.[67]

The attempted takeover of the outstanding shares was not without its problems. For one thing, James Murdoch's involvement created a conflict of interest. He is in the awkward position of representing both Fox, the potential acquirer, and Sky's minority shareholders, which is one reason why Hamilton Claxton, of Royal London Asset Management, holder of £50 million of Sky shares, found James's appointment 'surprising' and 'inappropriate'.[68] But just as Rupert developed independent editorial boards to overcome hurdles to his acquisitions of Times Newspapers and *The Wall Street Journal*, he found a way around the potential conflict problems at Sky. He agreed not to vote shares he already controls in Sky, either for or against the merger, leaving the fate of the deal to depend on a 75 per cent approval vote of the independent shareholders, who would receive a 36 per cent premium over the closing price on the day before the offer was made.[69]

The second problem is not so easily solved: the regulators. Ofcom decided that 21st Century Fox is a fit and proper company to hold a broadcast licence, even though it is headed by James Murdoch, about whom it some years ago expressed doubts after the hacking scandal, doubts not so great, however, as to prevent it from leaving the final decision on James's future with Sky's shareholders. Unfortunately for the deal's prospects, after Ofcom made its decision, Karen Bradley, UK culture minister, under pressure from politicians and voters opposed to allowing the Murdochs to complete their control of Sky, rejected the advice of Ofcom and unexpectedly referred not only the question of media concentration and diversity, but the 'fit and proper' issue, to the Competition and Markets Authority.[70] While the CMA studied the evidence, *The New York Times* revealed that Fox executives were aware when the company extended the contract of its star pundit, Bill O'Reilly – a four-year deal paying O'Reilly $25 million annually – that he had settled six sexual harassment cases. Only later was he dismissed. What it did not know until after the ink was dry on the contract was that one of the settlements with a Fox employee involved the payment of the staggering sum of $32 million. Payment was from O'Reilly's personal funds, but nevertheless allowed James's critics to argue that the contract negotiations provided an opportunity for Fox to learn the details of the settlements, and that a lavish contract for O'Reilly was not the way to change the culture at Fox News. To make matters worse, James told the press, 'I can't make sure that everyone in the business doesn't behave badly at times, right?' That is undoubtedly true, but to the regulatory ear it might sound as a confession of an inability to manage so vast an operation as Twentieth Century Fox/Sky. Besides, James knew that O'Reilly had behaved 'badly' when he renewed the commentator's contract. O'Reilly denied any guilt and would be accorded a presumption of innocence had the complaints gone to trial, but it was not company practice to accord such a presumption. It did not in the case of Roger Ailes, and therefore is not a reasonable excuse for executive inaction in the O'Reilly case which, in fairness, the CMA will have to weigh along with the substantial structural and cultural changes James has been pushing at Fox News.[71] None of these developments could have been anticipated by Rupert when he made the bid for complete ownership of Sky. He was once again demonstrating both his willingness to take risks and his persistence. Moving James back to the hostile environment from which he was forced to flee was the risk. Continuing to stalk Sky for more than five years after the hacking scandal reflected persistence.

Since the first, failed bid for Sky, cost pressures created by competitors' bids for sports rights have increased, and competition from such as Apple, Netflix and Amazon has emerged.[72] Apple, dipping into its $262 billion cash pile, will spend $1 billion on original shows during the next year, making it one of the leading tech-industry companies to become a content creator, but still not in a league with Netflix: CEO Reed Hastings announced that the company will spend $6 billion on original content in 2017 and a 'lot more' in the future.[73] Not to be left behind, Amazon will spend $4.5 billion on its Prime Video, according to analysts at JPMorgan.[74] John Landgraf, CEO of FX, 21st Century Fox's satellite channel, has a budget of $1 billion, and says of the new competition, 'It's like getting shot in the face with money every day.'[75]

My guess, which I like to think is an informed one, is that James has the skills and energy to compete successfully for audiences in countries such as those in Asia, where Disney is not much of a factor. An executive who reported to James for several years said that one of the frustrations of working for him 'was that he was always looking strategically, 10 years down-the-line, as part of a bigger family picture'.[76] Claire Enders, CEO of an important London-based media research firm, more recently commented that James 'is widely respected in European media circles as a pay-TV visionary ... emulated by rivals'.[77]

The fact that he is not so well-regarded by UK-regulators would count for less if he were Disney's man at Sky.

CHAPTER 4

ECONOMIC REGULATION

'The single constant in the American experience with regulation has been controversy ... Issues common to regulatory agencies are unlikely ever to be settled, once and for all' – Thomas K. McGraw in *Prophets of Regulation*, 1984[1]

'Why is it proper for the government to prohibit insalubrious foods and not sadistic movies, to control the pollution of the environment but not of the culture, to prevent racial segregation but not moral degenration?' – Gertrude Himmelfarb, 1994 [2]

'[We should] contemplate intervention ... not merely because a regulator armed with a set of prejudices and a spreadsheet believes that a bit of tinkering here and there could make the world a better place' – James Murdoch, 2009[3]

Rupert doesn't much like regulation, but he knows he must deal with regulators, and the Murdoch Method includes techniques he has developed to do just that. That aspect of the Method is best summarised as: inform, complain, compromise and cooperate. First, Murdoch always keeps regulators, and, when they are relevant, legislators, informed of his plans – not asking permission, or a favour, but simply not keeping them in the dark about important business moves that might eventually come up for review in their agencies. John Dingell, a powerful, long-serving Democratic congressman who believed government has a large role to play in the economy but who, as far as I can remember, never leaned on the Federal Communications Commission (FCC) to take an anti-Murdoch position, once told me that what he liked about Rupert was that 'Murdoch never took me by surprise'. Like legislators, regulators do not like surprises, to read in the morning papers an important move by the companies they are charged by law with following closely. It has been Rupert's practice to advise regulators of planned changes in business practices if they are of consequence – and to do so in person, even when dealing below the top level in a regulatory agency. Reed Hundt, a former chairman of the FCC, told *New Yorker* interviewer John Cassidy that Murdoch is 'just smarter about that than everybody else'.[4] When News Corp. was considering the purchase of a satellite television company, Murdoch travelled to Washington to see the relevant member of Hundt's staff. As Hundt describes it, 'Rupert himself came and sat down with that person. Rupert wanted to make sure that he understood on a personal level the direction of policy, but what he was also saying – and he never actually said this, because he didn't need to say it – was that he was open to this guy. That kind of thing has a huge impact on a government official at any level.'

Murdoch's critics undoubtedly see this visit as an unspoken warning to some dazzled official, a sort of 'I know who you are and my friends in the administration will know where to find you.' Rupert is, after all, a media mogul of some influence, some real, some more imagined, and with a reputation that precedes him whether he intends it to or not. Threats would be in bad taste, probably counter-productive, and anyhow unnecessary: reminding a regulator of his clout with that official's political masters is unnecessary. More likely, visits such as this reflect one of Rupert's dominant characteristics: rampant curiosity. In important matters, second-hand reports rarely satisfy him, often to the consternation of his own staff which would prefer clearer lines of authority. Just as he wants to size up politicians seeking his support by meeting them to learn not only their positions but to appraise their integrity and the likelihood that they will have the toughness to carry out the policies they profess to support, so he wants to make his own estimation of the possibilities of regulatory approval, or of a company accepting a takeover offer, or of an investment banker's willingness to love him in December as he does in May.

Rupert's desire to keep regulators informed is not the norm. A client once called me to complain about the rude treatment he had received from one country's regulator, a man I knew to be courteous and accessible. It seems that my client, nurtured in the deferential environment of his corporate headquarters, had sent this regulator a note announcing the date on which he would be visiting the country on business, and that he had an opening in his schedule at eleven that morning, at which time he hoped to drop in at the agency. Now, regulators and civil servants are well aware that in private conversations top executives hold them in low esteem – 'never met a payroll', 'don't understand the businesses they are regulating', 'too risk-averse to join the private sector'. Top regulators with whom I have consorted in the US, UK and the EU have mentioned that to me, some in anger, some with wry amusement. So, when my client treated an important regulator's schedule as subordinate in importance to his own, he did not get the appointment he sought. Rupert is unlikely to make such a blunder. Not that he drops in on most conferences with regulators. But when it is a good idea to do so, as in the instance described by chairman Hundt, he makes himself available.

I have had other clients, CEOs, who send subordinates to meet top regulators at crucial settlement conferences, to the annoyance of officials who feel slighted at the suggestion that they and the matters over which they preside are of insufficient importance to warrant the time of a CEO. This is especially true at the European Commission. I have still other clients whose first reaction to a regulatory move they find irksome is to complain to the press or their congressman. The latter dutifully contacts the regulator, knowing that such pressure will antagonise him, but wanting to be able to tell a constituent that he had made an effort on his behalf.

Beyond personally keeping regulators informed of his plans, the Murdoch Method includes complain, compromise and cooperate. Complain, because his free-market ideology, the cost of compliance and the need to show his troops that he abhors government intervention in business affairs, especially his, make such complaint ideologically and strategically necessary. Cooperate, if possible, because it is often more efficient to cooperate on matters such as data requests and, later, proposed solutions to problems deemed important by regulators. Cooperate, because defiance often begets problems far more damaging than cooperation, as Uber and some of today's more recent disrupters are discovering to their cost.

Rupert's complaints are most often voiced in the confines of the offices of News Corp. One such came my way and took the form of an instruction from Rupert to defy the Office of Fair Trading by refusing to fill out a burdensome questionnaire that marked the opening of an investigation into News' pricing of its newspapers. I knew I could ignore him because he was in the complain stage, the first of the 'complain, compromise, cooperate' stages through which he would pass. I understood the expected reaction of a recipient of such a Murdoch instruction: ignore it. This was not insubordination, merely the act of a long-time associate who had learned that Murdoch expected him to ignore instructions that, if acted upon, might do the organisation harm – a key ingredient of the Murdoch Method, used with safety only with long-time, trusted colleagues.

Next would come compromise. Along with News' in-house team and outside counsel I worked with the regulators to find out what they really needed and to pare down the routine initial data request. Even though the initial data request had been reduced, with non-essential items eliminated by the regulator after our discussions, News would incur compliance costs in the neighbourhood of £1 million on data collection and on ensuring several attorneys the early and comfortable retirements to which many of Britain's top-tier lawyers have told me, in weaker, alcohol-infused moments, they aspire. Rupert agreed to the compromise, data request and, through Jane Reed, his director of corporate relations, made available knowledgeable company personnel and free access to files and data and lawyers, the latter often in numbers dictated more by the financial requirements of the law firm than by the manpower requirements of the necessary filings.

Finally, the Murdoch Method moves on to cooperation by making such agreed changes in the operation as would satisfy the regulators without doing harm to the profitability of the business.

There is another lesson here for all managers in industries in which regulation is a factor – in addition to the importance of assigning appropriately titled executives to meet with regulators to keep them informed of important developments. Don't wait until a problem emerges to make contact with regulatory agencies. Rupert knew that when problems arose we would be dealing with regulators with whom I had interacted for years in academic seminars and other venues, for whose intellect and integrity I had considerable respect; and with whom I had agreed often enough to make them willing to give me a fair hearing at the important informal meetings at which regulators seek to understand the industry with which they are dealing. For me, they were teaching sessions, which Murdoch did not attend, for two reasons: they are best left to people with something like infinite patience, and he has better things to do. Better to rely on those such as Sir Edward Pickering, Rupert's mentor from the day he landed in Britain, a director and editor of Murdoch publications, well known for his integrity and for his access to Rupert, and on Jane Reed, whose authority and integrity were beyond question.

Most important, both for the regulators and for me as Rupert's representative, I had confidence that the game would be played by the rules. I can't pretend to have been involved in every regulatory matter in which any of the News companies became involved, but I participated in a considerable number, and it is fair to say that once the regulatory process was under way, Rupert generally resisted any temptation he might have had to complain to higher authority or to the press about the cost in management time and lawyers' and consultants' fees, although occasionally he shared rather sour views on the latter with me in private.

Does Rupert always succeed in resisting such temptation? Certainly not. When Senator Ted Kennedy pushed through legislation requiring Rupert to divest himself of properties in Boston and New York, Murdoch rang up every official who might help. All professed sympathy and promised to try to get the Kennedy legislation reversed, or an exception made. To no avail.

A few years earlier Rupert had also tried to use political influence to overturn a decision by the FCC. It seems that in 1985 the Commission had forced Rupert to cooperate with a statute limiting ownership of television stations to American citizens. His choice: take the oath of American citizenship or lose his television licences and stations. That was not an easy decision for Rupert, not least because it upset his mother, a formidable, patriotic Australian and fan of the British monarchy. 'How will I explain this to my mother?' he asked, reminding me of another incident in which Dame Elisabeth played a revealing role. In May 1981 Rupert gave a dinner party for Cita and me to celebrate the start of our honeymoon. In addition to Rupert, the Wyatts and Lady Elisabeth were present. When we emerged from Les Ambassadeurs a rather large limousine, summoned for him by his staff, was waiting. His mother expressed displeasure with such ostentation – in fact, Rupert would never have ordered such a car – and the vehicle was not seen again during Rupert's stay in

London. In the case of his US citizenship, he mollified his mother by promising not to sell his Australian holdings.[5]

That forced change of citizenship rankled. Some years after that bout with the FCC, the agency chairman, Reed Hundt, opened an investigation to determine whether News Corporation could lawfully retain control of several television stations he had acquired while constructing Fox Network. Those additions took Rupert's combined holdings beyond the statutory market-share limit, triggering the need for a waiver. Murdoch launched a vitriolic public attack on Hundt. Congressmen who control FCC budgets, many with their own reasons for wanting Hundt gone, joined the assault. Murdoch, who wanted the stations in order to strengthen his assault on the liberal oligopoly of ABC, CBS and NBC, genuinely felt entitled to a waiver from a rule that was designed to preserve competition, but was having the opposite effect. He also believed that the FCC chairman was a tool of his arch-enemy, Ted Kennedy.

In the event, Murdoch retained ownership of his stations,[6] but only because Hundt felt that, since his predecessor had allowed News to acquire the stations, it would be unfair to order their divestiture. One view of that decision is that it represented proof that Murdoch's massive lobbying effort, and alleged threats by his lobbyists to ruin the careers of FCC personnel, paid off. Another is that such threats are counter-productive, and that in this instance Hundt took the only fair position available, given his predecessor's approval of the acquisitions. I can't adjudicate that particular dispute, but I can say that in my considerable experience such attacks as the one Rupert unleashed on Hundt are ineffective. Most regulators pride themselves on immunity to political pressure. Things were a bit different in Britain, where the established procedure allows ministers and their staffs to intervene in competition-policy proceedings, as the culture minister has done in the Sky merger matter. I never did determine whether such a system helped Rupert by involving politicians who have exaggerated fears of the power of the press, or hurt him by involving politicians to whom his political positions were anathema, or who have personal reasons to resent his papers' coverage of their activities.

This does not mean that Rupert never attempted to influence the legislation that sets out the rules by which he would have to play: he has lobbyists who do that, as do most large businesses. It seems reasonable to assume that a legislator approached in America by a lobbyist for Fox News, in Britain by one affiliated with News International, or in Australia by a lobbyist for the Murdoch papers there, is inclined to be more attentive to his guest than he would be to a lobbyist for some industrial enterprise. I do know that Rupert has often said to me, 'Let them make the rules and I will play by them.' But that does not preclude him from attempting to shape those rules to his advantage. Once the rules are set, however, Rupert will play within their bounds. That is an important component of the Murdoch Method of coping with regulation. Whether Murdoch lieutenants so restrict their activities I cannot say, since one danger of the highly personalised Murdoch Method is that it at times inclines company employees to guess what Murdoch would want them to do – and to guess wrong.

I can say with certainty that Rupert never interfered with me or Jane Reed when we were working on difficult regulatory issues in the UK. Reed was my liaison with the News International staff in control of the data and the data runs I needed to determine whether the regulators had a legitimate concern, and, if so, how we should respond. Reed never asked me to ignore an unfavourable fact, or massage the data until its connection with the truth became more than tenuous, or yield to the lawyer-advocate's request to adopt the role of advocate rather than impartial expert in my reports and testimony. When I argued that media companies must be held to a more stringent standard than, say, a manufacturing company, Jane stood steadfastly with me as others in the company tried to persuade us that such a position might harm the company's chance of prevailing. That's why, in addition to deciding that News International did not have an excessive share of the relevant newspaper market, which I felt included regional as well as national papers, I requested studies of the influence of the company's media properties, measured by the amount of time spent with each company's products. She authorised the expenditure on the survey.

Murdoch's hands-off policy is a very wise one. Most regulators resent politicians' attempt to influence the results of their proceedings, as EU regulators did when American politicians tried to gain a more favourable outcome for Microsoft in its ultimately unsuccessful attempt to avoid fines levied by the European Commission. In Britain, investigations by the Office of Fair Trading (replaced in April 2014 by the Competition and Markets Authority and the Financial Conduct Authority) were always conducted with no apparent consideration given to the fact of News' special political access, my only complaint being the unhurried pace of the proceedings and the often ill-considered data requests that at times were more fishing expeditions than the gathering of relevant information. Policy debates and the hunt for such mutually acceptable changes as might be called for in corporate behaviour were almost always conducted in a professional manner. Of course, I wasn't paying the lawyers' bills and, in a sense, was a financial beneficiary by participating in the preparation of responses to regulators' inquiries, and by consulting on new methods of doing business to replace those to which regulators objected. So my patience with the process often exceeded Rupert's, who, as the legal bills mounted, at times regressed to the 'complain' stage.

I must confess, however, that my own patience with the regulatory process also reached its limits at times, as during one meeting in which the civil servant in charge of an inquiry into whether advertisements for Sky programmes in *The Sun* constituted an unlawful competitive practice, his copy of the day's *Guardian* on the table before him, confessed, with no hint of embarrassment, that his objection was not to any News business practices, but to the positions of Murdoch's newspapers on several issues. Or when the staff of one regulatory agency made it a practice to serve a very large data request on News' staff shortly before Christmas, with a due date of the first business day of the new year, knowing full well the commission staff would still be on, or recovering from, the Christmas holidays. This was intended to and did force some News staffers to cancel their own Christmas holidays, and was just the sort of behaviour that assured the request would be answered with the least possible usable information, a situation I always tried to avoid since multiple rounds of data requests are costly and prolong periods of uncertainty.

It is an important part of the Murdoch Method to allow people in whom he has confidence to make direct approaches to regulators, so I did not have to check with him for permission to visit the head of that agency, who was unaware of this bit of unpleasant gamesmanship that was reducing my ability to persuade the News staff to cooperate. I suggested to the head of the agency that civility is a two-way street, and that cooperation in solving the problem at hand required decent personal relations between the regulatory staff and the people at News who were detailed to help me. The practice ceased and we got on with the business of solving the regulatory problem to the mutual satisfaction of both parties, meeting the business needs of News and the regulators' view of what the law required.

Another problem I have with the regulatory process as we confronted it when dealing with issues raised in connection with Murdoch operations is its cost, especially in Britain where law firm fees traditionally exceed those in America. During one investigation of News' practices, I attended a meeting with a major London law firm. The senior partner and four young associates were at the conference table when I arrived. I asked why we needed such a large (and expensive) group. The partner's explanation failed to persuade me, so I suggested that my client, News, would object to such overstaffing. Incredibly, the partner called News' general counsel to complain; I called Rupert. The partner also invited me to a rather elaborate and liquid lunch in the law firm's dining room to explain that without the fees earned by assigning young, relatively low-paid non-partners to cases, the firm's profits would be far lower. That did not seem to me to be a problem that Rupert should be asked to solve, and future meetings were less fully staffed.

It would be naïve not to recognise the possibility that Rupert never had to intervene personally because regulators know that if they made him unhappy they would hear from the White House or No. 10 or The Lodge. We can rarely know what is in the mind of a regulator, but there are two reasons for suspecting that regulators generally do their jobs as they were supposed to, without fear or favour, or at least without the latter despite a bit of the former. The first is that the leakiness of government and the alertness of the media, which includes so many of News' competitors, to any show of favour to Rupert make it unlikely that any important politician would risk interfering in a regulatory process on his behalf, unless the law so required. The second is that the regulators worry about the reputational consequences of bowing to such political interventions. With very few exceptions these are honourable men who believe they are implementing laws enacted by democratically elected legislators, using procedures that are more or less transparent, and secure in the belief that there are times when markets do not work well, justifying their intervention. These regulators seek the approval of their peers and the academics with whom they interact, a point that should not be discounted when appraising their incentives to do what they believe is right. That does not mean they are always right: at times, they operate with an anti-business, anti-market bias that causes them to come down unduly hard on the companies under their jurisdiction. At others, their bias in favour of the companies under their control, as opposed to innovative challengers, what is known in the trade as regulatory capture, often leads them to excessive protection of the companies they regulate. If you doubt that, ask executives of Uber and other so-called disrupters. Absent a legislative mandate, regulators lack incentives to keep proceedings moving along at a rapid pace so that business uncertainty is minimised.

Of course, the Murdoch Method of coping with regulation must be adapted to the wide variety of types of regulation with which any international media company must cope. In America, there is the Securities and Exchange Commission to regulate financial activities and reporting; the FCC to supervise mergers and broadcast licences; the antitrust division of the Department of Justice to monitor business practices and the competitive impact of mergers; and the Internal Revenue Service to make sure that taxes legally due are paid. In Britain, there is the Competition and Markets Authority to ensure that markets work well: Ofcom to regulate the TV, radio and video-on-demand sectors and 'make sure that people in the UK get the best from their communications services and are protected from scams and sharp practices',[7] not to mention whether an applicant for a broadcasting licence is 'a fit and proper person' to hold such a licence; and various parliamentary committees to call attention to unacceptable practices. And in Europe there is the European Commission, which Murdoch sees more as an ally in his fight against what he contends are content thieves such as Google, rather than a body to be feared. Most countries now have antitrust authorities of one sort or another, many serious regulators, others established merely to collect fees from companies applying for their approval.

Books have been written describing these laws, regulations and court decisions,[8] but for our purposes we need know about two features that affect News. The first outlaws possession of an unacceptable degree of market power; the second prevents the use of unlawful business practices. To this observer it seems highly unlikely that any Murdoch operation possesses enough freedom from competition – market power – to extort unreasonably high prices from readers, viewers or advertisers. Newspapers face competition not only from each other in most markets for advertisers and readers, but from online services such as Google and Facebook, not to mention specialised advertising outlets such as realestate.com.au in Australia and Zillow in America, which have cut deeply into print advertising and forced Murdoch to set up and acquire competing online companies.[9] In Britain, daily and Sunday newspapers compete vigorously, moderated only by brand preferences often determined by the reader's agreement with the political stance of their favourite paper.

Which brings us to the second of the more traditional areas of regulatory inquiry: the propriety of a company's business practices. News' practices have at times been challenged by regulators, and at times have resulted in a modification of the way the company does business. The company's UK newspaper distribution system granted independent distributors monopolies in the areas in which they distributed News' papers. That put retailers at a disadvantage if they were dissatisfied with the service – late deliveries mean lost sales – or with margins between what the distributor charged and the printed price of the newspapers. After discussions with regulators, a system was set up that avoided the added costs of having competing distributors criss-crossing each other's territories, but provided a mechanism for acting on retailers' complaints and stripping distributors of their territories if they consistently provided poor or excessively costly service. That compromise satisfied the business needs of News and the obligation of the regulators to protect small businesses. More important, in a 345-page set of fact-findings and opinion, the Office of Fair Trading, as it then was, decided 'not to refer the newspaper and magazine supply sector to the Competition Commission'.[10]

In yet another inquiry, in 1990–91, I was News' witness along with Sir Edward Pickering.[11] The inquiry chairman, John Sadler, was tasked with determining whether the cross-promotion of Sky by advertisements for its television service in *The Sun* was anti-competitive. Fortunately, Andrew Neil and I had insisted that Sky pay the same rates for such ads as *The Sun* would charge Sky's competitors, so that, given the nature of the market, no one could reasonably accuse the Murdoch companies of subsidising Sky in its competition for television audiences. We prevailed. Better still, we prevailed despite an opposing study submitted by the consulting firm I had sold a decade earlier. But that was not my only pleasure. In addition to clearing News of anti-competitive acts, Sadler held that the BBC was leveraging the market power it possessed in the television market into the magazine market by promoting its publications on air, giving those magazines an unfair competitive advantage over independent competitors. So we had a double victory: exoneration of News and a bit of trouble for the BBC. The icing on the cake was a lovely note from John Edwards, a very able lawyer then with Clifford Chance: 'On my return from holiday I saw your kind letter of the 19th March. Your sentiment is much appreciated but I do not honestly feel that I can claim any reasonable proportion of any credit for the excellent result which you have clearly achieved for Rupert.' I hope he addressed similar notes to Sir Edward and Jane Reed.

In America, regulatory battles resulted in the approval of News' acquisition of companies producing advertising inserts, and of the sale of some magazines of the sort generally found at checkouts in American and British supermarkets. In the latter case, we demonstrated the competition faced by these checkout magazines from so-called celebrity magazines by bringing samples to the Justice Department staff to demonstrate the overlap. This proved much more effective than the traditional presentation of masses of data and computer models. The scrutiny the text and photos received from Justice Department attorneys and economists was a testimonial to the scholarly interest these publications aroused in people who would never dream of or dare to buy a copy in their supermarket.

It seems clear that what economic power News does have – and it is not very much given the competitive nature of the markets in which it operates – is sufficiently constrained by legislation and regulation, formal and informal. But it is equally clear that straightforward economic power, constrained or not by regulation, is not the only type of power we must consider when examining the role of a media company, especially one such as News Corp, with global reach and a chairman with very definite views on major public policy issues, and who does not live by profits alone. There remains the question of content regulation.

Such regulation is sometimes set forth in statutes, sometimes results from political and societal pressure and sometimes from self-regulation. For example, Britain relies on 'watersheds' to set hours before which material that might be inappropriate for youngsters cannot be broadcast. In the United States the market plays a key role. Advertisers have withdrawn sponsorship from Fox News Channel's programmes headed by 'stars' accused of sexually harassing employees. And they claim to be intolerant of half-time Super Bowl entertainment that they deem inappropriate for the young people watching the game, although that intolerance is not as quickly triggered as it once was. In addition, the Federal Communications Commission can fine broadcasters who cross some ill-defined line in their use of language or images.

This is a much more difficult area for Rupert and his management team to cope with than the more traditional economic regulation. Metrics that exist in the case of economic regulation – market share, pricing behaviour, competitive impact – simply have not been invented to determine the need for and impact of content regulation, leaving Murdoch and his executives to rely on what Rupert calls, 'editorial judgement ... conscience'.[12] Former Supreme Court Justice Potter Stewart's guideline concerning pornography includes the words: 'I shall not today attempt further to define the kind of material I understand to be embraced with that short-hand description [hard-core pornography]; and perhaps I could never succeed in intelligibly doing so. But I know it when I see it.' Unfortunately, 'I know it when I see it' is not a sure guide to separating the permissible from the offensive.[13] Murdoch, who has control over his content creators and distributors, must also frame a working definition of what is proper for his organisation, balancing the goal of assaulting elitist attitudes of propriety against the often competing goal of refusing to lurch into pornography or the 'dumbing down' of his products. The conflict between those two goals is obvious, but can be reconciled only by the man in charge, the person responsible both for exercising social responsibility and for maximising long-term profits. Which is one reason the role of self-regulation, of corporate culture, is every bit as important as any control by an outside body, especially in America, where the First Amendment to the Constitution guarantees freedom of expression. When the *New York Post* ran a cartoon in 2009 showing the bullet-riddled body of a chimp, with two cops standing over it saying, 'They'll have to find someone else to write the next stimulus bill', a storm erupted. Since President Obama wrote the first stimulus bill, and is African-American, the chimp was taken to represent the president. In response to complaints, Murdoch issued the following statement:

> As the Chairman of *The New York Post*, I am ultimately responsible for what is printed in its pages. The buck stops with me.
>
> Last week, we made a mistake. We ran a cartoon that offended many people. Today I want to personally apologize to any reader who felt offended, and even insulted.
>
> Over the past couple of days, I have spoken to a number of people and I now better understand the hurt this cartoon has caused. At the same time, I have had conversations with *Post* editors about the situation and I can assure you – without a doubt – that the only intent of that cartoon was to mock a badly written piece of legislation. It was not meant to be racist, but unfortunately, it was interpreted by many as such.
>
> We all hold the readers of *The New York Post* in high regard and I promise you that we will seek to be more attuned to the sensitivities of our community.[14]

In addition to such individual interventions, there is industry-wide self-regulation such as systems of rating movies and television programmes according to their suitability for audiences of different ages. These seem to work moderately well, although not in the case of youngsters not properly supervised at home or when they visit friends. Efforts by the Federal Communications Commission to distinguish which obscenities can be used in what circumstances provide more fodder for jokey journalists than effect on broadcasters. For our purposes, it is an area best left for consideration when we turn to how the Murdoch Method handles the company's drive to push the envelope of consumer taste, while not crossing the line into unacceptable vulgarity.

Which leaves open a final question – is there a dimension of media-company power that requires not only content regulation, but some form of regulation in addition to the run-of-the-mill competition-policy constraints under which all companies operate? There is little doubt that even loss-making newspapers convey more political power than do profitable non-media enterprises. Or that Fox News can influence voters on important issues, as it is believed to have done in America's 2016 presidential elections. Of course, influence is a two-way street: readers of newspapers and television viewers can and do influence the editorial and policy choices of media outlets seeking their patronage. Deciding whether it is the newspapers and the television programmes that influence the voters, or vice versa, is no easy chore.

No one, least of all Rupert Murdoch, denies that he has strong views on many important public policy issues, views some call biases. His Australian papers crusaded against the idea that the climate is changing due to human activity that produces carbon dioxide emissions, his *New York Post* and *Sun* back candidates of his choosing, although editors and reporters have voices to which he listens when making up his mind. Fox News is unalterably opposed to many of President Obama's legacy items, including Obamacare and the 2015 Joint Comprehensive Plan of Action, more commonly known as the Nuclear Deal between Iran and the permanent members of the UN Security Council and Germany. His undertakings prevent Rupert from dictating the editorial policies of *The Times* and *The Sunday Times*, and of *The Wall Street Journal*, but the independent boards that protect the editors would be foolish to insist he select and ask their approval of editors uncongenial to him in general lest his enthusiasm for funding those papers diminish. A bit of sense and sensibility in the application of these rather strange arrangements that dilute the power of the man who is paying the bills is required, and so far has prevailed.

Rupert is further constrained by market forces. Advertisers have no loyalty to any media product, scampering from one to another depending on ratings, circulation and effectiveness of their ads. And to what might be called the newer media – Facebook, Google and others. Consumers have a wide range of choices, and if they disagree with the opinions of a Murdoch media product will transfer their loyalty to a more agreeable source.

It seems fair to conclude, first, that the Murdoch Method of coping with regulation is about as workable a method as a media company can devise; and, second, that society has little to fear from News' economic power as that is traditionally understood by regulators – large market share that conveys power over prices charged to advertisers or customers – or from business practices that are out of line with what is generally acceptable. As for power, there is no doubt that Murdoch's exists, especially since the development of Fox News, but neither is there any doubt that it is severely constrained by market forces, by legislation and by regulation. The power of those constraints is different at different times and in different places, but nowhere does Murdoch have the power to drown out competing points of view.

Not everyone is convinced. In response to my argument that diversity of sources of news and views is our ultimate protection, a Member of Parliament sitting on a committee that was interrogating me on this subject asked, 'Do newspapers make errors?' Answer: 'Yes.' 'Have you considered therefore that the more newspapers we have the more errors there will be?' After a moment of stunned silence, I answered: 'I hadn't considered the possibility that in its day *Pravda*, the only newspaper in the Soviet Union, would produce fewer total errors than would occur in a multi-newspaper country.'

The remaining question is whether the Murdoch Method of handling regulatory problems will survive the departure of its author. Lachlan has so far restricted his comments in that area to an opposition to censorship, which in practice will require a situation-by-situation definition of just what that term means – surely any attempt to prevent the publication of opposing views or revelations of government misdeeds, not so surely an attempt to impose establishment views of the propriety of, to take one example, photos of partially clad women in mass-market newspapers. James seems to have more comprehensive views on the role of regulation, and they reflect less patience with regulation than do Rupert's. He used his MacTaggart Lecture to make an all-out assault on regulators, accusing them of being 'armed with a set of prejudices and a spreadsheet [who] believe that a bit of tinkering here and there could make the world a better place.[15] No economist who has had decades of dealings with regulators, least of all this one, would deny that James's charges are, in some cases, accurate. But that is not the question: it is whether such public attacks advance the cause of a major company that, like it or not, must coexist with a variety of regulatory agencies.

It is reasonable to ask whether the approach to regulation that is part of the Murdoch Method will remain so when Rupert is no longer around. My expectation is that, with James gone, and Lachlan in control, News's policy will move in the direction of continuing Rupert's approach.

But there is a lesson for managers to learn from James's somewhat different approach. When the bid to acquire the outstanding shares of Sky was announced James told the press that the merger would be approved without any 'meaningful concessions being made'.[16] Anyone who has been around the regulatory scene could have warned him that such a statement is an invitation to the regulators to demand concessions, if for no reason other than to establish their relevance and authority. In the event, the Murdochs have made concessions: they took Fox News off the air in the UK, allegedly because of low viewership but that has long been the case; given the timing, this was clearly a concession to regulators.

And they offered to assure the independence of Sky News by placing it in some form of well-financed independent trust.[17]

Then, when the government decided to take a closer look, James announced, in effect, that refusal to allow the deal would be an act of hypocrisy. He told a Royal Television Society conference in Cambridge that was also addressed by Ms Bradley, 'If the UK is truly "open for business" post-Brexit, approval of the merger would be an affirmation of that claim.'[18] Presumably, if the government disallows the deal, it would be abandoning its claim to be open for business.

Finally, James cited his own record as a manager. 'We owned 100 per cent of it for many years and there were no issues. When I was chief executive: no issues. And when I was chairman again: no issues. The record has to matter.'[19] Indeed it does. But given Ofcom's scathing comments about his management skills after the hacking scandal, and the minister's concerns about the sexual harassment incidents at Fox News, he might have been better advised to remain silent about any past 'issues', and defend his suitability to hold a broadcast licence by emphasising his lack of de facto control of Fox News prior to his vigorous intervention to depose Roger Ailes and clean up the scandal-ridden workplace there.

Dealing with regulation can be tedious and frustrating, especially for a hard-charging executive such as James. It is not unreasonable to expect that as time passes and experience accumulates James might react to regulatory challenges in a calmer, or at least less bellicose, manner. He will need an amicable relationship with a host of regulatory authorities: competition authorities to help him get his films into theatres in a timely and flexible way, to end 'those crazy hold-backs theatre owners put in place';[20] international regulators to help him protect his 'content', to crack down on firms from Beijing to Mountain View that 'steal his IP'; local authorities in California to make obtaining permits needed for facilities-expansion merely a brief nightmare; and regulators to assure that his films and other content have access to distribution. Like other executives he might, for these and other reasons, among them the need to minimise legal and other costs, decide that complain (in private), compromise and cooperate is the best available way of coping with regulators.

CHAPTER 5

CRISIS MANAGEMENT

'We must be prepared to take risks and accept that we will make mistakes, sometimes very large ones' – Rupert Murdoch, 2006[1]

'We ask our people to run at breakneck speed … We ask them to take risks and we know there will be failures … The failure … is bad enough, but it would be even worse if it crushed the creative risk-taking spirit that conceived the idea in the first place' – Peter Chernin, at the time president and CEO of News Corp., chairman and CEO of Fox Group, Sun Valley, 1998[2]

'Far from watching their empire crumble, Mr Murdoch and his family have more than doubled their wealth since the [hacking] scandal broke … The Murdochs' happy ending is a reminder of how forgiving the corporate world can be if bosses at the centre of a crisis act swiftly' – *The Economist*, 2014[3]

Richard Nixon chose to call one of his books *Six Crises*,[4] written well before the crisis he so badly managed that he was forced to resign the presidency. Some were indeed crises, some merely reflected Nixon's paranoia, his belief in that popular one-liner, 'infamy, infamy, they've all got it in for me'. Which, indeed, they had when his lack of talent for crisis management allowed the Watergate break-in to balloon into a career-ending scandal. As they might say in Las Vegas, Rupert Murdoch could see Nixon's six crises and raise him at least half a dozen more during the six decades in which he transformed himself into the media mogul he is today. The difference between Murdoch and Nixon – a man whose talents Rupert so admired that he invited him to be the keynote speaker at a corporate gathering after Nixon was forced to resign – was in their approaches to crisis management. Nixon whined, Rupert never does. Nixon hid behind subordinates, Murdoch puts himself in the firing line. Nixon denied complicity, Rupert confesses it. In short, the Nixon method led to disaster, the Murdoch Method to resolution and even new opportunities.

Start by distinguishing a crisis from the many other reasons Murdoch finds to intervene in specific events in which his companies become involved. At times, he intervenes because he loves the newspaper business. When Rupert rewrites a *New York Post* headline, as I have seen him do, and as Lachlan saw him do once too often for his comfort, he is intervening not because the paper is in crisis, but to pursue his first and most lasting love. When Rupert wanders into a staff meeting, he is intervening not because he has some crisis to solve, but because he is often a prisoner of his own curiosity and because he knows full well that the person on the other end of the conversation will carefully consider any guidance Rupert offers during what may have started as a casual chat. He does believe that these drop-ins are well received: 'I think people like it if I show interest in their work.'[5] Indulging a desire to pursue a first love, or satisfying curiosity while at the same time leaving an indication of his view on the course of action the staffer might take, are, in the context of the Murdoch Method, interventions, but they are not crisis management.

The Murdoch Method of confronting crises comes most clearly into play when one of two threats emerges: a threat to his personal or the corporations' reputation, or a financial threat that can bring down the empire. I have been with Rupert during some of the crises he has confronted, and watched him from afar during others, and believe that what has over time become the Murdoch Method – not because he read it in a management book, not because he suddenly thought it up one day – developed from individual responses to individual circumstances, forming a pattern worthy of the title 'Method'. To apply the Murdoch Method of crisis management one must:

- build reputational capital;
- take personal charge;
- prepare;
- accept responsibility and blame;
- pay for one's sins;
- convert crisis into opportunity.

A large stock of reputational capital is the key to all else when it comes to managing a crisis. And Rupert has a large balance in his reputational bank account, as even his enemies and critics admit. As far back as 1981, when the then owners of Times Newspapers Limited (TNL) were shopping for a buyer who would relieve them of the financial burden of a loss-making enterprise, they fixed on Rupert because, as Sir Gordon Brunton, managing director of TNL's parent company, put it, if Murdoch gave his word on a particular action, he would keep it.[6] He promised to and therefore would pour in the resources necessary to the survival of *The Times*, and would keep both *The Times* and *The Sunday Times* alive rather than shut them down and sell off the Gray's Inn Road building and other assets, and leave with a handsome profit, which under the terms of the purchase agreement he could have done. Or discontinue publishing the loss-making daily edition while continuing to publish the profitable *Sunday Times*.

I have had several experiences of my own with Rupert that permit me to testify that he is, indeed, 'a man of his word'. One is personal: never have I had to remind Rupert of some commitment. Others are anecdotal. After Rupert verbally agreed to a deal to purchase a media property, he reviewed it with me and, to my surprise, I found a way to make it a bit better deal for him without making it a worse deal for the seller. Rupert rejected the idea, not because he didn't recognise its advantage to him, but because, he said, 'I don't like to change a deal once I have agreed to it and left the room.' I have ever since been wary of a negotiator's version of *l'esprit de l'escalier*, the thoughts that occur afterwards.

Then, when purchasing *New York* magazine, Murdoch agreed to terms that his lawyers tried to improve upon when drafting the final documents. Lawyers will do that sort of thing, in part because they see it as their job, in part to demonstrate to the client how valuable they are. When counsel for the seller, a friend of mine and the man who relayed this tale to me, called Rupert and complained, Rupert reprimanded his lawyers and told them to prepare documents reflecting what he had agreed to, not what they thought they could wring out of the seller, which it turns out were items of office furniture of which the seller was inordinately fond.

Finally, there was a dinner at which I found myself seated next to Brenda Dean, now Baroness Dean of Thornton-le-Fylde, formerly head of the Society of Graphical and Allied Trades (SOGAT) print union during the so-called Wapping dispute, a fifty-four-week-long strike. Rupert had been chafing under the work rules imposed by the print unions, which required so much overmanning that one Saturday night as the presses rolled I saw more pay cheques being handed out than there were workers on the floor. According to Neil, one man sent his daughter to pick up his pay cheque.[7] Rupert complained that he employed six men per press in New York, not his most efficient operation, and eighteen in London.[8] He knew a showdown was inevitable, and so built and clandestinely equipped a plant in Wapping to produce all News International's papers. It would computerise the printing process, eliminate 'hot type' in favour of computers and reduce losses at *The Times*. When Dean responded by leading the printers out on strike, Murdoch fired them all, some 6,800, and the next morning produced all the company's papers in the new, computerised plant. Using 670 printers. The resulting strike turned violent, and mounted police had difficulty maintaining order in the face of mass picketing that brought back into action the rent-a-mob that had been used in the miners' strike. But the new presses rolled, and the papers were delivered by Peter Abeles' transport company when the railway unions refused to handle the papers, an illegal secondary boycott that resulted in fines that ultimately bankrupted Dean's union. Murdoch held on in the face of enormous political, social and trade union pressure. SOGAT folded. Rupert had saved not only his papers, but those of his more timid competitors who were then free to introduce cost-saving technologies in their plants without having to withstand a long strike.

It was then that I became a columnist for *The Sunday Times*. Several journalists – refuseniks – refused to move to Wapping, and I was enlisted to fill one of the blank spaces. When then-editor Andrew Neil sent me a proof of my first column, it was half as long as my draft, but had nothing of substance missing. The accompanying note advised that columns are for the readers, not the writers.

Baroness Dean, who by the time we met at a dinner party at Chequers during the Blair years had settled into a calmer life that included service on a board studying educational standards, knew that I had been a Murdoch consultant and friend during the strike, and had been seen accompanying Neil, the point man for Rupert during the bitter dispute, at dinners and other events. Which is why the prime minister expected fireworks at his dinner table. He was doomed to disappointment. Dean was quite pleasant as we talked over old times, and at one point in the conversation said that during the fraught negotiations, which ended in total defeat for the union, Rupert had kept every promise he had made. High praise from a defeated adversary.

But even a large supply of reputational capital is of little use unless its owner takes personal charge in a crisis – 'accepts ownership' of the problem is the more commonly used expression these days – which is what Murdoch did when confronted with three crises, each of which threatened to bring down all he had built: a financial crisis that almost caused him to lose control of his companies; the hacking scandal in Britain; and the sexual harassment suits at Fox News Channel. In such crises, anonymous or even well-known and highly regarded public relations spokesmen may be trotted out, lawyers consulted, but only the acknowledged man in charge can successfully call the shots. In a crisis, the all-clear sign is never clearly marked, and its location changes often and with dizzying speed. What seemed a solution in the morning is no longer available later in the day; escape hatches close, new ones must be found. The best person for that job must not only be quick-witted; he must have an overwhelming incentive to solve the problem in a way that preserves the viability of the enterprise, which bought-in 'crisis managers' often do not have; and he must see how every step along the way to a solution affects all other parts of the enterprise. Most important, Murdoch as crisis manager is known to have the power to have his companies honour any commitment he might make. Also, from Rupert's point of view, his personal management of a crisis puts him in an excellent position to decide who 'gets thrown under the bus', and who will be sacrificed to the gods of public opinion and the legal authorities should such a sacrifice be necessary, a thought that must at times in the heat of a crisis be unnerving to all employees who do not share his last name. Dynasts are rarely impartial in apportioning blame.

Rupert's reputation for doing as he promises, and being able to assure delivery of his promises, stood him and News in good stead when he made a losing bet that long-term interest rates were high and due to fall, and financed his expansion and costly effort to launch Sky Television with lower-cost, short-term debt. Rupert's first serious effort to break into British broadcasting in 1986 had been rebuffed in favour of a consortium that, in effect, planned to reproduce BBC-style elitist broadcasting from a satellite, using untried technology. In fact, the technology *was* tried: some of us who were racing to get Sky up and on air before BSB installed the latter's antenna, known as a 'squarial' because of its shape, in a Wapping office, and to our delight found that it did not work.

In June 1988 Rupert was given a second chance when a new satellite was launched, and he jumped at it, in typical Murdoch fashion and driven by a typically Murdoch incentive. 'Broadcasting in this country for too long has been the preserve of the old Establishment that has been elitist in its thinking and in its approach to programming,' he said at the time.[9] Rupert beat the establishment champion, BSB's limited four-channel service, to market with a four-channel service of his own, but one that could be easily expanded – Sky 1 (general entertainment); Sky News (a twenty-four-hour rolling news channel that Prime Minister Thatcher called 'the only unbiased news in the UK';[10] Sky Movies; and Eurosport. In fact, BSB never did get off the ground. It became clear that Sky and BSB would either merge or both 'spend themselves into oblivion', in the words of Sam Chisholm, eventual boss of the merged company.[11] Rupert, concealing the fact that he was just about out of money, in effect took over BSB – Chisholm fired almost the entire BSB staff – although the deal was dubbed a 'merger' to soothe the egos of BSB's establishment backers and to meet certain legal requirements as soon as the deal closed and got rid of dozens of high-end staff cars.

But making a television service available and getting people to watch it proved to be two different things. I remember with no pleasure that on frequent drives to Heathrow I forlornly counted the few, scattered satellite dishes, most of them in lower-income areas of London. The paucity of dishes resulted in part from actions by Labour-dominated town councils, which earlier had banned Murdoch newspapers from their libraries, and now barred the installation of dishes. All the while, money was pouring out of the door at the rate of £2 million every week, and debt was soaring. Rupert remained calm, or so it seemed when we spoke.

Then the world suddenly changed – war in the Gulf, liquidity squeezes, Japanese banks fleeing risk – and News Corp. was faced with the prospect of refinancing its short-term debt with much higher-cost loans – if the banks would permit. They wavered. Sometime during the crisis, on the evening before a meeting with the banks, I dined with Rupert and Lachlan. This was shortly after Lachlan, a few months past his nineteenth birthday, had joined his father's Australian company and flown with his father from Australia to witness the formal signing of the merger of Sky with BSB on 2 November 1990.[12] Anna Murdoch, always a source of strength and sound advice, was elsewhere. If the banks refused to roll over his debts – and the pattern of daring expansion and admittedly inattentive financial management made that outcome a real possibility – Rupert's dream of expanding his media holdings and passing them, intact, to his children would be the thing of which case studies in failure are made for the use of business school students.

It was a quiet dinner, with Rupert in a reflective mood. Among other things, he reminded us that his father had told him that the newspaper business is a potential tool for good, and that he hoped to remain a force in it. When we went our separate ways, I was touched to see Rupert and Lachlan stroll off into the London night, arm-in-arm, heading for Rupert's flat in St James's and, I guessed with certainty, a sleepless night. The next day, relief: Rupert's promises to reform financial management and cut costs carried the day with the lenders, in good part because of his reputation for keeping his word. With a little help from a friend, or so rumour has it.

Banks have a rule when dealing with a troubled creditor who needs a loan extension. The lead banks generally farm out pieces of the loan to other banks, to reduce risk. Banks agree that unless all of them consent to roll over the loan, none of them will. A small Pittsburgh bank, holding a tiny portion of the outstanding loan, was holding out.[13] The unverified rumour is that the president of that bank received a call from the White House suggesting that the Pittsburgh bank review its position. It did. That is one of those stories that is too good to check even if checking were possible.

In the course of these successful negotiations Murdoch also deployed another characteristic: his facility with financial data, what Andrew Neil calls 'an eerie grasp of numbers',[14] a fact of which I became aware in our periodic reviews of market conditions, interest rates and other empirical measures of how the economies of the world were doing. That facility with data combined with his willingness to do the hard preparation that every successful crisis manager must do to prepare for every twist and turn of the crisis. One lesson I have learned from years working on corporate litigation, consulting with lawyers and with their clients, is that it is difficult to persuade successful executives of the need for preparation, which is one reason I suspect that Bill Gates did so badly when deposed in the Microsoft antitrust case. Their superior position in often rigid hierarchies insulates them from criticism or close questioning of what they say or believe or remember. Regulatory and legislative bodies before which they appear, and bankers with large problematic loans outstanding, are not nearly as awed by top executives as are the executives' business colleagues, and the questioning is often hostile, in the case of politicians for no other reason than that such an approach will net the questioner a few precious minutes on the late television news programmes. Having worked with Rupert on several speeches, I know the value he places on preparation – trying out phrases, rewriting those that do not trip easily off the tongue, making sure he has his facts right.

In addition to having a store of reputational capital, and taking personal charge after careful preparation, the successful crisis manager must accept responsibility for the mess with which he is dealing. 'When mistakes are made,' Rupert's one-time chief finan-cial officer told Murdoch's biographer, 'he never kicks the dog and says you recommended it.'[15] Rupert did not try to blame the huge losses incurred in the Myspace acquisition and eventual sale on some outside event or unfortunate executive. 'We just messed up. The buck stops with me.'[16] In fact, there were millions of bucks, the loss of which were, in the end, his responsibility. Such apolo-gies do not eliminate all the reputational damage of the initial errors, but they do take the crises off the front pages, although not out of the archives sourced by historians and biographers.

Accepting responsibility, of course, is not the end of the road in most crises. The piper will be paid. After personal intervention and public apology Murdoch's next step in diffusing a crisis is to arrange compensation for injured parties, partly because that is the decent thing to do, partly as a sign of contrition, partly to avoid costly litigation and partly to convey the message that, the price of folly having been paid, it is time to move on. Not quite as dramatic as the Arab custom of paying blood money to compen-sate the family of a murder victim and thereby avoid punishment of the murderer, but it will do until some better means of putting paid to a crisis comes to hand. Victims of the hacking scandal were compensated, as were authors badly treated by Murdoch's publishing companies (see Chapter 6), and multimillion-dollar settlements paid to women accusing Fox News' executives and commentators of sexual harassment.

Having defused a crisis, Murdoch next turns to ways to capitalise on it. Perhaps the most famous crisis Murdoch confronted arose when some *News of the World* operatives hacked into the mobile phones of celebrities to obtain scoops. That story is too well known, and my knowledge only what I have read in the papers, to justify more than a sketchy retelling here. The hackers included some who gained access to the phone of Millie Dowler, a fourteen-year-old girl abducted and then raped and murdered.

Public revulsion resulted in parliamentary hearings at which James, in charge of News' UK operations, denied knowledge of the hacking, and Rupert, in a halting performance, expressed regret. Although never charged with direct responsibility for the hacking, or even with knowledge of it, Rupert arguably set the tone of the corporate culture that emphasised scoops as a competitive tool, especially in the tabloid segment of the newspaper market. That made celebrities and establishment figures fair game for reporters with an incentive to push the line between the legal, stories deemed to be in the public interest, and the illegal. And not only when celebrity hunting, but when onto a juicy crime story.

The hacking crisis threatened the very existence of the Murdoch media empire. Not because of the millions to be paid to aggrieved parties, many of them celebrities who had never before revealed an aversion to publicity, and indeed hired publicists to make sure they were not forgotten by the press. Rather, the threat arose because the Dowler case was such an insult to everyone's sense of propriety, because the subsequent legal problems might result in criminal action against the corporation in America, and because the hacking might induce the regulators to strip Sky of its broadcast licence. Which explains the dramatic nature of the action Rupert took, more dramatic than in other crises, but consistent with the Murdoch Method of crisis management. Unfortunately, the application was far from flawless.

Rupert did take personal charge, flying to London to manage the fallout from the hacking activities. But, unlike other crises, this one occurred where he did not have a deep well of reputational capital on which to draw. Members of Parliament drove the investigation. They are not bankers or business partners, who know that they are dealing with a man who keeps his word. Many MPs, past and present, have personal reasons to dislike Rupert because his papers had exposed some of the doings they would rather have kept private, or opposed their election. Others, members of the establishment that Rupert so disdains, saw the hacking scandal as the logical culmination of his willingness to discomfit their class. Still others resented the cultural effect of *The Sun*.

So Murdoch's decision to take personal charge, while unavoidable, did not advance the defence. Especially since for the first time I can remember he was not well prepared to confront his company's accusers. I have great regard for Joel Klein, the lawyer who accompanied Rupert to the hearings but might not have been in charge of his preparation, and can only guess that he suffered as he watched Rupert's appearance before the parliamentary committee: halting, disjointed and stumbling, so much so that rumours began to circulate that Murdoch had finally succumbed to old age.

But his acceptance of responsibility did accomplish one thing: by diverting some of the anger from James to himself, and arranging a hasty exit for James from Britain, Rupert prevented the scandal from ruining his son's future prospects. And by making a very public apology to the Dowler family, authorising payments to them and other affected parties, agreeing to complete cooperation with the police as they pursued their investigation, he diffused some of the public anger. As Sir Harold Evans, no fan of Rupert's, but a practised observer of his tactics, put it, 'Murdoch senior's bluntness had the effect of rendering James's testimony inconsequential ... James, the eager mollifier, was too ready to seek refuge in convoluted references ... and patronizing explanations.'[17] Not least of all, Rupert converted this hacking disaster into several opportunities. On which he pounced.

For many years Rupert indicated to me and others that he wanted to replace the *News of the World* with a seventh-day edition of *The Sun*. The circulation of the *News of the World* was falling, the taste for salacious stories was declining or being satisfied on television and on the internet, the cost savings would be significant, and News would have only one brand with which to familiarise advertisers. So although Rupert undoubtedly regretted the crisis that forced his hand, he closed the *News of the World*, and had his staff compose and get a *Sun on Sunday* on the streets in record time.

The second opportunity on which Rupert pounced was the opening to move James to America, something James had long resisted. As reaction to the scandal became more vociferous, it must have become clear to James that it was in his interest to get out of the firing line in Britain. Rupert had James step down as chairman of News International, in which post he had responsibility for the company's UK newspapers involved in the scandal, and parachuted him to the safety of America as soon-to-be CEO of what would be the 21st Century Fox Entertainment Group. Hands-off, which might have prevented Lachlan's departure, became hands-on in the case of James.

And then, in a move that amazed even me, and dents my pride in being unsurprised by any daring move by Rupert, he added the chairmanship of Sky to James's title and role as CEO of 21st Century Fox. Ofcom's decision to leave James's future with Sky to the discretion of the company's board was the opening Rupert needed. The eleven-member board, including its six independent directors, unanimously approved the move.

The third opportunity resulted from the fact that Murdoch found himself awash with cash. The hacking scandal made it impossible for him to obtain regulatory approval of News' acquisition of the remaining shares of BSkyB, at least at that time. That freed up considerable cash with which to pursue another opportunity – placating shareholders upset with the possible consequences for News, both in Britain and in the US. So Rupert announced a $5 billion share buy-back, shoring up his share price and calming nervous shareholders. He would have preferred to have won all of BSkyB, but better to turn crisis into

Murdoch in the offices of the *New York Post*, 1985, displaying a sample of newspapers and magazines published by News Corp.

New York Mayor Ed Koch shakes hands with Murdoch at a 1988 party marking the tenth anniversary of Murdoch's acquisition of *New York* magazine after a bitter takeover battle. Former Governor Hugh Carey (centre) looks on.

Murdoch talks with reporters during 1981 negotiations with print unions before purchase of Times Newspapers.

Murdoch at a press conference at the Portman Hotel in 1981, after finalising purchase of Times Newspapers. Harold Evans, editor of *The Sunday Times* (left) and William Rees-Mogg, editor of *The Times*, look on.

Murdoch announces 1993 expansion of Sky Television, first launched in 1989, to include more than 20 channels.

President John F. Kennedy meets with Murdoch in the Oval Office in 1961.

China's President Jiang Zemin greets Murdoch at the 1999 exhibition of treasures from China's Golden Age, six years after Murdoch's speech claiming satellite television would threaten dictatorships resulted in a ban on satellite dishes in China.

French President Nicolas Sarkozy greets Murdoch during a G8 meeting in 2011 of information technology leaders at the Tuileries Gardens in Paris. Christine Lagarde, France's economy minister and later managing director of the International Monetary Fund looks on.

Murdoch and presidential candidate Donald Trump on the latter's Aberdeen golf course in 2016. Trump's victory is said by many to have been facilitated by the support he received from Murdoch's Fox News.

Keith Murdoch in 1936. His views on the responsibility of journalists shaped his son's use of the media properties he controls.

Murdoch with his mother, Dame Elisabeth, in 2005, at Keith Murdoch House in Adelaide, Australia. She preached the importance of high standards: 'Making money is not greatness'.

Murdoch addresses a crowded newsroom at *The Wall Street Journal* in 2007 to reassure nervous staff of his intention to preserve the editorial independence of the paper and to invest funds needed to broaden its news coverage.

Murdoch testifies before a US congressional committee in 2010 that was looking into immigration policy. He has generally favoured a welcoming policy towards immigrants.

Roger Ailes is helped from his office to his car by wife Elizabeth Tilson in 2016. A few days later he was forced to resign as chairman and CEO of Fox News in the wake of accusations of sexual harassment, which Ailes denied until his death less than one year later.

Rupert Murdoch and Disney CEO Bob Iger announce sale of entertainment assets of 21st Century Fox to Disney.

opportunity than to settle for merely solving the crisis. And his existing control of almost 40 per cent of BSkyB's shares assured him that no one could gain control of it without purchasing the Murdoch holdings.

Most important of all, Murdoch finally agreed to do what many investors had long been calling for: a corporate revamp that pleased investors and suited his dynastic intentions. On 28 June 2013, he divided News Corp. into a growing entertainment film and television company, and a more static print operation, which he believes he can turn around. He is chairing both companies. Investors were pleased that part of Rupert's crisis management included paying greater attention to restless shareholders' interests. *The Economist* believes that 'The crisis forced Mr Murdoch, devoted newspaper man, to make difficult choices that he never would have in calmer circumstances.'[18] In a sense that is true, but in another sense it is not. Many businessmen, faced with a crisis of similar magnitude, decline to make difficult choices: car manufacturers had to be prodded by government to correct faulty ignition switches and pay restitution to customers; BP stumbled badly on its way to a response to its offshore oil spill; manufacturers of faulty airbags first blamed the problem on the weather, then refused to correct the fault in all vehicles, and eventually filed for bankruptcy; Volkswagen chose to subvert anti-pollution rules rather than make the necessary adjustments to its technology; a Murdoch rival, Robert Maxwell, may have solved his crisis by taking his own life.

Did the grasping of these opportunities offset the effect on Rupert, his closest colleagues and the company of the hacking scandal? Not with the legions of Murdoch-haters whose opinion was confirmed but not created by the scandal. For them the evil he does will live long after him. But for others, the new enterprise of Rupert & Son will be judged more by what it produces by way of profits and how it deports itself going forward.

Unfortunately for Rupert, that new enterprise was put to the test almost immediately upon its formation. On paper, Roger Ailes, the brilliant creator of the Fox News Channel that has contributed over $1 billion in annual profits to the entertainment company, was to report to James and Lachlan, rather than to Rupert, as he did before the corporate reorganisation. Ailes wasn't having it, for two reasons. First, there was bad blood between Roger and both James and Lachlan. Ailes had attacked James for allowing the hacking scandal to happen and for being slow to contain its fallout. And the Fox News boss had in effect forced Lachlan, who had responsibility for the Fox Television Stations group, out of the company when Lachlan refused to allot programming time to a crime series that Ailes was proposing. Rupert reportedly told Ailes, 'Do the show. Don't listen to Lachlan.'[19]

Second, there was the not small matter of Ailes' ego, and of his justifiable belief that he had been an important contributor to Fox News' success. He had bested CNN, an entrenched competitor in the rolling, twenty-four-hour news business, and was delivering $1.2–1.5 billion in profits,[20] 20 per cent of Fox's total. Fox News is so popular with viewers that cable companies pay dear for rights to broadcast it, and Fox has been able to use it as a bargaining chip when persuading cable companies to take other programmes, such as Fox Business Channel.[21] 'My job is to report to Rupert, and I expect that to continue,' Ailes claimed as a counter to the company press release announcing that he would henceforth report to Lachlan and James.[22] Caught between his sons and a much admired Ailes, Rupert first responded by confirming that Ailes would indeed report to James and Lachlan jointly. But he added that Ailes would 'continue his unique and longstanding relationship with Rupert'. Which, of course, included reporting directly to Rupert. A wonderful example of the Murdoch Method: Roger was unwilling to report to anyone other than Rupert, so Rupert satisfied James and Lachlan with a formal announcement that Ailes would report to them while at the same time assuring the Fox News supremo that his privileged position was unchanged. The net effect was to allow Ailes to avoid effective supervision by either Rupert or his sons. We might call this Rupert's pragmatic adaptation of formal lines of authority to the realities of the situation, in this instance with consequences that would contribute to a scandal that calls into question the efficacy of that part of the Murdoch Method that includes use of a large dollop of fudge to avoid a painful personnel decision.

Ailes seems to have felt secure that, despite the corporate reorganisation, he remained beyond the rules that govern other News Corp and Fox executives. CNN Money reports that what it describes as 'a long-time Rupert lieutenant' told its reporter, 'When you go well beyond your profit targets, the bosses don't comb through your spending',[23] especially when the boss is enjoying the sight of an enraged, overmatched media establishment's discomfort at Fox News' success, both financial and ideological. Gabriel Sherman, an Ailes biographer who persistently covers Fox and who has developed inside sources regarded in the business as highly reliable, reports that one source told him that when it came to Fox News' budgets, 'You didn't ask questions and Roger wouldn't entertain questions.'

Whether that sense of omnipotence led Ailes to feel free to indulge a taste for harassing or at least humiliating female employees, as charged in a series of lawsuits, but denied by Ailes, we cannot be certain, since the presumption of innocence has not been tested in a court of law and might never be: Ailes died shortly after the scandal broke. But Fox's willingness to pay out tens of millions in settlements suggests that its attorneys are not eager for such a test, either because they feel they would lose or because of the ongoing negative publicity for their client.

Ailes' woes began when Gretchen Carlson, television anchor on *Fox and Friends*, sued him for sexual harassment – for making her job contingent on the granting of sexual favours – and for wrongful termination. As has since become commonplace when one such suit is filed, some twenty other women followed with similar lawsuits, suggesting, according to *The New York Times*, always on the alert for new fuel for its anti-Murdoch campaign, that 'sexual harassment was a persistent problem in the [Fox News] workplace'.[24] Ailes denied any such behaviour, claiming that 'the [Carlson] suit is wholly without merit', initiated because she realised that 'her career with the network was likely over'. Similar denials followed the filing of copycat lawsuits.

Those denials were filed for Ailes by Susan Estrich, an Ailes friend, a sometime Fox on-air commentator, a distinguished attorney at the prestigious law firm of Quinn Emanuel Urquhart & Sullivan, and, most important, a feminist icon, a rape victim and author of seminal works pointing out that sexual harassment is a serious problem. Estrich was careful to distinguish what Sarah Ellison, a reliable chronicler of the doings at the Murdoch companies, called Ailes' 'crude and cavalier behaviour toward women [that] was well known inside the company' from sexual harassment.[25] In an interview with Ellison, Estrich pointed out that the issue in the Carlson case was sexual harassment, not 'crude and cavalier behaviour ... Tacky behaviour, inappropriate behaviour, overtures you'd prefer not to have – that is not sexual harassment.'

That distinction, important in a court of law, is less commanding when it comes to setting policy of a major company. James in effect took over the role of crisis manager previously assumed by his father. He quickly persuaded the more circumspect Lachlan – the two were attending an industry gathering at the Sun Valley Resort in Idaho when the news broke – to order an investigation. Rupert, who was in the air en route to Sun Valley, was not consulted, although in my experience in Rupert's aeroplanes he can be reached quite easily by phone. Paul, Weiss, Rifkind, Wharton & Garrison, a distinguished law firm, was retained and quickly rendered its report. Among other findings, the investigators reported that $3 million had been paid by Fox to settle similar charges brought against Ailes, and that the payment had been concealed from the board and the auditors by a bit of accounting legerdemain performed by the corporate treasurer, who promptly retired. Did Rupert know about the payment? Probably not. Should he or someone high up in management have known? Probably, yes, even though the sums involved in early settlements of sexual harassment claims amounted to little more than 'a rounding error' in a company producing more than $1 billion in annual profits, and subsequent settlements did not bring the total to a level that would have a material effect on its finances, according to the company. Few doubt that there were some executives who knew of Ailes' doings and the settlements, and that some subsequent 'retirements' were less than voluntary. Rupert sided with James, not an easy decision for him. Ailes was a friend; he had been instrumental in the creation of an alternative to the unbalanced coverage of the liberal news media; he had brought billions into News' coffers; and he was backed by several on-camera stars who were threatening to quit if Ailes were fired (they later withdrew their support as more facts emerged).

The back story to all of this extends far beyond any disgust by Lachlan and James at Ailes' alleged behaviour. One chapter in that back story is that the handling of the crisis proves Rupert's willingness to cede power to his successors – real power. 'A successful patriarch ...' writes *The Economist*, 'may be a bothersome back-seat driver long after relinquishing the steering wheel ... A striking number of patriarchs suffer from "sticky-baton syndrome".'[26]

Rupert did not succumb to the temptation to hold on to the steering wheel or, as *The New York Times* put it, the reins:

They [James and Lachlan] have shaken up 21st Century

Fox's profile in Washington, replacing their father's Republican lobbying chief with a Democratic one. They have jettisoned film executives, overhauled foreign TV operations and dug into the evolution of cable channels such as National Geographic.

Their father, Rupert Murdoch, handed them the reins of 21st Century Fox only a year ago. But since then, James and Lachlan have been remaking the company at break-neck speed.[27]

But, added the report, Fox news is 'one corner of the company ... where the generational shift has not been visible'. That was in July 2016. Before the year ended, that 'corner of the company' was no longer exempt from the generational shift. 'The New Age of Murdochs', announced the entertainment industry bible *The Hollywood Reporter*, is 'now firmly atop 21st Century Fox'.[28]

The second chapter in the back story relates to James's political and social views. Well before the Ailes imbroglio James had become appalled at the prospect of a Trump presidency, and the role Fox News was playing in making the Trump candidacy viable. Adding fuel to the anti-Trump fire was his wife, Kathryn, an active environmentalist and Hillary Clinton supporter, who tweeted before the election, 'A vote for Trump is a vote for climate catastrophe', and after it, 'I can't believe this is happening. I am so ashamed.'[29] Both James and Kathryn believed, and with reason, that Ailes had biased Fox News' coverage of the campaign in favour of Trump,[30] although such vigorously anti-Trump commentators as George Will, Charles Krauthammer and Megyn Kelly were given ample airtime in which to have their say. Nevertheless, a Pew poll revealed that 40 per cent of Trump voters and 47 per cent of conservatives relied on Fox News for their election coverage and as a main source of news.[31] No doubt that group included many predisposed to vote for Trump, but, if any of them wavered in the face of Trump's serial gaffes, they must have found Fox News' reporting and commentary reassuring.

Worse still in James's view, the Ailes problem extends beyond the immediate confines of the news operation. He believes that the reputation of Fox News 'casts an unfavourable shadow on other parts of the company, particularly in Hollywood',[32] the business and social milieu in which he operates. Not so different from Barry Diller's earlier concern, expressed at a gathering of corporate executives in Aspen, that the company's gossipy tabloids made life difficult for Fox by printing reports that movie stars found unpleasant, and by taking political positions at variance with the left-wing Hollywood worldview. That was in 1988. Rupert refused to rein in his beloved tabloids to please the Hollywood liberals. Almost three decades later, in an analogous situation, Rupert agreed to a house-cleaning at Fox, either to lessen James's Diller-like problem in Hollywood, or to bow to changing mores.

The law firm report in hand, James demanded what Winston Churchill, whom he is fond of quoting, called 'Action this day' – immediate dismissal. Lachlan soon concurred. The brothers rejected the argument that action should be deferred until after the presidential election in November so as not to jeopardise the quality of the coverage and the high ratings Fox was achieving. They eventually persuaded Rupert that Ailes had to go, immediately, and that ratings for Fox's coverage of the Republican convention would not be impaired. Only three weeks after the scandal broke, Ailes was unceremoniously escorted from the Fox offices and building by security personnel. He did receive a $40 million severance package that Ailes says was a golden goodbye for past services, and Fox contends was due under Ailes' employment contract, taking that position either because it was true, or to appease James, who opposed any severance payment.

There is some feeling at Fox News that the speed with which Ailes and others accused of sexual harassment were dispatched had as much to do with James's dislike of all the network stands for, and his desire to rid himself of the on-air Trump supporters, as it did with the nature of the offences charged. They point out that he treated a similar problem on his hometown turf, Hollywood, in a far different manner. One month before Ailes was fired 21st Century Fox put up billboards to promote the film *X-Men: Apocalypse*. They showed the villain strangling a woman, with the caption 'Only the strong will survive'. Women's groups were outraged. Actress Rose McGowan released a statement, 'There is a major problem when the men and women at 20th Century Fox [*sic*] think casual violence against women is the way to market a film … The fact that no one flagged this is offensive and frankly stupid … The geniuses behind this, and I use the term lightly, need to take a long hard look at the mirror and see how they are contributing to society … Since you can't manage to put any women directors on your slate for the next two years, how about you at least replace the ad?'[33]

Jennifer McCleary-Sills, director of gender violence and rights for the International Center on Research on Women, added, 'What really is the challenge here is the intentionality of it. You could have chosen any from the thousands of images, but you chose this one. Whose attention did you want to get and to what end?'[34] The powers that be at 21st Century Fox apologised and withdrew the ads. So far as is known, no law firm was hired to advise the company on what additional action to take. No one was fired.

In a final twist, all three Murdochs agreed that Rupert should assume Ailes' vacant posts as chairman and acting CEO of Fox News Channel and Fox Business Network until a suitable long-term successor could be named – a bonus for Rupert, who is delighted to serve as an editor of a news organisation, with hands-on responsibility for daily decisions. In typical fashion, Rupert announced an expansion of the channel's news operation, including more reporters and a new Manhattan studio, and a purging of sleepy commercials during prime-time broadcasts. 'He's one of us – he's a news guy,' enthused Brit Hume, the network's long-time and much-respected political analyst.[35] My long familiarity with Rupert's love of being on top of the news, of having information sources not available to most people, supports Hume's assessment. One Fox source told me that 'they will have to dynamite him out of that chair'. High-level Fox executives estimate that Rupert is spending 80 per cent of his time on programming and otherwise steering Fox News through the crisis created by the scandals and the departure of some of its leading stars.

So Ailes was gone, and an era was ending at Fox News. One unnamed executive told reporters at the *Daily Mail*, a rival British tabloid, Rupert 'can be done with people very quickly and he's not very emotional about it'.[36] Perhaps. But when taking over from Ailes, Rupert paid tribute to the man who 'has made a remarkable contribution to our company and our country. Roger shared my vision of a great and independent television organization and executed it brilliantly for over 20 great years. Fox News has given voice to those who were ignored by the traditional networks ... against seemingly entrenched monopolies ... Roger has defied the odds.'[37] After Ailes was deposed Rupert invited him to what the *Daily Mail* described as 'an awkward last supper luncheon at his upscale New York home'.[38] Shortly thereafter Roger Ailes was dead. A haemophiliac, he fell, struck his head and died a few days later.

I have seen the side of Rupert that the *Daily Mail* – a competing newspaper, remember – reports. But I have also seen him hang on to old loyalists long after mere commercial consideration dictated their departure. He was unable to do that in the case of Ailes, but his kind words and show of continued affection by inviting

Roger to lunch after all that had gone on encouraged others at Fox to remember Ailes for acts other than those that brought about his downfall. The outpouring of tearful regret from Fox staff, including many women telling stories of his support for their careers, and stars such as Brit Hume and Bret Baier relating his many kindnesses when they confronted devastating personal problems, revealed a side of Roger Ailes not widely known.

If Rupert has any regrets about his inability to protect Ailes from the wrath of James and Lachlan, he can take some satisfaction from the fact that their decisiveness proves the wisdom of his lifelong dream of turning over his empire to them, even though (or perhaps because) they bring a much-needed new sensibility to the management of their inheritance. Even if what Susan Estrich classifies as 'tacky behaviour' is not illegal, it can cross the line of what even a media empire based on pushing the envelope of acceptable behaviour can tolerate in a world in which it increasingly relies on selling the 'eyeballs' of consumers, male and female, to advertisers with a more modern sensibility. Even more important, the Murdoch enterprises need to attract talented women such as Megyn Kelly, and reports of the culture at Fox cannot be of much help in that endeavour.

Kelly, the talented Fox News commentator, was the star around whom James and Lachlan were planning to build a more modern Fox News, appealing to a younger audience. The average age of Fox viewers is sixty-eight,[39] and advertisers are only willing to pay lower per-minute rates for these older viewers than CNN captures for its younger demographic. In the event, with her contract due to expire, Kelly rejected a $100 million, four-year pay offer from Fox and moved on to NBC and the challenge of daytime television and of taking on CBS's long-running *60 Minutes* weekly news programme. Initial ratings are disappointing.

Hard on the heels of Kelly's move came the forced departure of yet another star presenter. *The New York Times* revealed that

Fox had paid $13 million to settle five harassment claims made against its star commentator Bill O'Reilly, the linchpin of Fox News evening programming. A cancellation stampede by sponsors of his programme followed. The number of commercials on *The O'Reilly Factor* fell from around forty to eight[40] (other estimates vary), although the financial impact on the network was softened by most advertisers' decision to shift their buy to other Fox programmes. James called for the immediate firing of O'Reilly, but Lachlan hesitated, reportedly deciding to go along with James only after his wife, Sarah, convinced him and Rupert who, like Lachlan, sets great store by her advice, that the FNC star had to go.[41] In the end it was O'Reilly vs Kathryn and Sarah Murdoch: no contest.

Observers predicted disaster for FNC. No Ailes. No Kelly. No O'Reilly. Rupert, declaring confidence that 'the strength of its [Fox's] talent bench' would assure that 'the network will continue to be a powerhouse in cable news',[42] immediately selected Tucker Carlson (no relation to Gretchen Carlson, who had filed the original complaint against Ailes) to replace the more centrist Kelly, and then moved him into O'Reilly's slot when O'Reilly was forced out. After some fluctuations in the ratings, the interim head of Fox News, and chairman of the board, proved to have understood his audience better than did his critics. In the quarter ending June 2017 the Fox network was first in prime-time viewers, increased its audience of the twenty-five- to fifty-four-year-olds that had previously eluded them by 21 per cent to take first place in that demographic. Carlson not only beat O'Reilly's ratings, he is a lot less expensive. And the talk show that replaced Kelly drew larger audiences than she did. Further tinkering by Rupert with the schedule is now an ongoing affair, with many of the changes taking the network further to the right, most recently by hiring right-wing talk-show host Laura Ingraham to fill the ten o'clock slot. Although MSNBC, the liberal counterpart to Fox, is gaining in some time segments, 'Fox News is still the full-day leader overall', according to *The New York Times*.[43]

Still, Fox News did not escape from the several scandals unharmed. MSNBC, its liberal counterpart, is growing faster in the young demographic, and its *Rachel Maddow Show* is number one in that key demographic. Its anti-Trump stance is attracting larger audiences than ever, making the Fox-vs-MSNBC battle a mirror image of the sharp political divide that characterises American politics. Rupert's success so far has probably increased the difficulty James faces in his drive to move Fox towards the centre of the political spectrum. If anything, with the removal of O'Reilly it has moved a bit to the right. In the longer run, any chance James has of realising his and his wife's desire to move FNC more to the centre-left of the political spectrum will depend very much on which buttons viewers will be pushing on their remotes in a new era in which Ailes' programming genius is unavailable to Fox, and a controversial President Trump dominates the news.

James's father is satisfied that this crisis, like others before it, has been turned into an opportunity: a new line-up with commentators more attractive to the younger viewers that have so far avoided Fox, salary costs reduced, his own 'feel' for what consumers want reaffirmed, and a continued although shrinking lead over CNN and MSNBC. The immediate future of Fox News is in Rupert's hands; the longer-term future will be determined by Lachlan, who tells me he is eager to preserve this important part of his father's legacy.

Eventually, of course, even greater change will come to what is now in important respects a Murdoch & Sons enterprise. No media enterprise dependent on advertiser goodwill, no matter how daring, and no matter how successful it has been in changing the culture of the market it serves, can long defy fundamental changes in societal mores. But one thing that will survive the change in generational control is likely to be the Murdoch Method of coping with crises. As Rupert had done in crises past, his sons took personal control of the response to the crisis at Fox News. They agreed to have 21st Century Fox foot the $45 million cost of settlements with Ailes' accusers;[44] they cleared the executive suite of those who allegedly enabled Ailes to behave as he was charged with doing, and those who allegedly concealed the settlement payments from the auditors and the board; they restructured the Human Relations Department so that employee complaints would receive a more sympathetic response.

The response of James and Lachlan to the unfolding crisis was, in a way, an improvement on the manner of implementing the Murdoch Method's proscription for dealing with crises – no dithering as with the Patten crisis or initial bungling as with the hacking crisis: Ailes was to go, and now, and be locked out of his office, replaced by Rupert, who by video and in person explained the matter and the Murdochs' chosen solution to Fox's worldwide staff. Call it the Murdoch Method, Marque 2.

The deeper roots of the crisis – the tolerance of a macho boys-will-be-boys atmosphere at Fox – is being addressed by the Murdoch empire's new generation. As Gabriel Sherman put it in an interview with National Public Radio (roughly equivalent to the BBC, but largely reliant on voluntary contributions rather than a compulsory licence fee), there has been a 'change in management … James and Lachlan Murdoch are very much modern individuals. They understand how corporate America works, and they don't want their father's company to have this sort of outlaw-pirate-like culture that … Rupert Murdoch encouraged in building it into the global media empire that it is.'[45] Although both James and Lachlan are very much 'modern individuals', and equally appalled at the work environment at Fox News, they would not have approached their new assignment with identical sensibilities. James is comfortable in the socially and politically liberal Hollywood milieu, ever eager to give voice to that town's views on everything from climate change to Donald Trump. Lachlan is less likely to run with any political crowd, and generally confines his public speeches to citing his grandfather's fears of and objection to censorship of the media. James's wife Kathryn is a prolific tweeter who trumpets her embarrassment with any association with Fox News. Lachlan's wife Sarah prefers to offer advice to her husband and father-in-law privately, which she did when advising that Bill O'Reilly should be fired. James wants to 'reimagine' Fox News, by which he undoubtedly means bringing it more towards what he considers the political centre. Lachlan, to whom caution comes more naturally, seems a bit more sensitive to the financial implications of such a move and has spoken of 'the unique and important voice Fox News broadcasts'.[46]

These are real differences of style and views, less relevant should the almost-certain departure of James becomes a reality.

CHAPTER 6

RESPONSIBILITY

Big Julie (a gangster at a crap game): I'm rollin' the whole thousand. And to change my luck, I'm going to use my own dice.

Nathan Detroit (the defenceless host and gambler): Your own dice?

Big Julie: I had 'em made especially in Chicago.

Nathan: I do not wish to seem petty, but may I have a look at those dice? But these dice ain't got no spots on 'em. They're blank.

Big Julie: I had the spots removed for luck. But I remember where the spots formerly were.

Nathan: You are going to roll blank dice and remember where the spots were?

Big Julie: Detroit … do you doubt my memory?

Nathan: Big Julie, I have great trust in you.

From Guys and Dolls, Frank Loesser, 1955[1]

'A paper must be fearless, and sometimes even offend its friends and supporters, but if it is founded upon truth, it will entrench itself more and more in the confidence of the public' – Keith Murdoch, 1921[2]

'Just produce better papers, papers that people want to read. Stop having people write articles just to produce Pulitzer Prizes. Give people what they want to read and make it interesting' – Rupert Murdoch, 2008[3]

Rupert Murdoch is well aware of the Rudyard Kipling/Stanley Baldwin jibe about power without responsibility, and believes it has nothing to do with him. He is right – sort of. Anyone who knows Rupert even moderately well knows that one of his greatest ambitions is to live up to the injunction laid down by his father, the legendary Sir Keith Murdoch, to use newspapers as a force for good, a force with which to challenge government overreach and 'establishment' orthodoxy. This was reinforced by his formidable mother, a force in Rupert's life until her death at the age of 103, who said she 'did long to be able to help Rupert prove worthy of his father in the newspaper world'.[4] Not to be ignored, as events were to prove, was Rupert's grandfather's exhortation to Sir Keith, 'Don't lack cheek.'

That Rupert has succeeded in the cheeky bit there is no doubt. Whether he has succeeded in discharging the responsibility laid on him by Sir Keith is a question the answer to which depends on the point of view of the observer. My belief is that he has, with certain exceptions. Dame Elisabeth once complained about 'all those horrid papers you're putting out' and urged her son to publish 'something decent for a change'.[5] Which, to her delight,[6] he proceeded to do the following year, 1964, creating *The Australian*, a serious national broadsheet, and the first newspaper Murdoch had created rather than inherited or purchased. Rupert told its editor, 'I want to be able to produce a newspaper that my father would have been proud of.'[7] 'It was my father's dream.'[8] Like the tabloid *New York Post*, which has rolled up hundreds of millions of dollars of losses, like Sky, like Fox News, the broad-sheet *Australian* burned money in its early years.[9] No matter: 'Publishing is not about making money; it's about achieving things and improving society,' Rupert announced to the staff when he regained control of the *New York Post*.[10] Almost twenty years later the existence of this serious broadsheet was cited as one reason why Rupert Murdoch, he of tabloid fame, could be trusted to buy *The Times* and *The Sunday Times*, and maintain them as quality papers different from *The Sun* and *News of the World*.[11]

Sir Keith's heroic defiance of authority at the risk of his journalistic career dominates not only Rupert's approach to journalism, but those of his children. It is over 100 years since Sir Keith penned the Gallipoli Letter, but it is as potent a force in shaping the behaviour not only of Rupert, but of the next generation of Murdochs, as if it were written yesterday. In 2014 Lachlan Murdoch took to the State Library of Victoria to deliver what is now the Sir Keith Murdoch Oration, and called on his audience to be true to Sir Keith's memory by resisting all efforts of governments to censor the press: 'We should be vigilant of the gradual erosion of our freedom to know, to be informed, and make reasoned decisions in our society and in our democracy.'[12] That is only one of the responsibilities that Lachlan's grandfather, Rupert's father, has laid on the shoulders of his progeny. Implicit in his directive is the responsibility of newspaper proprietors to decide at times that the government is wrong and that they are right, that the establishment that attempts to keep from the public news it finds inconvenient cannot be allowed the final voice in what the public learns. That accounts in part for the adversarial attitude towards authority that dominates every Murdoch media enterprise.

But no media enterprise can survive without profits and access to capital, a point James Murdoch quite properly makes when called upon to step back and consider the Murdochs' responsibilities. Media companies must attract viewers and readers, and appeal to advertisers who with increasing ease can take their money elsewhere. So the competition must be bested if the enterprise is to profit and survive. And in the case of News that victory must be won against entrenched competitors, in part by operating within a corporate culture in which it is considered desirable to shock, to push the envelope of taste and morals, to chortle when the establishment winces. At the same time as he attempts such market triumph and the fostering of News' unique cultural atmosphere, Rupert is hearing the voices of Sir Keith and Dame Elisabeth, speaking on behalf of 'responsibility'. The balancing of these pressures of heritage and commerce, not always but sometimes in conflict, is a difficult task, as the warring visions of James and his sister, Elisabeth (to be discussed later), demonstrate. Especially

when that responsibility includes a self-imposed dynastic requirement – Rupert's unalterable goal of passing on to his heirs a media
empire built on the principles believed to be consistent with the
wishes of one's father, and hammered home for decades by a very
determined mother, one of Australia's greatest philanthropists –
'Every time she calls,' Rupert once joked to me, and with considerable pride, 'it costs me $5 million.'

The Murdoch Method of sorting through these pressures is
rather like that of Big Julie in *Guys and Dolls*. Just as the gangster
was the only one who remembered where the spots are on his
spotless dice, so Murdoch is the only one who knows with
certainty the location of the line that separates responsible from
irresponsible journalism, decent from indecent entertainment. It
is his job to create a culture that provides thousands of employees
with guidance as to where that line is.

The Murdoch Method is an attempt to find the middle ground
between unworkable rigidity and equally unworkable anarchy.
Rupert knows he cannot impose identical limits on all the
products of his sprawling, multimedia, multinational company.
Workforce attitudes, the political situation, the legal environment
and society's cultural standards vary from country to country, from
media type to media type. Rupert knows, from over six decades in
the business, that the line also shifts as public notions of decency
evolve. To transmit his views on just where that line is located
he exerts hands-on control when necessary or simply because
it pleases him to do so, leaves things to trusted subordinates to
divine his views and to others to make good, informed guesses.
Not perfect, but it is difficult to imagine how it might be otherwise, how Murdoch might retain the 'outsider' and freewheeling
culture that has proved the cornerstone of his management style
and the company's success, while also institutionalising rules that
clearly set out the limits to how far the so-called envelope can be
pushed.

The problems Rupert has with attempting to apply his parents' interdictions are obvious: they were crafted in a day when Sir Keith's, and later Rupert's, main concern was with newspapers. The newspaper industry has always had its raucous elements: in colonial and post-colonial America newspapers were typically one-party advocates capable of the most scurrilous attacks on political opponents. And neither in the US nor in the UK were newspapers of yore models of objective reporting: from Northcliffe (much admired by Keith) to Beaverbrook (an admirer of Keith) to Hearst, proprietors managed reporting to suit their political positions, a tradition followed by Rupert with his tabloids. Legend has it that when Rupert was asked if he would tell his first UK acquisition what to print and what to say, he replied, 'I did not come all this way [from Australia] not to interfere.'[13]

Rupert has two advantages when trying to meet the standards set for him by his parents. The first is a deep understanding of the newspaper market and of its separate segments: to say he has printer's ink in his veins is not too much of an exaggeration. The second is that he can follow the rules laid down for him using what were once broadsheets (since the reduction in size of *The Times* the more accurate description is 'the serious press') for serious reporting, discharging that part of his public responsibility, and the tabloids both for fun and to honour his perceived obligation to bring news to the non-establishment masses, to harry the establishment and to be 'cheeky'.

When Rupert moves from newspapers to book publishing, and on to film and other entertainment, his inherited guidelines become somewhat less applicable, his confidence when applying them less sure, his colleagues less certain and less accustomed to responding to a little touch of Rupert in the night, rather than a direct order. As is demonstrated by a separate consideration of the three broad areas of his companies' operations: newspapers, in which he finds Sir Keith perched on his shoulder, book publishing, in which his parents' voices are present but less clearly applicable, and the multimedia world of entertainment, in which their voices become almost inaudible, leaving this self-styled 'prude'[14] adrift in a sea of the modern cultural products that are the stuff of Hollywood.

In the newspaper business Rupert is sufficiently confident in his judgement to rely heavily on hands-on control, especially in the case of his tabloids – the *New York Post* and, in Britain, *The Sun*. Rupert believes that having his name on the masthead is truth-in-labelling: readers who buy the *Post* do so in full knowledge that what they read has the imprint of K. Rupert Murdoch stamped clearly on it. In Britain, where such masthead identification is not used, Rupert's control of *The Sun*'s policies is well known. Indeed, he told a parliamentary committee that he has 'editorial control' over which party *The Sun* will back in a general election.[15] If some of the content of his tabloids is offensive, so be it. 'A paper must be fearless, and sometimes even offend its friends and supporters,' wrote Keith Murdoch in a leading article in praise of Northcliffe and published in Australia's *Herald* in 1921.[16] And in cases in which readers take justifiable offence, Rupert takes responsibility, as with the chimpanzee cartoon mentioned in Chapter 4. More amusingly, when asked by Barbara Walters, the celebrated television interviewer, if it is true that he interferes in what gets reported in the *Post*, Murdoch replied, 'I can't be said to interfere. I own it.'[17]

So much pleasure does Murdoch take from his control of the *Post* – Andrew Neil writes that Rupert is willing 'to sustain open-ended losses at *The New York Post* because of the enjoyment the paper gives him'[18] – that he was not willing to cede de facto control to his son Lachlan. Rupert was in the habit of 'cropping up visibly a few times a month',[19] one of the reasons – but only one – that Lachlan fled News Corp. headquarters in New York to spend more time with his family and to establish an entrepreneurial business operation in Australia.

Some years ago, one of Murdoch's associates asked me how he might approach 'the boss' to discuss closing down the loss-making *Post*. I told him that was a bad idea, for several reasons. First and foremost, getting the paper out every day is one of the incentives for Rupert to show up at the office. Second, the losses are manageable given the scale of the entire News enterprise, the equivalent of the cost of the executive washroom in a tiny firm. Third, the *Post* provides an important intangible – political clout. In short, leave well enough alone. Which he very wisely did.

Rupert, being more in New York than in London in recent years, with the exception of a protracted stay in Britain immediately after his marriage to Jerry Hall, has to exert his influence on *The Sun*, News' UK tabloid, somewhat more remotely, with numerous telephone calls not only to whoever is sitting in the editor's chair, but to individual reporters and columnists. No *Sun* editor is under the illusion that there is a chain of command that runs from Rupert through him and on to staff, and from staff upward through the editor and on to Rupert. Instead, whenever circumstances seem to require or when the spirit moves him, Murdoch will contact any staff member to give his views on the previous day's paper or provide suggestions for tomorrow's. Rebekah Wade (now Brooks) understood that, as well as the rollicking culture of the company and *The Sun* and, in addition, what it takes to insert oneself into the inner circle of the Murdoch family. The only time Rupert ceded control of *The Sun* (or seemed to while continuing making surreptitious calls to journalists) was when he gave control of all UK operations to James, even allowing him and the editor to agree to support the Conservative David Cameron over Gordon Brown in the general election of 2010. James not only abandoned Brown, but announced that shift in *The Sun*'s support from Labour on its front page on the very day that Brown succeeded Tony Blair as leader of the Labour Party, a thrust of the knife that Brown has never forgiven.[20] I often discussed with Rupert his affinity for Brown, a high-tax, government-intervention politician. It came down to Brown's work ethic, his detailed knowledge of issues, his Scottish son-of-the-manse background, similar to Rupert's grandfather's. Rupert's delegation of authority over *The Sun* ended when James was removed to the US during the hacking scandal and its aftermath.

Rupert is happiest in the editor's chair. From there, he can choose stories that not only boost circulation, but provide the public with information often ignored by the establishment press, the latter being a feature of Fox News as well as News' tabloids. He can also attack those who would take the nation in what he sees as the wrong direction by raising taxes, cutting defence spending, increasing the regulatory burden on business, failing to protect its citizens, closing the door to immigrants and otherwise deviating from a generally conservative agenda, spiced with a bit of libertarianism.

There is more to this hands-on approach than the pleasure Rupert derives from it. He firmly believes that a good executive has to understand just about everything on the operating level before he or she can be given executive responsibility. He receives weekly reports from which he can discover such details as when a press is underperforming, and expects his top managers to know the business from the ground up. That is one reason he did not parachute Lachlan and James into their current positions until they had proven, at least to his satisfaction and presumably that of his board, that they could turn a profit at one or another of the company's operating units. It is why Les Hinton – serially copy boy, newspaper and magazine reporter, executive, meeting organiser willing to take saw and hammer to build a podium, Wapping supremo, CEO of Dow Jones and Company – was such a favourite. And why Rupert named Rebekah Brooks CEO, with authority over all UK newspapers, only after she had satisfied him that she could succeed as editor of the *News of the World* and then of *The Sun*.

When hands-on is impossible, Murdoch delegates, most usually to long-serving executives who followed him from country to country in the newspaper business and who share his worldview. The recipients of this delegated authority understand that the gift of delegation can be revoked at any time, either temporarily or permanently, or overridden on a whim. One executive told me that to survive he had to recognise that the newspapers he managed were 'Rupert's train set, and Rupert can play with the trains any time he pleases'. That is an exaggeration: Murdoch delegated absolute authority over *The Weekly Standard* to its editor, Bill Kristol, both because that was the only condition under which the talented Kristol would take on the assignment, and probably in part to shield himself from the criticism that would inevitably result from some of Kristol's publishing decisions. He delegates authority to the editors of *The Times* and *The Sunday Times* because he undertook not to interfere with their decisions as part of the deal that allowed him to acquire those UK properties without a monopoly investigation, and to *The Wall Street Journal*'s opinion-page editor pursuant to his deal with the Bancrofts. Given the fact that Murdoch bears financial responsibility for the decisions of those editors, it is unsurprising that the division of authority is at times murky, and that some critics, most notably deposed *Times* editor Harold Evans, say he honours that undertaking more in the breach than in the observance.[21] My observation is that a self-confident editor can have very substantial independence, which Andrew Neil, then editor of *The Sunday Times*, proved by supporting Michael Heseltine's leadership challenge to Margaret Thatcher, and surviving to edit for years thereafter.

Add to that two incidents that I observed at first hand. One morning I was taking breakfast with Rupert when a call from

London interrupted our conversation. It was 'the Palace', pro-
testing about an article it had learned – I assume from some leak
at *The Sunday Times* – would be appearing in that paper and
asking Rupert to order the editor to kill it. I asked Rupert what he
planned to do. 'Nothing' was the terse reply.

Then there was the time in 1994 that I received a call from
Woodrow Wyatt. Woodrow had been extraordinarily welcoming
to Cita and me from the day we arrived in London – he would
take Cita on regular tours of the betting shops he oversaw as
chairman of the Tote, adding visits to buildings designed by his
ancestor, the eighteenth-century architect James Wyatt – and we
had become quite friendly with him and his wife, Verushka, and
their talented daughter, Petronella. Woodrow told me 'Margaret
is terribly upset' at *The Times*' reporting on the activities of her
son Mark, whose business affairs she refused to recognise were
becoming a potential embarrassment to her. Woodrow wanted to
know how to contact Rupert, who was then in Australia, reach-
able at a number I reluctantly (and it turns out unwisely) gave
him. About an hour later Woodrow called to report, with some
annoyance, that Rupert had refused to intervene. Woodrow also
said that he had woken Rupert because 'they have strange times in
Australia, where Greenwich Mean Time is not good enough for
them'. With an eye on history and his legacy, in his journals he
records a different outcome: 'I told Margaret that Rupert agreed
to do something about the negative reports.'[22] Which is what one
would expect of a courtier unwilling to report the limits of his
influence.

Finally, in his memoir, hardly a paean to Rupert, Andrew
Neil tells of the time when Mohamed Al-Fayed complained
to Neil about a story in *The Sunday Times* criticising the then
Harrods owner's renovation of the Paris house once occupied
by the Duke and Duchess of Windsor. Al-Fayed demanded an
apology and retraction. Neil refused, and Al-Fayed threatened to

pull Harrods' advertising. Neil responded that there was no need for the Harrods owner to do that as he was banning Harrods' advertising from the paper lest other advertisers get the idea they could dictate editorial content. Rupert, of course, received the news, if I recall correctly, from an irate Al-Fayed, or perhaps from Neil, and called Andrew to inquire just how big the paper's biggest advertiser was: £3 million annually was the nervous reply. Pause. 'F*** him if he thinks we can be bought for £3 million,' Murdoch said and hung up.[23]

Unlike editors, who have the protection of Rupert's undertakings, other executives do not. But their risk of incurring his wrath is reduced in most cases by their long experience with Rupert. That experience has taught them to exercise their delegated authority in general accordance with Rupert's wishes, even absent specific instructions – or not to exercise it all. His best executives understand when to submit those demands to what in American parlance is called a pocket veto – don't refuse to go along, but as Ronald Reagan, a Murdoch favourite, once advised, 'Don't just do something, stand there.' One such executive was the aforementioned Les Hinton, whose rapid climb up the corporate ladder began with the unglamorous and potentially dangerous chore of fetching sandwiches for Rupert in Australia. Legend has it that Les could not remember whether Rupert had ordered ham or roast beef, and so bought both. When asked, 'Where is my roast beef sandwich?' by an always impatient Murdoch, Hinton promptly reached into the correct pocket and produced it. This is yet another story that is 'too good to check'.[24]

Fortunately for me, Hinton was one of those executives who knew when to do as Rupert instructed, and when to let the instruction die of natural causes, which is what Murdoch often intends. At one point, I antagonised Rebekah Wade, at the time editing *The Sun*, by telling an interviewer with another newspaper that Rupert would be giving David Cameron a second look, after being unimpressed at an earlier meeting. Rebekah felt I was intruding on her turf, which included keeping Rupert's, and therefore *The Sun*'s, intentions under wraps until immediately before a general election. She was right, of course. I am told that Ms Wade complained in such vigorous terms about my intrusion that Rupert, in quite forceful language, instructed Hinton to put an end to my consulting relationship with News. Hinton called me in and asked, 'What the f*** were you thinking?' I agreed that I was off base, and had no excuse, but felt that one such error in my decades of consulting with the company should be tolerable. Hinton advised me to stay out of Rupert's way for a day or two. End of incident. Hinton allowed Rupert to make his point – don't step on the toes of my editors – while at the same time treating me fairly and preserving for News what I like to believe was an occasionally useful asset.

When it comes to book publishing, rather than newspaper publishing, Rupert seems somewhat less sure-footed. He controls one of the world's largest publishing houses, HarperCollins, the result of a merger of several publishers and only one of several imprints in News' stable of book publishers. Rupert retains an interest in this middling-margin business,[25] with margins continually under pressure from new sales methods and offers from Amazon,[26] for two reasons. The first is his belief that he has a competitive edge in competing for talented authors by being able to offer them book contracts, television and newspaper promotion of their books, and possibly a film adaptation. In short, synergy, something I have always believed to be elusive given the ability of literary agents to cut separate deals with publishers and film studios, deals they claim in aggregate equal or exceed the value obtained from a single, comprehensive deal. I have no convincing empirical evidence supporting either point of view, and since Rupert is in a position to act on his belief, and does so, see no point in developing any, since nothing would be likely to change his instinctive view of the matter.

Second, Rupert cannot be insensitive to the power conferred by his ability to publish the memoirs of politicians with whom he deals when they are in office, or contemplating retirement. Or who, having retired, receive royalty cheques and an ego boost that hints of things to come for their still-active and important colleagues. In one case of a US senator who was still in office, HarperCollins paid a $250,000 advance a few weeks before he cast a key Senate vote against a bill damaging to Rupert's interests. Rupert's critics see a link between the advance and the vote; Murdoch representatives call it a coincidence.[27] It should be noted that Murdoch imprints – publishers of memoirs of Margaret Thatcher, John Major, Peter Mandelson and David Cameron – can reasonably argue that it is not influence but profit they seek, in competition with other leading publishers. For example, rights to Florida Senator Marco Rubio's memoir, at the time not even a declared candidate for the Republican nomination, were acquired by a division of Penguin only after a six-company auction.[28] As *The Washington Post* summed it up, 'The publishing and political worlds appear awash in the belief that every candidate must have a memoir, a political tract or both, despite the lack of any indication that the public is clamouring to buy them. Books by politicians continue to appear with stunning regularity and frightening alacrity, not so much written as belched.'[29]

As Rupert learned, it is one thing to keep up with the daily headlines and stories of a family of newspapers, and quite another, and probably less exciting, chore to keep himself informed of the planned output of a giant publishing house. It is also one thing to imbue the managers and editors of newspaper properties, many of whom have grown up with Rupert and followed him from Australia to Britain to America, with Big Julie's knowledge of where the spots on the dice are – where Rupert draws the line between the acceptable and the unacceptable – and book publishers who operate in an inbred industry with its own set of standards. Standards of how to treat authors who claim advances and don't deliver manuscripts, standards of what to publish and what to reject, accounting standards for treatment of unsold copies – all are less the stuff on which Rupert was reared than the culture of the newspaper industry. Which might account for the inter-related histories of Rupert's attempt to crack the Chinese television market, the publishing of a book by Deng Rong, politician and daughter of Deng Xiaoping, and the decision not to publish a book by Chris Patten.

In July 1993 Rupert bought STAR China TV (Satellite Television for the Asian Region) for what would eventually turn out to be $1 billion[30] in order to gain a toehold in a potentially massive market for media products. Economic reforms were improving the lot of China's masses, the regime seemed to be interested in attracting foreign investment, and reforms that would convert an export-led economy into a consumer-led economy were in the wind. There were fortunes to be made if the political risks could be managed. As it turned out, they couldn't. In 2014 21st Century Fox sold its remaining 47 per cent stake in STAR for a relative pittance, ending a failed two-decade effort to penetrate a media and entertainment market that a repressive Chinese regime would not open to dissenting voices. I had always argued to Rupert that economists who believe that greater economic freedom and prosperity inevitably create a middle class that would press for and obtain greater political freedom are wrong. A sufficiently repressive regime that believes power grows out of the barrel of a gun, or possession of a Gulag, can and will preserve its monopoly of political power, as Xi Jinping has demonstrated. Indeed, increased prosperity can lead to an implicit deal between the governed and their governors – the latter provide a more comfortable life, the former refrain from challenging the regime. That proved to be the situation Rupert confronted when he attempted a major entry into a market of increasingly affluent customers and a determinedly authoritarian regime.

Murdoch had told me of his deep satisfaction at being informed by anti-communist Poles when he visited that country how valuable his satellite service had been in bringing them news that the communist regime sought to deny them. In September 1993, a few months after his acquisition of STAR TV, Rupert organised a gala gathering at the Banqueting House in London's Whitehall, one that included performances by the original cast of every West End musical. His speech at this celebration of the tenth anniversary of his purchase of Sky Television included his now-famous claim that satellite television was 'an unambiguous threat to totalitarian regimes everywhere'. Bruce Dover, a journalist with wide experience in Asia, reported that China's then-premier, Li Ping, 'was incandescent with rage ... [He] took the comments not just as a personal insult but as a premeditated and calculated threat by Murdoch to Chinese sovereignty.'[31] So, only two months after Rupert purchased STAR, which he hoped would increase the global reach of his burgeoning television network, Li Peng, dubbed 'the Butcher of Beijing' for his role in suppressing the Tiananmen Square protests, banned the distribution, installation and use of satellite dishes everywhere in China, dashing Rupert's hopes for early access to the nation's promising market.

Rupert knew that I was responsible for shaping his thoughts into the offending speech he gave at the Banqueting House – he identified me as the author to Bruce Dover – but nevertheless made no effort to blame me for the ensuing disaster. He took responsibility, telling Dover, 'I read through it in the afternoon before the speech and didn't pick it up – not in the context of China. I was really thinking in terms of all that happened in the Soviet Union.'[32] There the matter rested, even though Rupert's colleagues later remembered the sentence as the costliest ever uttered by a modern businessman.[33] Rupert never criticised me for my contribution to this commercial misstep, partly because that is not his style, more importantly because he remained proud of what he had said and of satellite television's role in making life difficult for Poland's communist regime. Woodrow Wyatt claims in his diaries to have told Rupert, 'All the unelected governments are terrified of the democracy you are blowing into the area',[34] presumably Eastern Europe and Asia. The *News of the World* columnist and old Murdoch retainer had it right when it came to the Chinese regime.

Murdoch then took several steps that can reasonably be taken as efforts to placate the regime in order to regain access to the growing Chinese television and film markets, subordinating his distaste for communism to his taste for conquering new, lucrative markets. The first, in April 1994, was to refuse to renew the BBC's contract with his five-channel STAR network in 1994.[35] The BBC had initially upset the Chinese by its extensive reporting of the regime's bloody suppression of the Tiananmen Square protest, using force that resulted in the deaths of about 2,500 people and injuries to more than 10,000. In the regime's eyes, the BBC compounded the insult with a 1993 documentary, *Chairman Mao: The Last Emperor*, in which it claimed that Mao had 'a sexual appetite for young women',[36] preferably 'very young with a low level of education' according to his long-time physician.[37] Or, as one writer delicately puts it, 'rather unusual sexual predilections'.[38] To add to what the Chinese took as a direct assault on its legitimacy, the BBC some years later ran graphic images of the Tiananmen Square massacre.

There is no question that Murdoch wanted to reduce the hostility to him of a regime that controlled so large a potential market for all sorts of media products. Like many American businessmen, he had visions of billions of Chinese consumers eager for his products. He told his most reliable biographer,

William Shawcross, 'that in order to get in there and get accepted, we'll cut the BBC out'.[39] But he also complained to others that STAR was losing money, some $100 million per year,[40] including $10 million paid to the BBC,[41] that the BBC wasn't paying enough for the use of STAR's channel, and that his decision was 'primarily a financial consideration', before adding, 'But it might have occurred to me, this might not hurt relations with Beijing.'[42]

So the hunt for a single motive is an exercise in futility: Murdoch himself could not disentangle his multiple motives for ending STAR's relationship with the BBC. He was undoubtedly aware that the ferocious Chinese regime would dearly love to have the BBC thorn removed from its paw. He was aware, too, that the men he had assigned to take STAR from loss to profit were clamouring for control of the BBC's channel, which they wanted to use for profitable Mandarin-language programming. And, based on my many conversations over the years with Rupert, I can say with certainty that in the background was his continued loathing of the BBC, not only a quintessentially establishment institution, beloved of Britain's great and good, but 'state-funded' and a 'competitor'. 'Establishment', 'state-funded' and 'a competitor' are three strikes and you are out in the Murdoch rule book. My own guess (and it is only that) is that the desire to regain programming access to the fifth UK channel and reduce STAR's losses, and his long-standing dislike of all that the BBC stands for, would have been enough for him to replace the BBC on his satellite. But it is equally probable that Rupert's vision of a massive Chinese market was also an important factor in leading him to decide that the responsible course, balancing commercial and ideological considerations, would be to recover the favour of the Chinese dictators. Unfortunately, the decision to remove the BBC from the satellite deprived millions of Chinese of the principal source of news that the communist leaders did not control.

This brings us to Rupert's use of his publishing houses to attempt to restore himself to the good graces of China's rulers. In the winter of 1994, Basic Books, a division of News-owned HarperCollins, published and vigorously promoted a hagiography of Deng Xiaoping, the most powerful leader of the People's Republic of China for more than a decade starting in 1978. It was written by his daughter and secretary, Deng Rong, also known as Deng Maomao, a not unbiased biographer. There followed promotional dinners and all the trappings accorded an author of a sure bestseller. To no avail. The book's reported success in China was not duplicated in the West. 'Fawning, cliché-riddled',[43] 'Reads like an official history … based on the orthodox party view … unable to evoke personal insights'[44] capture the tone of most reviews. HarperCollins described the advance as 'somewhat modest';[45] Bruce Dover guesses it was less than $1 million, 'but perhaps not much less'.[46] No matter. Weighed against the possibility of access to the Chinese market, the financial cost of what might or might not have been toadying was negligible. Its non-financial cost, however, was not insignificant. Intended or otherwise, the book deal and lavish promotion sent an unfortunate signal through the Murdoch organisation: quality of product is not the standard when News' other commercial interests are in play, and the boss might, just might, like to see similar displays of appreciation of the sensibilities of China's leaders. It also sent a message to the Chinese leaders: Rupert Murdoch will go to considerable lengths to gain access to our markets, so we have a strong bargaining position vis-à-vis Murdoch and his companies.

Fast-forward four years to the Patten affair, and the use of HarperCollins in a further attempt to gain entry to the Chinese market. I was sitting in an anteroom to Rupert's office at Fox Studios in Hollywood, waiting to see him, when I overheard a new public relations executive, fresh from his efforts on behalf of the cigarette industry, if recollection serves, telling a colleague that

Rupert had agreed to cancel plans for HarperCollins to publish *East and West: China, Power, and the Future of Asia*, by Chris Patten, a Conservative politician who had served as Governor and Commander-in-Chief of Hong Kong. Patten had been one of Margaret Thatcher's colleagues whom Rupert believed had been complicit in her dethroning.[47]

When I saw Rupert a few minutes later I suggested that cancellation was an enormous mistake, that it would be a long-running news story, and that he should cancel the cancellation. Rupert said that his public relations people had assured him this decision would not attract much attention – I know that his staff in Britain provided no such assurance, so it must have come from his US team, some of whom might actually once have read a British newspaper. Rupert ended the conversation with a curt 'Too late'. He then compounded the problem by attributing the cancellation to the fact that the book was boring and would not sell, as if he had belatedly curled up with the manuscript one evening and decided Patten's book would not be a commercial success.

HarperCollins duly cancelled the book, in the process suffering the resignation of one of the most talented editors in the business, and provoking a firestorm by Murdoch's newspaper competitors. Soon after, however, the publisher backed down and in a public statement declared that it had 'unreservedly apologized for and withdrawn any suggestion that Chris Patten's book *East and West*, was rejected for not being up to proper professional standards or being too boring ... These allegations are untrue and ought never to have been made.'[48] After a bit of waffling and blame-sharing, Rupert publicly called his decision to cancel the Patten book 'one more mistake of mine ... it would have made a whole lot less fuss if we just let it go on. A mistake.'[49] He would repeat this statement years later at the Leveson Inquiry: 'one more mistake of mine. It was clearly wrong.'[50]

HarperCollins agreed to pay £50,000 in damages.[51] All in all, this was not Murdoch's finest hour, a blunder compounded by the fact that sales of the book, which received a predictably glowing review in *The New York Times* – 'a book we need to read'[52] – could not have been hurt by the controversy surrounding its publication. Indeed, it went on to sell well as 'The book Murdoch tried to ban'.

Onward and downward. In an interview with *Vanity Fair*, Rupert then criticised the Chinese communist regime's bête noire, the Dalai Lama: 'I have heard cynics who say he's a very political old monk shuffling around in Gucci shoes.'[53] And, not to be left out of efforts to satisfy the Chinese regime, some five months later James Murdoch used a talk at the Milken Institute in Santa Monica, California, to attack Falun Gong, a meditation and quasi-religious group, members of which were prominent in the 1989 Tiananmen Square protests. He called it a 'dangerous' and 'apocalyptic cult' that 'clearly does not have the success of China at heart'. He also advised Hong Kong's advocates for democracy to accept the fact that they now lived under an 'absolutist' government, and criticised Hong Kong and Western media for unfairly depicting China in a negative way.[54] This from an executive of a company living by Sir Keith's admonition to 'be fearless', and whose brother, in a talk honouring their grandfather, would later enjoin his colleagues to resist censorship of every kind.[55]

The China foray proves three things. First, Rupert did indeed elevate commerce over principle when the prospect of access to the Chinese market was at stake. Second, Rupert makes mistakes, and rather big ones, as with the Patten book, reminding me of a statement by Fiorello LaGuardia, mayor of New York from 1934 to 1945, 'When I make a mistake, it's a beaut!' Third, Murdoch does not have the power to prevent the publication of any book he happens to dislike simply because it runs counter to his business interests. So long as HarperCollins has no monopoly power, and there are other publishers more than willing to publish any worthwhile and potentially profitable book, Murdoch cannot prevent books critical of the Chinese or any other regime from seeing the light of day, which means his handling of the issue has implications for Murdoch and News, but not for public policy. Macmillan was delighted to match HarperCollins' $200,000 advance for a book that had enough advance publicity to make it likely bestseller,[56] and Crown published the Patten memoir in the US.

As with the Deng Rong affair, the real costs of the decision to drop the Patten book were borne by News Corp., especially in Britain, where several News executives discussed its implications with me. Brought up in an atmosphere that fearlessly spoke truth to power, that cheerfully and cheekily risked antagonising governments and enduring libel suits from celebrities who crave favourable press coverage but abhor exposures of their weaknesses, their conversation turned to an apparent change in their leader. No more damn the critics and the consequences, full speed ahead. Once a corporate culture that encourages no-holds-barred journalism is modified even a little, the result is greater caution, a reaction that it takes a considerable time to dispel. My observation a few months after the Patten affair died down was that Rupert's confession of error and apology, and the absence of any repeat of that confessed mistake, calmed many fears.

To be fair to Rupert, the question of how a media company, with profit-making responsibilities to shareholders, should attempt to deal with totalitarian regimes has no easy answer. Google, Apple, Facebook and other new media companies are struggling with exactly the same problem: whether to withdraw from China or attempt to accommodate the regime's restrictions. Apple, for example, chose the latter course, and, at the regime's insistence, removed from its China store apps that allowed customers access to uncensored foreign content. Other American companies that offer services allowing users to bypass the so-called 'Great Firewall of China', its barrier to Internet access, did the same.[57]

My conversations with American executives and with British politicians suggest that the lure of a market with more than a billion consumers only now emerging from poverty is simply too great to ignore. Manufacturers agree to turn over intellectual property to gain access to that potential market, only to find that within a few years their Chinese partners have stolen their intellectual property and launched competitive enterprises in the nuclear, auto, solar, wind and other industries. Media companies, visions of hundreds of millions of viewers to wave before advertisers, find compromise with principles acceptable. Facebook's Mark Zuckerberg has been desperate to take a crack at China's market. He has made several trips to China, cultivated high-level officials, including President Xi Jinping, and is reported to have developed software to suppress news feeds. Facebook has also 'restricted content' in other countries 'in keeping with the typical practice of American internet companies that generally comply with government requests to block certain content after it is posted'.[58] Google's search engine is hampered by that 'Great Firewall of China', but Google nevertheless does business in China, as do Microsoft and Amazon. In 2005, Shi Tao, a Chinese poet/journalist, was sentenced to ten years in prison for sending an email to the US after Yahoo! China provided the regime with account holder information. LinkedIn has been 'willing to compromise on the free expression that is the backbone of life on the Western Internet'.[59] In early 2017 Apple agreed to remove *The New York Times* English- and Chinese-language apps from its stores, thus eliminating the ability of Chinese customers to read the paper without resorting to special software.[60]

Recent meetings in Washington have persuaded me that there is no easy answer to the choice of withdrawal or accommodation. It is not clear which approach is in the interests of the media companies and of the democratic countries in which they make their homes, or even whether those interests are coincident. Many foreign-policy experts, which this writer is not, believe engagement is essential to eventual liberalisation in non-democratic countries. That was the theory behind President Obama's decision to engage with Cuba rather than continue the US embargo until the ruling Castros demonstrated a greater willingness to release political prisoners and loosen their grip on Cuba's economic and political lives. And his decision to go beyond the terms of the accord with Iran by making dollars available to the Mullahs in the hope that such tangible gestures would result in a warming of Iranian–US relations. America's commercial enterprises, so this theory has it, in deciding that withdrawal is better than cooperating with despotic communist governments, are foregoing any opportunity to influence the course of reform in those countries. The failure of Cuba to liberalise and Iran to end its support for terror has thrown doubt on the 'engagement' thesis.

The contrary view is that the incentive of despots to retain power is so great that no amount of commerce, no demonstration that a relaxation of control would benefit the populace, will allow an economic opening to morph into a democratic opening. Indeed, by making the benefits of Western technology available to authoritarian regimes, Western companies actually strengthen them. All this is complicated for media companies because a willingness to accept restrictions on what information is made available to the public can make those companies complicit in providing the populace with a distorted view of the truth. I know executives on both sides of this argument, and believe them to be sincere, but my guess is that those who think they can make a satisfactory long-term deal with a regime determined to repress dissent with all the considerable means at its disposal – and along the way steal the intellectual property of the companies they allow to do business in their countries – are wrong, and they would do well to allocate capital and management time elsewhere. That seems to me to be true in all cases, but especially for media companies, which at their best produce the one thing that terrifies repressive regimes – news unadulterated to suit the needs of the regime.

We now come to the saga of Judith Regan, who, under the eponymous imprint of Regan Books, was employed as an editor for Murdoch's HarperCollins. Her sensationalist publications included Jenna Jameson's *How to Make Love Like a Porn Star* and 'shock jock' Howard Stern's *Private Parts*. These and others – nearly one hundred bestsellers in all by one count[61] – had made her imprint one of the most financially successful in the business, and an important contributor to News' profits. With no complaint from Murdoch.

In 2006 Fox announced that Regan had interviewed O. J. Simpson. According to the announcement, Simpson had confessed to the murders of his wife, Nicole Brown Simpson, and her friend, Ronald Goldman, crimes of which he had been acquitted in a racially charged trial in 1995. The interview was to be aired on Fox, and Simpson's book, *If I Did It*, was to be published by Regan Books, an example of the synergy Rupert believes his multimedia company possesses. Regan paid $3.5 million for the rights, the money, she said, to go to Simpson's children. Interest was intense, as it had been since the verdict was announced more than a decade earlier. I had been at the Labour Party conference in Brighton in 1995 when, on 3 October, the jury verdict acquitting him of the murders came through, and was surprised that, although Tony Blair had delivered his party leader's speech that afternoon, all talk that evening was about the acquittal, with most of the delegates incredulous that Simpson had got off. (He has since served nine years of a nine-to-thirty-three-year sentence for a crime unrelated to the murders and was paroled on 20 July 2017.) Tony Blair's speech could not compete for comment and attention with the verdict that seemed to defy all evidence, including then-novel DNA data.

Regan claimed the book was a confession, which Simpson of course denied, although it is difficult to read it as anything other than that. Regan told the press she was publishing it 'to release us all from the wound of the conviction that was lost on that fall day in October of 1995'.[62] The reaction to the proposed Simpson book was one of widespread disgust, both within the industry and among the public. 'It's so outrageous and flamboyant and audacious that part of you almost laughs while the other part of you wants to puke,'[63] said Little, Brown editor-in-chief Geoff Shandler, a view presumably unaffected by his desire to do down a competitor. Sara Nelson, the editor of *Publishers Weekly*, wrote, 'Judith Regan is a very smart and very savvy publisher. But this is just different. This is just ... really awful.'[64]

In response, Rupert announced: 'I and senior management agree with the American public that this was an ill-considered project. We are sorry for any pain that this has caused the families of [the murdered] Ron Goldman and Nicole Brown Simpson.'[65] One month later Regan was fired by HarperCollins' then-CEO Jane Friedman, allegedly for making anti-Semitic remarks, after which a spate of lawsuits followed, resulting in a payment to Regan of $10.75 million, and a withdrawal of accusations of anti-Semitism. That sum, along with 'a generous but undisclosed sum of money from the billionaire Leon Black', has put Regan back into the publishing business, where possible projects include a joint venture with Wendi Deng, Murdoch's former wife. Regan says of her experience with News, 'I have no hostility.'[66]

It is not unreasonable to have Rupert share some of the blame for Regan's excess. Having created an environment in which shock is acceptable, having hired a team that has seen him chortle over the discomfort of the establishment, he cannot be surprised if at times his team guesses wrong at what he considers beyond the pale. It is possible that Regan was emboldened to publish Simpson's book by Rupert's silence when she published what many outside the company considered outrageous material. It is also possible that the self-confident Regan gave no thought to the question of Rupert's limits. And if she had, in the absence of clear guidance and given her experience with HarperCollins, could she have divined the limits that would eventually lead to the Regan–Murdoch rupture? Not likely. After all, Murdoch did not decide that she had crossed the line between responsible and irresponsible publishing and broadcasting until public outrage goaded him to act. It is, of course, possible that, given the vast scale of the Murdoch enterprises, Rupert did not know of Regan's plans until the uproar following their announcement. On the other hand, it seems unlikely that Regan could have had a $3.5 million cheque written, and booked airtime on the Fox Network, without Rupert knowing about it. In the end, I lean towards the view that, had Rupert cleared the project in advance of the public uproar, Regan would have cited that prior approval when the storm broke. So far as I know, and I have not been through the probably confidential documents that shot back and forth between the parties, she did not. In the end, her book was published by Beaufort Books, which styles itself 'an innovative publisher', and briefly went on to become a number one bestseller on *The New York Times* non-fiction list.[67]

Rupert's views on his responsibility for more than maximising shareholder value are less clear when we turn to the entertainment side of his empire. And probably less relevant than in the past, now that control of 21st Century Fox's entertainment assets is passing to Disney. But they remain relevant for two reasons. First, Rupert remains in control of the world's largest print operation. Second, and looking to the future, Lachlan's views are not wildly dissimilar from those of his father.

'Rupert Murdoch is a bit of a prude – "I guess it's my Scottish blood",' he told Ken Auletta, a long-time commentator on matters Murdoch, who also notes that such prudery did not affect Rupert's decisions concerning television programming.[68] Rupert has often tried to explain how he exercises his responsibility for what his company puts on the air and in: 'We want Fox films to produce movies ... without crossing that hazy line that separates genuine mass entertainment from culturally degrading appeals to the darker side of man's nature.'[69] ... 'Although we cater to our audiences, we do not pander to them.'[70]

That the man who was quite comfortable featuring bare-breasted young women for many years in his favourite tabloid assents to the tag 'prude' comes as no surprise to me. I recall a company gathering in Sun Valley, at which Murdoch announced to his several hundred guests that the evening's entertainment would include a preview showing of a new Fox movie, *There's Something About Mary*. Pause. 'Er, it is a bit raunchy and some of you might find it embarrassing, so we won't mind if you skip it and avail yourselves of the many other facilities here.'

'A bit raunchy' might have been an inadequate warning to potential viewers of *There's Something About Mary*. One reviewer put it this way: 'The nauseating, R-rated shenanigans in this film don't just *push* the envelope, they crumple it up and set it on fire.'[71] 'Another described it as 'a comedy of errors, with penises accidentally caught in zippers and sperm mistakenly used as hair gel'.[72] Still another saw advantages for the stars of a film that tested 'the limits of political correctness and viewers' threshold for witnessing one man's struggle to keep his heart (and nether-regions) from being broken ... [and] catapulted Ben Stiller and Cameron Diaz's careers'.[73] Many agreed then with Phelim O'Neill's later reflection that the film's 'hitherto lowbrow laughs are elevated to almost graceful perfection'.[74] Most of the guests found the R-rated film very funny; Cita and I left; Rupert, who could have killed a film that clearly made him uncomfortable, instead deferred to the Hollywood crowd's preference for envelope-pushing. In this case, uncertainty about his own view, pragmatism, an attempt to accommodate the Hollywood ethos and an eye on the box office, and a desire to discomfit the elites trumped his self-professed prudery.

The Murdoch Method of managing the Fox entertainment operation – roughly, film and sport – necessarily differs in some ways from the Method applied to the print operation. Imposing some sense of responsibility on journalists is one thing, and no easy chore; imposing it on creators of what is called 'content', with its enormous cultural impact, is quite another – equally important, but a very different challenge and for Rupert a less familiar and in a sense more difficult one. His parents' instruction to do good and behave responsibly was laid down when print was king: its application to the multimedia world of entertainment requires skills not imagined by Sir Keith.

Rupert's difficulty is compounded by the fact that at the time of the acquisition of the film studio he did not have a substantial cadre of executives who had grown up with him in Australia, many familiar with the legend of Sir Keith. Not only were key Fox Studios players unfamiliar with Rupert, his legacy and his Method; many did not share his political and social views, and had a very different definition of the location of the line between socially responsible and irresponsible products. Conservatives are a rare sight in the tonier restaurants and high-level executive suites of Hollywood and Beverly Hills – which is why California is known in political circles as 'the left coast'. Indeed, conservative actors who have come out claim they are discriminated against when casts are assembled for movies, a charge that many executives do not deny. What remains true today was even more the case when Rupert purchased half of Fox Studios in 1985. Fred Pierce, the president of ABC in the 1980s, told an interviewer, 'It is very difficult for people who are politically conservative to break in' to television. Conservatives stay 'underground'. Another producer told an actor auditioning for a part, 'There's not going to be a [President Ronald] Reagan asshole on this show [*St. Elsewhere*]!'[75]

For Rupert, responsibility includes patriotism, a muscular foreign policy and a dollop of prudery. What he sees as patriotism, more liberal studio executives see as irresponsible flag-waving; what he sees as an appropriately muscular foreign policy Hollywood generally sees as doomed attempts at imperialism and 'nation-building'; what brings out the prude in Rupert would not be given a second thought by many in Hollywood. It was 20th Century Fox Television that produced the successful and avowedly anti-war, pacifist television series *M*A*S*H* for CBS long before Murdoch came on the scene. At one corporate get-together Rupert, tongue-in-cheek, asked one of the studio's executives why Fox did not make more movies like *Rambo*, the adventures of a super-patriotic super-hero armed with enough weapons to wipe out the entire army of Viet Cong who try to prevent him from rescuing American soldiers they hold prisoner. After the shock had worn off, the executive managed a response, the gist of which was 'We don't like that sort of film'. 'Is it because in this film America wins?' asked Rupert, indulging his taste for pot-stirring.

A more significant demonstration of the fact that Rupert was seen as not-one-of-us when he arrived in Hollywood – indeed, at the time he said he considered himself an outsider[76] – came at a meeting of his executives he asked me to attend at the Fox Studios. It was shortly after he had purchased the studio, and Rupert was in learning mode. He sat quietly off to the side, rather than at the conference table, with his usual biro in hand and yellow pad on his lap. At one point he asked for details about some decision being taken. The executive running the meeting bridled, and snapped, 'You can't come into our town and tell us what to do.' That explains one aspect of Hollywood that is far different from the newspaper business. Les Hinton, a shrewd observer of the industry's mores during a not entirely happy stint at Fox, told me that few work for a film studio. Instead, most top executives in Hollywood work for the

Hollywood entertainment industry. They have talent, earning power wherever they choose as their professional home, and are willing to move on if they feel put upon for whatever reason. That denied Rupert the degree of control over the Fox film and broadcasting operation that he had over the newspaper part of his empire, a situation that should not be a problem for James, who is more in tune with the social and political worldview of the dominant Hollywood majority.

Despite the tension between Rupert, the new kid on the set, and old-line Hollywood executives, Rupert was able to assemble a talented executive team and master the commercial aspects of running a film studio. Barry Diller, who worked reasonably well with Rupert before leaving to become his own boss, compares the unimaginative executives who run most of the conglomerates that own formerly independent production companies with Murdoch: 'A rare instance is Rupert, who is such a builder and risk-taker it keeps him always edged and fresh. The rest of them are suits', the Hollywood pejorative for pencil-pushers, bean-counters and other lower forms of life.[77]

The new, talented team included the magnificently mustachioed Chase Carey, whose tenure benefited from the Murdoch Method. Carey wanted to commit billions to make Fox a major presence in sport, his passion.[78] Murdoch, generally willing to back a daring move by a talented executive with buckets of hard cash, did just that. The benefits were many, not least Carey's loyalty. When Rupert extricated James from Britain during the hacking scandal, and parachuted him into Hollywood and Fox, Carey agreed to take James on as an apprentice, and then turn over his CEO position to him, remaining as a consultant should further education prove necessary.

Even in more routine circumstances, Murdoch will hear his executives out, respect their judgements, agree with them on budgets to be reviewed at the annual meetings which many executives approach as one would a cross-examination in court, and then let them do their jobs.

It is when it comes to politics that the Hollywood team, in most cases far to the left of Rupert, was most pleasantly surprised. The Murdoch Method of dealing with executives who do not share his political views is simple: if they choose to devote a part of their generous compensation to the support of candidates Rupert opposes, so be it. Political support from the show business contingent generally flows to Democrats, and the most liberal ones at that. In the most recent elections, Hillary Clinton raised $19.4 million from Hollywood, Donald Trump $255,000 going into the last month of the campaign.[79] Given James's deep-seated and widely expressed antipathy to Trump, he probably is counted among Clinton's supporters. He certainly sides with environmentalists rather than the climate-change sceptics Rupert unleashed in his Australian newspapers in a campaign that is believed to have been responsible for the repeal of the nation's laws limiting carbon emissions. James is involved in a variety of environmental causes,[80] and Sky's headquarters in Osterley, west London, are a green's dream: the first naturally ventilated television studio, a 67 per cent reduction in energy use and just about every green design feature known to man.[81] But James also has a libertarian streak which might not in the long run prove entirely consistent with his new colleagues' more expansive view of the proper role of government in Americans' lives with the exception of theirs.

No matter: in the end the Murdoch empire is a big tent, politically, which adds to the spice and zest of life within it, to the benefit of all parties. I have never witnessed any animosity between Rupert and his entertainment team resulting from political differences, which are generally treated by him in an accepting, lighthearted manner. It is only when one of the News tabloids springs an exposé on some celebrity with whom the studio executives must deal that there is murmuring in the ranks, something never heard when the same newspaper publishes a favourable review of the studio's latest release.

The difficulty created for Rupert by his expansion into the film business stems from something far different from his more conservative political views. News Corp journalists search for failings on the part of what they regard as the elites – royalty, celebrities, politicians – and try to bring them down. Filmmakers often share the journalists' iconoclasm, but direct it at the culture. They are as eager to put a thumb in the eye of the bourgeoisie as tabloid journalists are to make the elites uncomfortable. Just as tabloid journalists reject limits on what they might write about the great and the good, so studio executives reject limits on the use of profanity and explicit depiction of sexual activity in their entertainment products, and generally portray members of the clergy and successful businessmen in a bad light. In short, they push the cultural envelope – hard. Anything that is not hip, modern, secular, gender-neutral is a target for the Hollywood left. Although they disagree on many things, not least of which is the candidates to back with hard cash and publicity, the common attitude of Murdoch executives, be they from Fleet Street or Hollywood, is dissatisfaction with the status quo, although for very different reasons. The journalists are unhappy with elitist control of the media and the economy, and the flaunting of societal norms by celebrities; the filmmakers are unhappy with the constraints of the currently accepted cultural and societal norms. Rupert is responsible for converting these views into workable company policy consistent with his own ideas of where the limits of the behaviour of both groups are to be found. But when it comes to translating the elastic concept of 'responsibility' into management policy in Hollywood, he must rely less on the voices of Sir Keith and Dame Elisabeth, and more on his own instincts and experience.

Until, that is, things get out of control, which they did at a corporate meeting at which Stephen Chao, a rising Murdoch executive, decided to test the limits of acceptability before an audience of the corporation's major executives and important guests, some of whom had brought families to the meeting. I was asked by Rupert to participate in drafting a suggested agenda for his review – something that the company's executives, editors and reporters from around the world would find stimulating and informative. The gathering was to be held at the Silver Tree Inn and Conference Centre in Snowmass, Colorado, adjacent to Aspen. As always, I took my assignment to be to come up with real substance: Rupert intensely dislikes a meeting consisting of platitudes, self-congratulations by successful executives – the usual love-in that so many corporations favour. The Murdochs and Cita and I had homes in nearby Aspen at the time, and Cita and I maintained offices there as well, a portion of which we allocated to Rupert and his long-time assistant, Dot Wyndoe. (Rupert has since sold the Murdoch Aspen home.) I managed to have the agenda allocate a session to the fraught topic of censorship.

My purpose was to acquaint the politically liberal, censorship-averse creative teams at Fox with the limits some conservatives, in and out of government, were pressing to have imposed on their assaults on existing American cultural norms. Food for their thought, I thought. Rupert readily agreed – and we constructed a panel that included the inventive Chao, a Harvard classics graduate who had been a reporter on the *National Enquirer* and later, with Fox, the creator of such highly profitable television reality programmes as *Studs* and *America's Most Wanted*. Chao was a Murdoch favourite who had moved up the corporate ladder with uncommon speed. Rupert had named him head of Fox News Service and then of Fox Television Stations. As a counterweight to Chao, a person who could be counted on to call for maximum freedom for the company's creative team, I persuaded neoconservative intellectual Irving Kristol to serve on the panel, which was chaired by Lynne Cheney, then chairman of the National Endowment for the Humanities, and wife of the then-Secretary of Defense Dick Cheney, who was scheduled to speak later in the programme. I knew Irving's views on censorship: he favoured former New York mayor Fiorello LaGuardia's decision to close the strip/burlesque houses in New York, and to make porn magazines more difficult for young people to access on newsstands. He believed this balance between individual freedom and govern-ment intervention to be about right. Potential audiences could frequent strip joints or buy off-colour magazines – neither was banned – but would have to try a bit harder to get access to those art forms, stripper aficionados by ferrying across the Hudson to New Jersey.

Kristol's views on the importance of preventing degradation of bourgeois culture and on censorship were not what the Hollywood crowd wanted to hear: to these studio executives censorship of cultural materials was an infringement on their rights and creativity. Never mind that they wanted Rupert to intervene with his editors to repress tabloid revelations that embarrassed the movie stars with whom they had to deal. A few complained that Arnold Schwarzenegger, then a hot property, was understandably upset when the *News of the World* published a story about his father's Nazi connections, and famous actors Danny DeVito and William Hurt took umbrage at stories in other Murdoch publications. My recollection is that Rupert was unperturbed, and when the head of Fox Studios broke an ankle when tackling a mountain on a motorbike, turned to his tabloid editors and said, 'I hope none of you did this.' The movie makers' objection to tabloid celebrity coverage was based on more than merely a business calculation – it was a matter of style, of a desire for continued acceptability in the circles in which they travel, circles in which association with Murdoch's conservative political positions is viewed with a mixture of incomprehension and disapproval.

That was not the only flash point at the meeting. His broadsheet editors were more than a little annoyed when their boss, objecting to an attack by the broadsheet team on the quality of tabloid journalism, said, 'There are two kinds of newspaper. There are broadsheets and there are tabloids. Or, as some people say, there are the unpopular and the popular newspapers.'

This butting of heads between print and film, between broadsheets and tabloids, between conservatives and liberals, was no accident. At News' corporate gatherings there is nothing tame, no holds barred, no pointless self-congratulation, except when a bit of history is needed to inform newcomers to the executive ranks of the company's achievements and its culture. Indeed, it was not unusual for Rupert to invite rivals to speak, among them John Malone, the cable tycoon who had bested Rupert in a fight for News' shares. Or controversial figures such as Richard Nixon, who had been forced to resign the presidency, and Mike Milken, the brilliant inventor of so-called junk bonds who had served a prison term for securities fraud.

At this particular meeting tensions ran higher than usual, and not because of intra-corporate disputes. Security was tight. Just one day earlier I was with the Cheneys at a meeting convened by the American Enterprise Institute, a Washington think-tank, in Beaver Creek, Colorado, a resort town that served as the part-time home of former President Gerald Ford. Ford chaired these annual gatherings of public intellectuals, corporate CEOs, former officials of the Ford administration and foreign leaders who had held office during his years as president. One of these was Valéry Giscard d'Estaing, formerly president of France, who characterised my defence of free markets as advocating 'the law of the jungle'. The meeting was marred by an unpleasant incident: we had to evacuate our hotel because of a bomb threat, presumably aimed at Secretary Cheney by anti-war activists. The fact that the threat proved to be no more than that did nothing to relax the

Defense Secretary's already tense security team.

From Beaver Creek, on to Aspen/Snowmass. Cita and I showed up early on the morning of the meeting to see whether Les Hinton needed any help with the preparations (he didn't), and to fetch coffee for the Secret Service contingent, which had made the short trip from Beaver Creek with Cheney and in fact didn't need caffeine to enhance its edginess. Kristol's presentation, in which he defended some forms of censorship, was greeted with a loud protest – banging of coffee cups – by the Hollywood and television crowd, especially when he answered the question 'Just who will do the censoring of cable television fare that you propose?' Kristol, fully aware that he was playing the role of agent provocateur, replied, 'Oh, the local police chief.'

Chao decided to rebut this by proving that sex and violence were of great interest and had huge entertainment value. He hired a male actor to stroll through the audience and onto the stage, positioning himself directly above the seated Lynne Cheney. Then the actor slowly began to strip while Chao, who did not acknowledge the male stripper's presence, continued his talk, hoping to prove that nudity is so riveting that no one would pay any attention to *him*. Murdoch had not been warned about this. The striptease stopped shortly before completion when one of the panellists said, 'I don't know what's going on here, but I have an eight-year-old daughter in the audience.' Cita recalls that the always sensible Anna Murdoch stood up, as if to leave, and that Rupert then put a halt to proceedings. A photographer attempted to take a picture of the semi-naked actor hovering over Mrs Cheney, but Cita knocked his arm to prevent him from achieving his fifteen minutes of fame and a large sum of money for photos that editors of Murdoch's tabloids, all in attendance, would, under other circumstances, dearly love to publish. Competing newspapers gleefully reported the incident, demonstrating that he who lives by the tabloid dies by the tabloid. Murdoch later told me he viewed that as fair play.

It is fortunate the strip show, and with it Chao's presentation, ended when it did. I was later told that the striptease was designed to show that people find such sexual display riveting, and that sex was merely part one of a two-part drama, the second part to be an example of the equally or even greater riveting effect of violence on audiences. According to some of the Fox people who were present, Chao next planned to have another actor run down the aisle waving a gun and pretend to assassinate the stripper. Chao had an explanation for this: he was trying to show that American television is more skittish about nudity and sexuality than about violence.[82] I never did find out if that was Chao's intention. Rupert stopped the show. Had he not intervened, Secretary Cheney's edgy security people would have intercepted the would-be assassin in a less than gentle manner, or quite possibly blown him away.

Rupert, who admired both Chao's creativity and his ability to produce hit shows on minimal budgets, now had a problem. He came by my Aspen offices for a chat, to consider what action he should take. We talked for a while. I explained that it would be easy for me to recommend firing Chao. But with the huge debt burden the company was carrying, and Rupert's responsibility to his shareholders to maximise profits, he had a more difficult calculation to make, since Chao was an important producer of profitable programmes. Spoken like an economist who often forgets that a cost:benefit analysis cannot always provide the answer to a difficult question.

We went our separate ways, but an hour or so later Rupert called. He said that the issue was not economics and profits, but leadership and limits. If he could not impose limits on the behaviour of his executives, nobody could. That afternoon Chao was dismissed.

Rupert publicly apologised to the Cheneys, and the next

morning announced to his executives and guests that he had no choice but to fire Chao if News Corp. were to operate within responsible limits. Rupert continued, 'One thing this company has to stand for is that there are limits.' And, quoting Othello's sacking of his lieutenant Cassio, he added with considerable emotion, 'I love thee, but never more be officer of mine.'[83] It is fair to say that the effect on the audience was electrifying: some sat in silence, others cheered, others heaved sighs of relief at this exercising by their boss of his responsibility to draw the line, somewhere, somehow, to demonstrate that indeed there are limits to bashing the culture. But this was not a life sentence for Chao. Sometime later, Rupert offered him a producer contract. 'Oddly we have remained friends,' Chao told an interviewer from *Village Voice*. 'I was offered a producer deal shortly after getting fired … A Hollywood ending to a Hollywood incident.'[84]

For Rupert, the incident provided a lesson preached by Kristol's wife, Gertrude Himmelfarb, who also was in attendance: '"Pushing the envelope" may also have the … effect of inuring people to … excesses so that they come to accept as normal and tolerable what would once have been shocking and repellent.'[85]

CHAPTER 7

PROTECTING HIS ASSETS

'I would say that if you're going to work for somebody, work for him. He's the best ... straight, supportive, honest and clear' – Barry Diller, former CEO of Paramount and Fox, 1992[1]

'[Murdoch] has had (with a few notable exceptions) a record of appointing smart lieutenants' – *The Economist*, 2011[2]

'[Our] executives ... define themselves by what they are not – they are not corporate bureaucrats, turning out memos, attending endless meetings, and drawing up organization charts' – Rupert Murdoch, 1999[3]

'Personally, Murdoch is a gentleman. He treats executives as part of his extended family: he invited them to his son Lachlan's engagement party, he remembers spouses' names, he rarely raises his voice' – Ken Auletta, *New Yorker*, 1995[4]

'Give the man credit ... for picking smart people to run his various properties – and allowing them to work without undue interference' – Richard A. Viguerie and David Franke in *America's Right Turn*, 2004[5]

News Corp owns several printing presses, capital-intensive immovable necessities if it is to remain in the newspaper business. It owns thousands of desks, movable but not worth much in the used-furniture market. It owns a few buildings around the world, fixed assets like the others. 21st Century Fox owns some valuable California real estate, some cameras, lights and equipment of all sorts. With the possible exception of the real estate on which the studio sits, and perhaps the new headquarters buildings in London, none of it would be worth much on such markets as exist for this stuff.

News Corp's most important assets are its talented people and the brands and revenue streams they create. 'I know that in my company what are traditionally thought of as "assets" – bricks and mortar and desks and printing presses, are worthless when compared to the people who use them, and who never appear on the balance sheet,' Rupert told an audience of student, faculty and guests on 1 December 1999, at Oxford's Sheldonian Theatre in a talk to commemorate the 175th anniversary of University College. Murdoch knows that these human assets are highly mobile – they go down the elevator every evening and, if the company plays its cards right, come back up the following morning. These assets are nowhere listed on the companies' balance sheets. Among other things, they create its intellectual property, an asset to be protected by the best or at least the most highly paid lawyers money can buy. Baz Luhrmann, the super-creative and risk-taking filmmaker affiliated with Fox, maker of *Strictly Ballroom*, *Romeo + Juliet* and *Moulin Rouge*, put it this way at a company conference: 'Our currency is not dollars-and-cents, our currency is really ideas and stories, of which the happy by-product is dollars and cents.'[6]

We live, as the renaming of News' entertainment arm attests, in the twenty-first century. Intellectual property (IP) – loosely defined as any product of the human mind – by one estimate is equivalent to 45 per cent of US GDP,[7] by another (methodologies and years studied not consistent) 34.6 per cent[8] and by still another 38.2 per cent.[9] Industries reliant on intellectual property pay higher wages and are growing faster than those rooted in exploitation of natural resources or in manufacturing all the tangible stuff we see and use. The growth of the Chinese economy since liberalisation in 1978 has been built at least as much on stolen IP as on cheap labour. Apple and Samsung spend tens of millions of dollars every year suing each other to find which one has legal title to valuable intellectual property rights. And Rupert Murdoch, who has accused Google of 'plain theft' for making his companies' IP, in this case its 'content', available to users of its search engine without paying royalties to its creators, is quite willing to use a team of lawyers to protect his companies' intellectual property.

With IP now the most valuable asset his companies own, it is inevitable that an important part of the Murdoch Method is devoted to its creation and preservation. This is a two-step process: attract and retain the best talent; and develop weapons to protect what these talented people produce – television shows, sporting events and broadcasts, news stories and features, books, technology.

The creative talents Rupert must hire and then retain if his empire is to prosper and expand must be persuaded not only to show up at work, but to spend their waking hours dreaming up new ideas for stories, programmes, technological advances and profit-making ventures. To acquire such talent involves, first of all, money, and often large dollops of it, and other financial rewards. But offers of money are much overrated as an incentive for creators of intellectual property to join any specific firm. Top talent can earn just about the same with any company, or at least close enough to the same so that at the high compensation such talent commands, in most cases the difference between offers cannot be the major motivating force behind a move from one company to another.

It is often the non-monetary features that attract or repel already well-compensated talent. And it is those features on which the Murdoch Method concentrates. As *The Economist* put it, 'Every company that employs creative people must think about how to harness their strengths for commercial gain without strangling their free-spiritedness.'[10] One way to do that, says James Murdoch, is to give the creators considerable freedom from what Hollywood derisively calls 'the suits'. 'I was once asked what goes into greenlighting a movie,' James told an interviewer, 'and the answer is, we never actually greenlight a movie. We just don't hit a red light long enough to stop it.'[11] Recognition that creative people relish such support when they dare is a key ingredient of the Murdoch Method, which at least partially explains why Rupert never hit the red light on *Titanic*, despite production cost overruns that had accountants gnawing on the pencils they were pushing. Following his instinct proved to be a good thing, as *Titanic* became one of the most profitable movies ever made, attendance buoyed by teenage and even younger girls paying for multiple trips to the cinema to swoon over Leonardo DiCaprio[12] and enjoy the music and stunning special effects made possible by Rupert's greenlighting of a budget that, by one estimate, made the film's cost greater than that of building the ill-fated liner.[13]

Oddly enough, the Method of attracting and retaining the sorts of people any company that relies on the creativity of its staff must have is so intuitive that I doubt Rupert could articulate it if asked. Based on decades of observing him in action, I believe I can. It has six major ingredients.

The first is that *loyalty is a two-way street*. To get loyalty flowing up to Rupert and the company it has to flow down from him to staff. And it does. I have seen Rupert make a round trip from New York to London to attend the funeral of one of his chauffeurs. I have seen him drop everything to arrange medical care in America at the best specialist hospital in the world for successful treatment of a rare, usually fatal disease afflicting a London employee who remained happily with the company for decades until his retirement, working as productively as ever. I have seen him arrange generous payment to the widow of a columnist and loyal retainer who had foolishly waived his pension rights to increase his cash take-home compensation. With Rupert's permission, I met with her and approved a plan that went beyond what was required of him, something in the order of payment equal to what her husband's pension would have been had he not waived it – if recollection serves. The story did not end there. Rupert felt it would be only proper to call on the widow and, after that condolence call, a cup of tea and, I am told, not a few widow's tears, he raised the amount he had originally instructed me to offer – even though the woman was actually entitled to nothing. I have seen him move a long-serving employee from a job he could no longer adequately perform to a specially created post, rather than pension him off, in order to preserve that person's dignity.

Second, *manners and courtesy matter*. At company retreats Rupert personally assigns quarters to his hundreds of staff and guests. A man with difficulty getting about gets accommodation requiring no stairs. An unexpected cold snap hits an otherwise palm-lined resort, and you wake up in the morning to find a jacket in your size outside your door. Here is Andrew Neil, whom no one can consider a Murdoch sycophant and who left the company after a disagreement with Rupert, on his treatment by Murdoch: 'I only ever had a few harsh words with Rupert on the phone in eleven years: he nearly always treated me with respect, courtesy and sometimes even kindness.'[14]

Third, it is important to *understand and respond to the needs of the people around you*. When my wife Cita was working for the governor of New York and the Murdochs lived in a nearby house in upstate New York (long before I met Rupert), Cita and the Murdochs alternated in picking up the cheque at their regular dinners together. Without mentioning it, Rupert always made certain that when his turn to play host came around, the restaurants he selected were in the same price range as those Cita, her New York State salary a small fraction of his income, could afford. And he has always deferred to my schedule if I was under pressure to be in more places than I could possibly manage, no small thing given the pressures on his own schedule.

Fourth, it is important for a leader *to provide support in a crisis*. When Rebekah Wade, then editor of *The Sun*, spent what must have been a rather long night in jail after a dispute in which she gave her tough-guy husband, television star Ross Kemp, a fat lip, Rupert came to her rescue. As fate would have it, the marital scuffle occurred on a day when Rupert was in London. Wapping was buzzing with rumours about who Wade's replacement at *The Sun* might be. It turned out to be a temp: none other than Rupert Murdoch, demonstrating his loyalty to an employee in considerable and widely publicised difficulty – Wade, a vociferous campaigner against domestic violence, had to be more than a little embarrassed at having done bodily harm to her spouse. Murdoch's assumption of the editor's chair – he announced to one and all in *The Sun* newsroom that they 'should bloody well make sure you get a good paper out … I don't want any crap copy' – silenced speculation about a replacement for Wade.

To make sure that such speculation remained spiked, on Wade's release Murdoch told her to book a table for two at a restaurant at which they were certain to be seen together. While Wade was at home preparing for the evening out, Rupert edited the paper. Of course, Wade is a Murdoch favourite – witness her return to a top position after her gruelling trial and acquittal in connection with the hacking scandal, and it is not certain that, if called upon to do the same for another employee, he would act as he did in this instance. But my guess, based on long experience, is that he would.

Fifth, *kindness matters*. Whether in anticipation of a quid pro quo, or merely as a result of his mother's training and his own instincts, Rupert has an ability to let those around him know that he can act with great kindness when the situation requires it. Once, when we were all in Aspen, Rupert, famous for his recklessness on the slopes, blew out a knee and needed surgery. The evening before he was due to be operated on, Cita had received a call telling her that her father was seriously ill in Baltimore. Rupert had arranged for me to fly back to New York in his plane, which was being repositioned while he recovered from his knee surgery. I reached him on his mobile while he was en route to hospital to ask permission to take my wife along on the New York flight so we could catch a train to Baltimore to see to her father. He agreed. When we settled into our seats the pilot announced that Baltimore would be our first stop rather than New York, an instruction the pilot had received from Rupert as he entered the hospital. Both because it is not Rupert's practice to advertise such gestures, and because he undoubtedly considered it a routine matter to make such an arrangement en route to a surgical procedure, this, like similar incidents, was neither reported nor widely known.

Finally, *humility matters*. With a frequency that often belies his reputation for ruthlessness, a reputation not totally undeserved, Rupert more often than not behaves with humility bordering on diffidence. This might be a subset of the other characteristics I have mentioned, but, even so, it deserves special mention. Rupert, for all his ability and willingness to exercise power, seems to do so in the context of consideration for others. At least, that has been our experience. Once, when I was in Los Angeles, Anna invited me to join her and Rupert for a quiet dinner at their home. Rupert was scheduled to give a talk the following day, which I could not attend because I was booked to catch an early flight to New York. Just before dinner Rupert handed me a draft of his talk, scheduled for delivery the following day before an audience of some 250 analysts, investors and financial types on a soundstage at the Fox lot. A quick reading suggested to me that this was one of those rare instances in which Rupert had been too busy closing an important deal to tell his public relations staff what he wanted to say. The result was a dull, banal recitation of business platitudes, a boring predicate to a blockbuster announcement of a major acquisition. After dinner we sat in the study, Anna as usual doing her needlework, listening as Rupert asked me what I thought of the talk. After I told him why I thought it was not up to his standard either intellectually or stylistically, there was a long silence. 'Perhaps Irwin might be persuaded to stay for an extra day, darling,' said Anna. Rupert, with a humility I had come to expect of a client who with very few exceptions had never asked me to adjust my schedule to his, mumbled something that sounded like he thought that would indeed be a good idea. As was most often the case, Rupert was too considerate to ask me to change my plans to suit his immediate needs. And, as usual, Anna had very politely intervened and given her husband a bit of good advice. So I stayed, and together we replaced most of the pap with a more substantive discussion of the issues that were on Rupert's mind at the time. I have always felt that when Anna was tossed over the side, the good ship Murdoch lost some of its ballast, and took a considerable amount of time to return to an even keel.

These traits underlie the Murdoch Method of managing people; they are reflected in his daily interaction with his staff and associates. But not always and not in all circumstances. At times he loses his temper, sometimes as a premeditated tool of terror, at other times because impatience overwhelms him. Any employee who becomes the object of his temper or impatience is likely to remember it long after the incident is closed. Rupert is capable of suddenly changing his view of an employee, no matter how long-serving, from favourable to unfavourable. Barry Diller put it best: 'Rupert's force of personality, charm and seduction is so great that they [employees] convince themselves his attention is given forever. In fact, it's a loan … People need to understand that.'[15] And when the time comes for a Rupert-induced break, he will most often delegate the chore of informing the employee of his or her fall from grace and its consequences to someone else. Not exactly a profile in courage.

When he decided to part with Richard Searby, a friend of fifty years with whom he shared a room at Geelong Grammar School and who served as chairman of several News entities for more than a decade, 'he sent Searby a curt note' through a subordinate.[16] Views differ as to whether Searby had provoked the rupture, or Rupert merely no longer saw any reason to keep his former friend and associate around. No matter: it is an unattractive feature of the Murdoch Method, to be balanced against its many advantages. To borrow from singer-songwriter Bob Marley, 'He's not perfect … because perfect guys don't exist.' But the large number of long-serving colleagues, and the many, like Diller, who speak highly of him after parting company, suggest that Rupert's personal relationships with his employees are a net asset to the organisation.

The Murdoch Method of luring and securing top talent also includes awe-inspiring displays of corporate success. He believes that employees, especially talented and productive ones, prefer to work for a successful company, one with clout as well as an ability to pay top dollar. 'People want to feel proud of who they are working for,' Murdoch told interviewer John Cassidy,[17] so it is his practice to show his staff that News counts and, by extension, so do they. Corporate gatherings are lavish in the extreme, one of the few examples of Rupert's willingness to issue a money-is-no-object instruction to the responsible executives. Prominent politicians and newsmakers are invited and featured. Movieland celebrities are sprinkled among the guests.

- At one corporate retreat, in Aspen, Colorado, former President Nixon was invited to deliver the major address, and dazzled reporters from all over the world with a seventy-five-minute, no-notes geopolitical *tour d'horizon* (marred only at the conclusion when, after taking several questions, Nixon looked at Anna and Cita and asked if 'the girls' had any questions).

- At another, in Sun Valley, Utah, all recipients of Olympic gold medals for ice skating were retained for an evening performance to the music of hit tunes from Fox movies. As if that were not impressive enough, the conference impresarios enlisted the entire Cirque du Soleil for another evening's entertainment.

- At yet another meeting, this one at the famous golf resort at Pebble Beach, California, Rupert demonstrated the reach of a global media company for some six hundred executives, editors, reporters and guests by inviting Tony Blair, Bill Clinton, Nicole Kidman, Arnold Schwarzenegger, Al Gore, Shimon Perez and a host of other celebrities. Memories of this conference, which emphasised substance as well as glitz, flooded back when I returned to Pebble Beach in 2014 to give a speech to an international group of hoteliers. Although eight years had passed, almost everyone on the staff recalled the News Corp. conference both because of the celebrity list and because of the large gun-toting security squad that patrolled the grounds and the hotel. I was reminded of Bill Clinton's star turn, when he thanked Rupert for inviting him: 'I had a great time. I don't have that much fun any more. When I was in politics, we always tried to invoke Clinton's First Law, which is: "Whenever you are having a good time, you probably should be somewhere else."' The audience loved it, not only the large contingent of liberal Hollywood Democrats. Unfortunately for Al Gore, who had served as Clinton's vice-president, his performance – a slide-show about global warming (it is now called 'climate change', a more elastic concept) – was presented in a manner so wooden that one wag remarked that Gore was fortunate that a dog was not passing by.

- At still another, on Hayman Island, the prime minister
  of Australia and several of his predecessors were invited
  and, given the importance of his media properties in their
  country, attended, impressing the large contingent of News'
  Australian reporters and executives. And, of course, Tony
  Blair was there to size up his prospects of winning Rupert's
  support at the next British general election, and be sized up
  by Rupert. When Rupert ignored urgent pleas of his staff
  to limit invitations to the number of rooms available, and
  invited more guests than the island's hotel could accommodate, he simply hired a large cruise ship, docked it offshore,
  and used it to accommodate staff and the overflow of guests.
  Hayman is the only venue in which my cigar proved an
  attraction rather than a repellent, as the smoke seemed to
  ward off the huge fruit bats that circled overhead. When
  I visibly recoiled at the sight of swarms of these truly ugly
  creatures, Rupert arranged to have a basket of bat-attracting
  fruit left on my balcony every morning, a joke I did not
  appreciate quite as much as did the housekeepers who were
  the ultimate beneficiaries of those baskets.

All these meetings had as one of their purposes a demonstration of the organisation's power, its success, its access to the ideas
of top newsmakers, all the while somehow convincing those
attending that Murdoch's stance as an 'outsider' remained intact.
That it succeeded in attracting and keeping talents with a taste for
upsetting the status quo is perhaps best illustrated by reference to
a man called David Hill, an Australian genius of a special kind.

Hill provides a case study worth reporting in detail because it
illustrates why Rupert has been successful in finding and retaining
executives, creative as well as managerial. I met David when
Rupert brought him to London from Australia to save Sky Sports,
then gushing red ink.[18] The joke among Murdoch haters was

'What is the difference between the Loch Ness monster and Sky Sports? Some people have seen the Loch Ness monster.' At our first meeting Hill demonstrated for Rupert, myself and selected guests how he thought cricket should be telecast, in contrast to the traditional shot, using a single camera stationed behind the batsman (at least, that's where I think it was stationed). I am no cricket fan, and can't vouch for the complete accuracy of my description of the production mode Hill quickly made obsolete, but I can attest to the riveting nature of the on-screen matches Hill produced. David had wrangled a budget that allowed four cameras. After watching the match, or part of it, Rupert asked David how many cameras he had used. 'Eight' came the reply. 'Great pictures,' said Rupert.

Few remember how poorly sport was presented on television in Britain and in America. Then came David, who claims he briefly considered becoming an economist, but, as he likes to say, 'Thank God that didn't take.' Backed by Murdoch's willingness to take huge risks by bidding for rights, and Chase Carey's enthusiasm, sports broadcasting changed. Hill's innovations included continuous display of the score, round-table pre-game shows, expanded use of technology to include wired-for-sound managers, multiple cameras, the yellow superimposed first-down line in American football, the strike zone in baseball, the streaking hockey puck, imaginative broadcasting of auto races, on-field reporters, and much more.[19] The importance of turning sport into not-to-be-missed-television events was crucial to Sky's and Fox's success; so crucial that when Murdoch and Chase Carey finally decided to challenge ESPN for supremacy as a sports broadcaster, taking on not only that dominant broadcaster but NBC and CBS as well, they brought David back from other assignments in the company to manage the creation and launch of Fox Sports 1 which, along with Fox Sports 2, remain Murdoch properties.

The decision to launch the new channel was based on the attract-
iveness of sport to young viewers and therefore to advertisers.
Advertisers crave access to young consumers – customers for cars,
couches, all manner of goods already owned by older consumers.
And young people have an almost limitless appetite for sports
programming. The result of a sporting event is in doubt until the
last whistle or bell. Recording the event and then zipping through
the commercials is not very satisfactory, since it is the suspense
of the unknown result that makes watching sport so exciting.
Young viewers, unable to avoid commercials, make for high ad
rates, and lots of adverts.

That is the market that David Hill brought to Sky and Fox,
and more than once. Rupert's management method kept him
on board for nineteen years, despite the offers that flooded in to
Hill as his fame grew in industry circles. Then, too, there was the
competing lure of entrepreneurship and a saner existence. At one
point David told me he was thinking of giving up the pressure
of so many broadcasts – including championship matches in
many sports – in favour of buying a television station in Tucson,
Arizona, and settling down there with his family. He must have
been more exhausted than usual at the time. David never did seek
that quieter life, despite becoming increasingly bored with sport,
something of which I was unaware until he confessed that to me
recently when we got together for a drink in Washington.

Hill stayed with Rupert for several reasons. He was well compensated financially; he had access to Rupert whenever he asked for it,
or took the privilege without bothering to ask; Rupert gave him
what he needed to be a success, which included not only resources
but lots of room to be what Chase Carey described as 'a once-in-
a-lifetime force of nature'.[20] That he was such a force was brought
home to me the one time David and I butted heads.

Rupert had asked me to put together for his consideration a
draft agenda for an upcoming corporate gathering. David had

talked eloquently about the importance of building brand loyalty, so I pencilled him in for an hour-long presentation on that subject. David never had much use for these meetings, and turned me down. I appealed to Rupert, who urged David to accept, which he did. I had won, or so I thought.

The agenda was duly drawn up to include David's presentation. When we – some six hundred executives, wives and guests – returned from lunch for David's talk, he walked onto the stage and told us to remove the envelopes he had had stapled to the bottoms of our chairs – simply leaving them on each chair or on the desks would not have been theatrical enough. We did as we were told. 'Open them.' We again did as we were told, and found baseball caps emblazoned with the Fox Sports logo. 'Put it on.' We did, hundreds of us. Hill looked around the room, announced, 'That's branding', and walked off the stage – to return after what seemed to me a long delay, and delivered an informative talk. Game, set and match to Hill over the doubles team of a laughing Murdoch and a slightly chastised Stelzer.

Little wonder that David stayed with Sky and then Fox for almost two decades and, as he left to set up his own production company, told an interviewer, 'Working for Rupert Murdoch, Chase Carey and [former News Corp COO] Peter Chernin is as good as it gets.'[21] Murdoch financed Hill's start-up.[22]

Rupert's success with Hill and others equally talented and sought-after is the more remarkable because his plan to have his children succeed him is so well known, meaning that the top spot was not to be available to even the best executive. That was a problem Murdoch could not entirely solve, as a consequence eventually losing several extraordinarily talented executives who chose to set up their own shops, which in most cases proved enormously successful in financial terms. Barry Diller left Fox Broadcasting and 20th Century Fox because Murdoch's dynastic plans would prevent him from ever having a controlling position.

'He told me, not coldly or meanly, but just realistically, "There is in this company only one principal".'[23] So they parted, but not before their collaboration produced the innovative television series *The Simpsons*; the television miniseries format; and the launch of the Fox Television network to challenge the big three of ABC, CBS and NBC, an oligopoly that at least until the end of the twentieth century 'dominated the dissemination of national and foreign television news'.[24]

After leaving Murdoch, Diller established IAC/InterActive Corp., which comprises more than 150 brands, including several online dating sites publicly traded under parent company The Match Group, has important stakes in travel sites Expedia and Orbitz, and has a net worth estimated by Forbes to be around $3.1 billion.[25] Peter Chernin, who headed both the Fox film and broadcasting companies, now heads his own investment and consulting group and has a net worth of $200 million.[26] Former editors and Sky executives Andrew Neil and Kelvin MacKenzie are both active in the media industry and it is safe to assume have few financial worries.

Of course, not all people Rupert decides are no longer of use to him leave to become millionaire entrepreneurs. Nor do all leave on pleasant terms, no surprise given the hard-driving environment at News, Rupert's sudden reappraisals of their value and the need, perceived or real, to replace top executives of acquired companies, as he did at Myspace and British Sky Broadcasting, in the one case disastrously, in the other as a predicate to great success.

The Murdoch Method of protecting assets applies not only to talented executives, who are wooed with charm, displays of corporate strength and, of course, money, but to intellectual property. Using the courts, if necessary. When Rupert made his early foray into the US media business, he could not find a law firm willing to represent him. He has no such difficulty now, although he relies heavily on his in-house legal team in most routine matters.

A recent challenge to News' IP came from none other than Barry Diller, former chairman and CEO of Fox, Inc., parent of Fox Broadcasting and Twentieth Century Fox.

Like Rupert, Diller prefers 'a situation where he'll be the principal and make his own rules', in the words of Fox Studios chairman Joe Roth.[27] As one of several ventures after leaving Fox, Diller founded a company called Aereo, which retransmitted signals picked off the air from television broadcasters. Diller claimed that Aereo was not required to pay fees for taking and then selling these programmes from its own antennae. Unlike Google's alleged theft of the content of Murdoch's print properties, which nips at the margins of those newspapers' advertising revenues, Diller's attack went to television broadcasters' very business model. These broadcasters collect something like $3 billion annually from cable and satellite companies doing essentially what Aereo was doing without any payment. Rupert and other broadcasters sued – and won in the Supreme Court.[28] Aereo is now bankrupt. A clear demonstration of what was at stake was Fox's threat, if it lost, to end its twenty-six-year run as a free, over-the-air channel (actually, viewers are providing their eyeballs free of charge as payment to the broadcaster, who resells them to advertisers), and move its programmes to a 'subscription model'. That proved unnecessary.

In the end, the protection to Murdoch's intellectual property and 'content' by the law is less important to his success than is the Murdoch Method of attracting and retaining talented colleagues. New technologies and distribution methods, and globalisation, increasingly put illegal copying beyond the effective reach of US law, making it more difficult to defend IP in court. And the efforts to persuade China's regime to end its countenancing of IP theft are of little avail. It is said that you can buy a DVD of the latest Fox movie on the streets of Beijing, one block from the Apple store, for $1 before the film goes on general release in America.

Fox and other content creators spend considerable sums lobbying politicians to put a stop to such theft, with limited success.

If I had to sum up the Murdoch Method of retaining creators of intellectual property, I would say it is to *compensate* generously both with cash and perks, one of which is access to Rupert; to *motivate*, relying more on the attraction of an exciting, thrusting corporate culture than on mere money; to *liberate*, by making clear Rupert is aware that risk-taking can lead to failure, but that as a general matter failure will not be penalised; and to *separate*, dismissing employees who don't produce.

This latter step is one from which Rupert prefers to distance himself, a trait apparently common to executives who otherwise thrive on confrontation. Charles Moore, her official biographer, says of Margaret Thatcher, a Murdoch idol, 'Although she was happy to have fierce arguments with colleagues about issues, she disliked personal conflicts.'[29] So, too, Rupert, who has a strong preference for avoiding the one-on-one confrontational unpleasantness of firing an employee. His old friend Woodrow Wyatt, then in a dispute with the editor of the *News of the World* over the change of his weekly to a monthly column, summed up Rupert's aversion to confrontation rather harshly but not incorrectly: 'He's such a coward. He'll never tell you anything unpleasant to your face.'[30] Woodrow, of course, was a person of whom Rupert was extraordinarily fond, and so had never been exposed to Murdoch in full fury. He once enlisted my aid in his fight to retain his weekly slot, apparently unaware that, when it comes to the wishes of an editor, advice from a consultant and friend takes a distant second place. 'Dear Irwin said he would speak to Rupert about my position again', which I did, but only to convey his old friend's pain rather than to seek a stay of execution.[31] The axe fell on the weekly column at the end of 1995. Never again would Woodrow appear at our flat on Sunday mornings before eight, in a robe, dripping wet from his swim at the RAC, to ask what we thought of his column.

To sum up, Rupert's failings as what we might call a personnel manager are not a deterrent to self-confident, talented executives when set against the combination of money, access, and willingness to provide the resources needed for success that Rupert has on offer. Join us, he in effect says, and you will have a career filled with excitement as part of a very unique culture in an extraordinarily successful company that seeks to unseat entrenched competitors who are underserving their customers, whose 'establishment' worldview it is our challenge to replace with our own idea of how to provide news, entertainment and sport to the world. If that sounds attractive, sign on the dotted line or, in many cases such as mine, just agree and 'get on with it', a favourite Murdoch phrase. But know all ye who enter here, that you are committing to a lifestyle as much as to a job, to an employer who is omnipresent in your mind even when thousands of miles away, and one capable of generating excitement, at times of a sort you would wish he hadn't.

CHAPTER 8

THE SUCCESSION
AND THE PIVOT

'So long as I can stay mentally alert – inquiring, curious – I want to keep going ... I'm just not ready to stop, to die' – Rupert Murdoch at seventy-seven, 2008[1]

'One of Rupert's children will take his place one day ... I do think it shouldn't be made too easy for the children to go into the company ... They have to be worthy of their hire' – Dame Elisabeth Murdoch, 1994[2]

'I shall define a dynasty as three successive generations of family control. All dynasties are alike ... Father, later grandfather, rests his authority on age, love, the habit of accepted power, the advantage of experience, the legal possession and control of assets' – David Landes, *Dynasties*, 2006[3]

'Are we retreating? Absolutely not. We are pivoting at a pivotal moment' – Rupert Murdoch , 2017[4]

Rupert Murdoch is at the top of his game. This 'conventionally henpecked husband'[5] is newly and happily married. The horrible hacking scandal, although not yet completely a thing of the past, is receding in memory. Fox News, under Rupert's direction, is maintaining its top ratings as it works its way through the buffeting of multiple sexual harassment claims. The UK newspapers seem to have stemmed and perhaps even reversed declines in circulation. *The Sun* and *The Sunday Times* helped put Brexit over the top in the UK referendum, and Fox News's support for Donald Trump has given Rupert easy access to the White House.

He is at the peak of his perceived political influence. This might not be the best of all possible worlds for Rupert, but it has to be very close to whatever is.

At the age of sixty-nine, after a successful recovery from prostate cancer, he famously said, 'I'm now convinced of my own immortality.'[6] I was working in the office next to his at Fox Studios during part of the time he was being treated, and was amazed that he maintained his breakneck schedule: after early-morning visits to the hospital he showed up at the office well before 8 a.m., and we often had a late dinner at his house in Beverly Hills after one of those hair-raising drives that were a regular feature of Rupert's move from office to home.

The guards at the studio gate knew me as 'Dr Stelzer', and I couldn't persuade them that my title was misleading them. So every evening when I left the studio the hushed question was the same: 'How is he, Doctor?' I gave up trying to explain the limits of my competence in the medical field and finally settled for 'great', to the relief of the guards.

On one level, Rupert, of course, knows he is not immortal, that he will die one day. But not yet, and probably not soon, given his genes (his mother, as we know, died at the age of 103) and the care he takes of himself – no tobacco, sensible diet, vigorous workouts. Jean-Robert Barbette, the Aspen gym-keeper with whom Rupert worked out when in town on protracted stays, tells me that Rupert always added an extra count to every exercise – ask for twenty push-ups and he did twenty-one. He consumes very little alcohol, a fact he referred to in his address at the memorial service of Sir Edward Pickering at St Bride's church on 1 December 2003: 'I fear he [Sir Edward] did not approve of my changing lunchtime habits. I am reliably told that he once lamented, "Rupert used to take wine with lunch – until the Americans got to him."'[7] Even though he is now the proud owner of the Moraga Vineyard Estates, set in the hills above Bel-Air, purchased for $28.8 million in 2013, Rupert consumed very little of his wine at a recent dinner with us at Lachlan's Aspen house. At that dinner he demonstrated one of his most appealing traits, a desire and ability to participate in just about everything going on around him. He simultaneously paid attention to Jerry Hall and his several grandchildren, kept an eye on Fox News on a huge television screen, discussed with Cita the 'old days' in Old Chatham, New York, responded with a snort to my criticism of some Fox News commentators, discussed the future of print with Lachlan and me, and attributed a few added pounds to 'happiness'. Because everyone had a piece of his attention no one had it all. But no one seemed to object.

Through all the successes and failures, all the international goings and comings, all the dinners and musings I shared with Rupert, I never doubted one thing: Rupert's children would inherit the News empire, although I did not anticipate the surprise 'pivot' that changed the form of that inheritance. Meritocracy and nepotism live comfortably side by side in Rupert's mind. Rupert has always said they would have to prove themselves, and I do believe he meant it. Fortunately, all the children he and Anna produced are able (this was obvious at an early age), and James and Lachlan have survived what one observer calls 'a brutal form of on-the-job training ... an executive assault course'.[8] But a Murdoch 'proving' him- or herself within the confines of News is rather different from a non-family member 'proving' himself in that same environment, an important difference being that major missteps by a Murdoch do not result in a permanent fall from the succession ladder. Nothing unique about that. Henry Ford's heirs proved themselves at the car company, Ralph Roberts' and Charles Dolan's heirs proved themselves in the cable business, Arthur Sulzberger's heirs proved themselves in the newspaper business, if by 'proved' we mean performed to the satisfaction of their fathers. Never mind the reputational problems created for James Murdoch by the hacking scandal, the failure of Ford's Edsel,

James Dolan's mismanagement of the New York Knickerbockers, owned by his cable company, and the Sulzberger heirs' ongoing difficulty coping with changes in the newspaper industry. Some critics say that inheritance after failures is mere nepotism, others that the overall performance of the heirs to these enterprises was indeed more than adequate, the inevitable consequence of genetic inheritance and lifelong exposure to the business.

In any event, the die is now cast. In the summer of 2013, as we have seen, stockholders happily approved Rupert's decision to split his entertainment and print properties into separate companies. He had been under pressure to do this so that shareholders seeking growth would be relieved of the drag created by the print properties. The print group inherited the name News Corp, and 130 newspapers, including *The Wall Street Journal,* and the *New York Post* in America; *The Times, Sunday Times* and *Sun* in Britain; and seven of the top ten newspapers in Australia. In addition, Lachlan will have responsibility for publisher HarperCollins, News America Marketing, *Barron's* magazine, and several television properties and the top residential property site in Australia. These properties put the new News Corp among the top ten global media companies in terms of revenue generated.[9] 21st Century Fox includes the Fox Entertainment Group, which owns the film studio, the Fox broadcast network, Fox News, Fox Sports, National Geographic, and a 39.4 per cent share of Sky Plc. Sky has assets in Germany, Austria, Italy, Ireland and Britain.[10]

This corporate reorganisation demonstrates Rupert's ability to convert problem into opportunity, something he has told me he considers one of his strengths, demonstrated during the hacking scandal. The scandal had given him the opportunity to close the *News of the World* and replace it with a *Sunday Sun,* as he had long considered doing. It enabled him to bring a previously reluctant James back to America and place him in a future leadership slot. It provided him with reason and opportunity to recapture the

interest and talents of Lachlan, who returned to active participation in corporate affairs to stand by and advise his father in a
time of crisis. In short, the hacking crisis provided Rupert with an
opportunity to push ahead with his succession plan.

Whether by design or good luck, Rupert was similarly able
to convert the problem created by shareholder pressure to split
his company into a largely print–sports enterprise (News) and
an entertainment company (21st Century Fox), into a series of
opportunities.

First, it enabled him to solve a pressing problem caused by the
emergence of a new breed of disrupters, many based in Silicon
Valley. The development of 'streaming' has enabled owners of
what the industry calls 'content' – programmes of all sorts – to
bypass cable companies and reach consumers directly. They are
prepared to outspend 21st Century Fox by five to eight times in
creating such content, which would put them in a position to
outbid Fox for 'eyeballs', dooming it to eventual extinction. Or at
least, that is how the Murdochs see it. But a combination of Fox
and Disney content and brands creates a formidable competitor
to the disrupters. And increases the global reach of Disney, now
not what its management would like it to be.

Which is why Disney was willing to bid $66 billion (including
assumption of debt) for some of 21st Century Fox's entertainment
assets, a figure the Murdochs found irresistible compared to the
prospect of taking on the better-heeled disrupters. With the entertainment assets already neatly parked in a separate company, it was
relatively easy to structure a deal that passed ownership to Disney.

A deal that presented an opportunity for Rupert to solve
still another problem: James. Just as many years earlier James
expressed unhappiness with Rupert's decision to pass his crown
on to Lachlan, so he chafed at the decision to make him subordinate to Lachlan in the newly organised Murdoch companies. That
made Rupert's original succession plan inherently unstable.

James is intelligent, a quick learner, understands the digital world, is at times surer of himself than he perhaps ought to be, and, in the words of Murdoch chronicler and critic Michael Wolff 'excruciatingly boyish'. He often uses bad language, admitting to an interviewer from *Der Spiegel*, 'I try very hard not to use expletives. Sometimes I do not quite meet that objective', adding by way of exculpation, 'like many of us'.[11] But more often than not he follows an outburst with a display of his extraordinary charm, part natural, part calculated. When arranging an afternoon get-together, James took pains to inform me that he had gone to some lengths to find a London venue that would permit me to smoke a cigar – which I never do in the afternoon – and immediately lit a cigarette when he arrived.

James often shoots from the hip and has at times been reckless, as when he stormed into the offices of *The Independent* on 21 April 2010 to protest that competitor's treatment of his father in its reporting.[12] At some point while the crown was being sized for Lachlan, James barged into his father's office demanding that he be allowed to enter the succession race. The air turned blue. That would involve him dropping out of Harvard and, as a first step on the ladder to the top spot, establishing and making a success of a record company, the one area of the media/entertainment business in which News was not represented, in part because Rupert regarded it as drug-ridden. I was included in the family gathering to discuss James's plans, and when asked my opinion sided with James, the first time I can remember advising anyone to cut short a college education. James didn't need a degree to bolster his résumé or his employment prospects, and deserved to be given a shot at the succession when age might temper his impetuousness with a bit of patience for the failings of others.

James's Rawkus hip-hop record company succeeded in introducing some successful artists, if that is the right word for the musicians it attracted, but ran into financial difficulties and in

1996 was sold to News Corp., which soon shut it down. So ended James's days as a tattooed, goateed executive, a poster of Chairman Mao on his office wall[13] – mimicking Rupert's famous display of a bust of Lenin in his Oxford rooms.

Rawkus might not have been the success James, and later News Corp. shareholders, hoped it would be, but no one questions the fact that between 2000 and 2003 he was successful in turning Murdoch's loss-making Hong Kong-based STAR business around,[14] and then topped that achievement with a successful run as non-executive chairman of BSkyB after being appointed to that post by his father. That appointment unleashed the anti-Murdoch press, delighted to have a new Murdoch target, and upset some experts on corporate governance. Key players in the City of London worried that so valuable an asset was to be placed in the hands of so young an executive, at thirty-one the youngest CEO of a FTSE 100 company.[15] Appointing a Harvard dropout to such a position was nepotism at its worst, claimed the press. Shareholders were initially dubious, worried that all James had to recommend him for the position was his last name. James saw it somewhat differently. At one point in the row he complained to me that the name 'Murdoch' was a heavy burden. However, he had the good sense not to respond when I asked him, 'James, all in all, is the name an advantage or a disadvantage?' The not-naturally-Murdoch-friendly *New York Times* suggested some years later that James has 'the Murdoch brand advantage. When people speak to him, they believe – and rightly so – that they are speaking to the strategic thinker who connects the dots at the mothership.'[16] That belief had to be an asset that outweighed any disadvantages of the Murdoch name, and contributed to the willingness of the Sky board, its independent membership augmented by the addition of Jacob Rothschild as deputy chairman, to approve James's appointment.

At Sky, James combined his father's feel for what viewers want to see with his own understanding of the technology that delivers that programming, and a shrewd sense of how best to price the service, often more art than science when dealing with a novel product or offering. Better still, he proved expert at bundling services that BSkyB could offer, driving up per-customer revenues and the company's profits, winning over shareholders and the City, no small achievement for a Murdoch in the often-unfriendly UK political environment. And then, onwards and upwards to the post of deputy chief operating officer and head of international operations of News Corp., in charge of the UK newspapers and television operations in Europe and Asia.

James had one advantage denied Lachlan – a 3,000-mile barrier between himself and his father, not all the time, but enough of the time to give him considerable autonomy, or as much as was possible given the nature of his father. An old friend of Rupert's from their Geelong Grammar School days pointed out to me that Rupert's daily telephone calls are nowhere near as unnerving as his impromptu, unannounced visits, his penchant for 'going walkabout', as the Australians call it, in whatever office he finds himself. Besides, Rupert was determined not to make the mistake he had made with Lachlan by overriding James's decisions.

James reinvigorated the journalists by refusing to concede that theirs is a dying industry; he moved from triumph to triumph at Sky, driving earnings and per-customer revenues steadily upwards. Then James scored an own goal, almost as consequential as the hacking scandal. He shattered the much-valued family unity, in the process creating a rift with regulators.

In 2009, James delivered the broadcast industry's most important address, the MacTaggart Lecture, a talk that would come back to haunt him. He intended to challenge his audience – I have seen him do that successfully in other venues – but also managed to antagonise his sister by attacking the industry of which she was a member, and the ethos she shared, at least in good part. He also exhibited a scorn for regulators, which those of us who deal with them regularly know can only mean trouble in the future, in contrast with the more cooperative approach of Rupert, who accepts that both Fox and News Corp must live with regulation and regulators as long as they are in business.

His essential argument in the MacTaggart Lecture was that profits are needed if the broadcast industry is to be successful, and that regulation was inhibiting innovation.[17] Both unexceptionable observations, but, presented in James's typically direct and unadorned style, designed in part to startle the broadcast-industry audience, he left himself open to charges of extremism in the pursuit of profits; ignoring the special public-interest nature of broadcasting; and failing to recognise that broadcast regulators have a difficult job dealing with a complex, fast-changing industry affected with the public interest. This contrasted with his father's more nuanced MacTaggart Lecture in August 1989, in which Andrew Neil and I had a hand in shaping Rupert's ideas into speech format. Rupert combined attacks on the elitist programming of the BBC with a recognition that 'in a market-led TV system there is still room for a public-service element to provide programming that the market might not provide.'[18]

Three years later, James's sister was offered the same prestigious platform afforded James, and used it to rebut him and separate herself from his views in a manner that must have made her grandmother proud. 'A hunger for excellence and a passion to resonate with our audience is far more motivating than money… Profit without purpose is a recipe for disaster … We need to … reject the idea that money is the only effective measure of all things or that the free market is the only sorting mechanism.'[19] James had alienated two sources of possible support that he would need when the hacking scandal broke: Liz and Ofcom, his sister and his regulator, and in the latter case other members of the international regulatory community, which is more close-knit than outsiders realise.

Michael Wolff, whom James characterises as a man 'carving out a career for himself by writing about a company that he doesn't really know',[20] claims that Liz said James had f***** the company[21] and should be fired, not very different from the position James would later take towards Roger Ailes, Bill O'Reilly and others when the sexual harassment scandal broke. And Ofcom was to do considerable damage to James's reputation when it reported on its investigation of the scandal, although if asked the regulators would deny any relation of their comments on James's manage- ment skills, or lack thereof, to James's assault on them in his MacTaggart Lecture.

James's insistence that Fox News apply high standards of behaviour in dealing with the sexual harassment claims against Ailes, Bill O'Reilly, Jamie Horowitz, president of Fox Sports,[22] Charles Payne, of Fox Business Network[23] and other 21st Century Fox employees, and his generally admired managerial moves at Fox probably counted in his favour when, in June 2017, Ofcom concluded that 21st Century Fox was a fit and proper company to hold a broadcasting licence. As mentioned earlier, that decision is under review by the Competition and Markets Authority.

So James would make a rich addition to the Disney executive corps. But he 'never seemed comfortable with print' [24], and 'does not relish the newspaper culture the way his father does … [and] seems to take no delight in the company of reporters and in the sort of gossip that … his father both traffics in and relishes.' [25] Which brings us to Lachlan.

Any doubt I harboured that Rupert planned to name Lachlan his successor was dispelled when Rupert invited me to lunch at company headquarters in New York shortly before the announce- ment of the roles to be assigned to James and Lachlan. In the course of our conversation he told me that for the next six weeks Lachlan would be shadowing him; going wherever he went, attending all meetings, and generally getting a better understanding of the chairman's role.

When Lachlan spent part of his school years at the Aspen Country Day School, where he indulged his passion for rock climbing and the outdoor life, Cita and I got to know him as a thoughtful, quiet and widely read young man with very considerable backbone. Later, at our dinner parties in Washington, we watched as the then-Princeton student held his own with senior historians in discussions of Burke and other great figures in British history. When his father appointed him deputy chief operating officer of News Corp., his rise to the top chair seemed a certainty. But Rupert's lieutenants were having none of it – they mocked him as 'the prince'. Rupert not only did not stand by Lachlan but, I am told, would tear up the front pages Lachlan had approved for the *New York Post*, an experience familiar to and tolerated by other editors, unburdened by any father–son overlay that I leave to amateur psychiatrists to describe.

When Rupert intervened once too often by overruling Lachlan's decision not to air a programme Roger Ailes was proposing, Lachlan said enough is enough, and returned to Australia. One hot summer day I spent about two hours with him at tea in a hotel in London, at which meeting he told me of the humiliations inflicted upon him, and his desire to spend time with his wife and family, rather than 'spend my life on an aeroplane between New York and Sydney'. Many years later Lachlan attributed his departure to the fact that it was a time in his life when he wanted to 'take a big risk', and said, 'It's one of the very best decisions I ever made in my life, leaving the company, and I'd do it again.' I am inclined to stick with the contemporaneous account he shared with me.[26]

Rupert was upset, but, consistent with his parents' teaching about the importance of family, appointed himself chair of News'

Australian operations, 'Keeping the seat warm for Lachlan,' wrote Mark Day in Murdoch's *Australian*. And a good thing it was, as it facilitated Lachlan's return to active participation in the company. As David Landes, Emeritus Professor of History and Economics at Harvard, notes in his study of business dynasties, 'Emotional clashes seem to be almost unavoidable, gaining force from both success and failure … and it is the family's ability to deal with such clashes within the structure of the business that helps determine their success.'[27]

I recall trying to persuade Rupert, shortly after Lachlan announced his departure, that the move was testimony to Rupert and Anna's ability to raise strong-minded children in the home of very strong-minded parents. I am not certain that thought offset the father's regret at the departure of his eldest son – a departure that, fortunately for both Rupert and Lachlan, proved reversible, thanks to Rupert's open-door policy towards his children, and the irresistible attraction to Lachlan of inheriting control of one of the world's great media companies. Lachlan now says he is delighted to be 'working more closely than ever with my father'.[28] Furthermore, he has indulged his taste for the great outdoors by buying a forty-five-acre ranch in Aspen, not far from where Cita and I live, and a town of which he has fond memories.[29]

Lachlan has a reputation for calm judgement, a love of the businesses for which he has major responsibility and a decent although mixed record as an entrepreneur that includes failures at a mobile phone company and Ten Network Holding,[30] more than offset by his success at converting a $10.75 million investment in an Australian property portal into one valued at $3.65 billion.[31]

He will be presiding over a very substantial enterprise. In addition to News, the world's largest publisher with powerful brands in the US, UK and Australia, the new pared-down Fox (shorn of the 21st Century name), will have $10 billion in annual revenue and $2.8 billion of earnings before interest, taxes, depreciation and amortisation (EBITA in the jargon of the financial community). It is a testimonial to the scale at which the Murdochs operate that Lachlan has described this entity as being about 'returning to our roots as a lean, aggressive challenger brand, focused at the beginning on must-watch news and live sports.'[32] The interesting things about this statement are its emphasis on the important roles of Fox 'must-watch' News, and the lucrative rights the new company will hold to air National Football League (NFL) and Major League Baseball across the sports networks it retains. And, of course, the idea that the focus on news and sports is only 'the beginning'.

The companies' shareholders will, of course, have to approve all of these moves, and lawyers being available, some may object that their interests were somehow not being served, although the handsome price received for the 21st Century Fox Entertainment assets makes that unlikely. No matter.

The corporate structures of News and Fox give the Murdochs voting power disproportionate to their share ownership – 39 per cent of the votes despite owning only 13.6 per cent of News Corp and 14.5 per cent of 21st Century Fox. Southeastern Asset Management, a Memphis-based fund manager that is known for its reluctance to intervene in the management of firms in which it invests,[33] at one time News Corp's second largest shareholder, sold off its position after it failed to eliminate the pro-Murdoch voting structure.[34] But not before it was joined by other share-holders to produce a 47.4 per cent vote in favour of replacing the existing system with a one-share, one-vote arrangement.[35] It should be noted that there was strong demand from institutional investors for the shares Southeastern put on the block, suggesting that many institutions are quite willing to live with the current control arrangements. In a belt-and-braces move, Rupert had the board approve a 'poison pill' that allows existing investors, including the Murdoch family, to buy new shares at half price if another buyer acquires more than 15 per cent of the voting shares. In effect, anyone acquiring more than 15 per cent of those shares would face an immediate loss of half his investment.

That makes it difficult for anyone to repeat cable magnate and financial engineer John Malone's threat to Rupert's control of his empire in 2005. Malone acquired 16.3 per cent of News stock that became briefly available when Rupert was delisting News Corp. in Australia so that the shares could be listed in New York. Rupert was reported to be 'furious',[36] and eventually eliminated what he described as a 'cloud over the company'[37] by recapturing those shares, but only by turning over to Malone some $11 billion in assets consisting of $550 million in cash, three regional sports networks and his 38.5 per cent controlling stake in DIRECTV, known as the Deathstar because of its threat to the monopolies of local cable companies, Malone's principal assets.[38] Malone graciously terms this deal a win–win, giving Rupert 'hard control of News Corp where nobody could threaten him', and Malone's Liberty 'a good deal'. In fact, there was only one winner, and it was Malone. In the course of a long interview with the cable magnate, journalist Matthew Garrahan commented, 'Mr Malone is a rarity in media in that he once got the better of Rupert Murdoch.'[39]

None of this jockeying for assets and billions seems to have affected Murdoch and Malone's mutual respect. Rupert has invited Malone to address News' executives at corporate meetings, calls him 'the most brilliant strategist I know', and Malone reciprocates the compliment: Murdoch 'is not just trying to get big … He sees the nexus between programming and platform.'[40] These shows of mutual respect are quite common in an industry in which rivals in one venture become partners in another. Occasional efforts by one titan to tread on the toes of another are 'nothing personal, it's just business', to borrow from Mario Puzo. After the courts supported the successful effort by Murdoch and his allies to shut down Barry Diller's Aereo, Diller said, 'We are absolutely still friends.'[41]

Although the one-share, one-vote alternative to the governance system of News Corp sounds eminently reasonable, and is supported by a sixteen-member coalition of money managers who, combined, manage more than $17 trillion in assets,[42] the issue of which voting system produces maximum value for shareholders is not at all clear. The dual-class share arrangement, which allows the owner of a significant but minority stake in the voting shares to control the entire operation has been common in the media business for some time, and is used by other companies such as Ford and Wal-Mart, and by the much-revered Warren Buffett at Berkshire Hathaway, among many others. It is now the corporate-governance structure of choice in several high-tech companies such as Alphabet, Zynga, Facebook, Fitbit and Box Inc. The founders of these companies, like the Murdochs, want to maintain control of the future of their creations while at the same time raising capital from outside investors. According to data-gatherer Decalogic, 13.5 per cent of the companies listing shares on US exchanges in 2015 have set up dual-class share structures.[43] In 2015, 15 per cent of US IPOs had dual-class structures, up from 1 per cent ten years earlier.[44]

Rupert is convinced that secure family control eliminates the need to concentrate on short-term earnings so important to investment analysts for whom he has often made clear to me he has little regard. Voting control allows him and his team to focus on the long-term, which he contends is in the best interests of all the shareholders. This view has become more widespread since the success of Jeff Bezos in turning Amazon into a dominant force in retailing. Bezos gives no thought at all to short-term profits which, according to Colin Sebastian, an analyst with the investment firm of Robert W. Baird & Co., accounts for Amazon's spectacular success. 'When you have such a long-term perspective that you think in decades instead of quarters, it allows you to do things and take risks that other companies believe would not be in their best interests.'[45]

Several academic and consulting studies side with Murdoch. A McKinsey study found that sales of family-controlled firms have grown at an annual rate of 7 per cent since 2008, compared with 6.2 per cent for non-family-owned firms. 'McKinsey see these trends continuing for the foreseeable future,' reports *The Economist*.[46] Another study, by Ronald Anderson and David Reeb, compared the one-third of the S&P 500 in which families are present and found that 'family firms perform better than non-family firms ... and that when family members serve as CEO, performance is better than with outside CEOs'.[47] Another, by finance professors at the University of Singapore and Temple University respectively, concluded that it is hard work for family enterprises to 'prosper over the generations ... but the evidence suggests that it is worth the effort for the family, the business, and society at large'.[48] A study by scholars at the IE Business School in Madrid for Banca March found that 'Family businesses do better than non-family firms in stock returns. €1,000 invested in 2001 in the market capitalisation-weighted portfolio of listed family businesses in Europe would have generated €3,533 by the end of the decade compared to €2,241 produced by the portfolio of non-family firms. This is 500 basis points of additional income per year.'[49] And a statistical study by David Audretsch (Indiana University) and Marcel Hülsbeck and Erik Lehmann (University of Augsburg) concludes that 'more family control is beneficial to all groups of investors'.[50] Finally, a study by the Center for Family Business at the University of St Gallen, Switzerland, concludes that private firms with better than 50 per cent family ownership of voting rights and public firms with at least 32 per cent of family ownership of the voting rights 'tend to be focused not on the next quarter but on the next generation ... [and] are very good at being efficient at innovation'.[51] Dorothy Shapiro Lund, a teaching fellow at the University of Chicago Law School, puts it differently. She writes, 'There may be companies that are made worse off when all shareholders vote. Some shareholders ... have no interest in learning about the company.' She concludes that consolidating voting power in the hands of holders of voting stock would allow informed decision-making, to the benefit of all shareholders.[52]

This is not to dismiss the arguments of shareholder advisory services that favour one share, one vote. A study commissioned by the Council of Institutional Investors provides 'no support for the assertion that the degree of control wielded by holders of superior class shares influences long-term company performance'[53] but could find no damage to performance of companies with two. It is possible, of course, that the superior performance of firms relying on dual-share structures is due less to the corporate structure of family-held firms than to the fact that the better-performing group is overweighted with companies in the newer, most explosively growing sectors of the economy. Also, it is important to remember that one shareholder, one vote allows all owners of the business, or their representatives at pension funds and the like, to select the people who will manage their investments, and attracts to the company ambitious and talented executives who do not want to work in companies in which their route to the top is barred by nepotism. After all, one (but only one) reason the extraordinarily talented Barry Diller left Fox was because he wanted to own and run his own enterprises, something, as we have seen, that was never going to happen in the Murdoch empire.

From a public policy point of view there remains a question of the effect of family ownership on the overall performance of an economy. Here the evidence is ambiguous. Against the seemingly superior performance of closely held companies must be laid the tendency of those firms to invest less in risky R&D and more in supposedly safer physical assets.[54] Also, if too numerous, or too well connected politically, family firms can form cartels that create barriers to innovation and to opportunity for non-family members. But that fear does not seem to apply in the case of News

Corp or 21st Century Fox. 'The secret to healthy family power', opines *The Economist*, 'is competition. In an open system of free markets, governed by the rule of law and held to account by a free press, nepotism matters less.'[55] In both Britain and America, where the rule of law prevails, where regulation ensures that competition remains vigorous, as it now is in the dissemination of news, family enterprises pose no worrying threat to the democratic process.

In the end, there are credible arguments on both sides of the corporate governance controversy. Some studies suggest that firms that are family-controlled or have two classes of stock are the better performers. Others find no performance difference that can be traced to the ability of a founder or major shareholder to exert control using shares with greater-than-ordinary voting power. In the case of closely controlled companies, especially those controlled by founders using shares with superior voting rights, financial performance will depend on the quality of the founder and his long-term ability to retain the talents that put his firm on course to success, and on his ability to select from his offspring and nurture the one or ones with the special talent required at the time he, or less often she, inherits the founder's mantle.

So Rupert can look with some satisfaction on what he has wrought and what he is handing on. Lachlan is in a business he loves. And James is positioned to do just about anything he pleases. But Lachlan will have to reverse the downtrend in newspaper advertising, James cope successfully with the technological changes sweeping through the entertainments industries. Both are operating in highly competitive industries. Ever heard of Studebaker, Collins Radio, National Sugar Refining, Armstrong Rubber, Cone Mills? Probably not. They were Fortune 500 companies in 1955. By 2014 only 61 of the 500 companies on the list of those with the highest sales in 1955 remained among the elite. Almost 88 per cent of the companies on the list in 1955 have either gone bankrupt, merged, or still exist but are no longer in the top group.[56] Capitalism is, as Joseph Schumpeter famously pointed out,[57] characterised by a perennial gale of creative destruction, a gale that at times even the most talented managers cannot survive. The Murdoch children are as driven as their father. Whether they are as talented, or whether those talents equip them to be able to cope with the pace of technological and financial change that is in store for them, remains to be seen. My guess is that they will prove up to the challenge.

That, I hasten to add, is not the view of all students of the media business. Peter Preston, who wrote widely about the media sector, contended one year after Murdoch announced his intention to divide his empire into two separate companies: 'He [Murdoch] hasn't a son who can take on this burden. Hacking finished James's ambitions in that direction. There is no frontline succession.'[58] Since Preston was editor of *The Guardian* for twenty years, a newspaper not exactly sympathetic to Rupert, his wish might well have been father to his thought. But in a reluctant recognition of Rupert's contribution to the survival of the UK newspaper industry, Preston also wrote that if the sons cannot match the contribution of their father, the 'stability' of the media industry will suffer. 'Dad's buccaneering devotion to print has been one of the props of the press worldwide for two decades. Expect some horrid, all-too-normal collapses if it's gone.'[59]

Preston was not alone in believing that the Murdochs will go the way of the Bancrofts. Serial Murdoch critic Michael Wolff predicted in 2011 that James 'absolutely cannot survive ... The Murdochs will be moved out of this company. James will go into some form of exile and Rupert will be put out to pasture and an outsider not named Murdoch will be put in charge.'[60] Don't bet on it. James is no longer in exile and the distant pasture that can hold Rupert has not yet been discovered.

The final question is whether Lachlan and James go the way of the Bancroft family, too distracted by the diversions wealth can bring to watch the store. From what I have seen of these young men as they have grown up, I would rate that highly unlikely. But if Disney does not have a place in, or better still, at the top of its hierarchy, he might find the lure of politics irresistible: after all, if a billionaire property mogul can move into the Oval Office, so might a billionaire media mogul. He has established his liberal credentials by railing against Fox News and President Trump, by being the principal engineer of Roger Ailes' enforced departure. And he has established his green credentials in many ways, not least by his lavish personal and financial support of Fox's National Geographic channel, which covers issues he identifies as of great concern to him, 'the environment, conservation, exploration and education'.[61] One leading environmentalist, who recoiled in horror when 21st Century Fox acquired National Geographic, tells me of the satisfaction his community now feels about the acquisition and James's role in the operation of the channel. Greens are relieved that the sins of the father, who believes, or once believed (which is still not clear), that climate change is a hoax, have not been visited upon the son. As for Lachlan, he might decide that charities, family and the call of the wild take top priority.

Each one improbable, but the Murdochs specialise in the improbable.

EPILOGUE

The Murdoch Method worked for Rupert. He created a great media empire. But that leaves unanswered a broader and more difficult question: would the world be a better place if Rupert had stayed in Adelaide, bowing to the competitors who wanted to buy him out, rather than following the calling set out for him by Sir Keith? After all, a media company is a special thing: the effects of its activities are not confined to its balance sheet. It can enrich or debase the culture. It can increase access to news and diverse opinions or, like the major television enterprises in Britain and America in pre-Murdoch days, represent a single point of view. It can widen the reach of its entertainment products, or content itself with staying within the bounds of what controlling elites deem acceptable. In short, a media company produces what economists call externalities – costs and benefits that are not reflected on its financial statements, but costs that are borne by and benefits that accrue to society as a whole.

Rupert is well aware of his responsibility, or, as he puts it, his companies' 'special powers':

> We can help to set the agenda of political discussion.
>
> We can uncover government misdeeds and bring them to light.
>
> We can decide what television fare to offer children on a rainy Saturday afternoon.

We can affect the culture by glorifying or demonizing certain behaviour, such as the use of drugs …

Can we increase our profits by making and distributing pornographic films? Probably. But we won't …

Might we boost the ratings of our wonderful and objective Sky News by 'dumbing it down'? Perhaps. But we won't.

Might we be more welcome in some countries if we offered to spin the news to please the government? Perhaps. But … we will not distort what we are permitted to broadcast.[1]

It is, of course, impossible to measure the costs and benefits of News Corp's impact, to do an empirical weighing-up, and reach a firm conclusion about whether we wish Rupert had been content to stay in Adelaide, or are overjoyed that he chose to share his special talents and worldview with us. Much will depend on whether we share that worldview, or prefer a media company with a less adversarial relationship to what I have called the establishment. That Rupert is hostile to that establishment, and that his hostility has not been tempered by his success, there is little doubt. No amount of success, no invitations to this or that social event, no strolls down the red carpet to an Oscar awards ceremony with a dazzling woman on his arm, no lavish apartments, no invitations to chat with high-ranking political figures have persuaded Rupert to see himself as an insider rather than an outsider. As his power has grown, so it seems has his personal obligation to remain outside the establishment – to refuse a knighthood and a peerage, if offered – to produce films and television programmes that upset well-entrenched views of what it is culturally acceptable, to expose politicians who cheat on their constituents or, better still for circulation, on their wives, to produce screaming headlines denouncing famous sexual predators.

Because the products turned out by Murdoch companies are a result of his anti-establishment worldview, anyone who finds that view not to his liking need go no further in an appraisal of the costs and benefits to society of Murdoch's expansion from his Australia base. Content with the status quo, they will find that the costs imposed upon their world by Rupert Murdoch exceed any benefits from his activities. Others must look further.

Start with the proposition that, for better or worse, Rupert is responsible not only for his direct orders, but for the actions of his subordinates. Those whose proximity or access to him enable them to take direct orders from him do just that, with the trusted expected to ignore any that might be damaging to the company. Their lives are easier than those not so placed. Those who have less contact with 'the boss' must imagine what those orders might be, and act accordingly. To his credit, Murdoch never denies that his responsibility for what is done extends to the latter group, although at times – relatively few times as they should be counted over a career bordering on seven decades – he has engaged in unattractive finger-pointing. Generally, News executives understand where the outer limit of what Rupert will deem responsible is located. But they have no rule book, no clear set of do's and don'ts. The Murdoch Method specifically rejects the utility of such rigid rules: they would make it difficult or impossible to permit budget overruns of the sort that allowed the production of *Titanic* when the director blew the budget; or prevent launching the very raunchy (in its day) and successful *Married With Children* during family-watching time on network television; or risk hundreds of millions establishing a conservative news channel in America.

But the absence of rigid rules and a Method that often leaves executives to guess what Rupert would do, combined with an anti-establishment atmosphere hostile to existing norms, also gave us the hacking scandal, the work environment at Fox News that produced the sexual behaviour that, when revealed, was found to be abhorrent, and entertainment products all of which Rupert himself would not care to defend.

No picking and choosing among this truncated list: what I regard as benefits of the Murdoch Method and its disadvantages, or costs, cannot be unbundled. All are products of a single view: the elites deny the majority access to the news and entertainment that it is the obligation of Rupert's companies to provide. You can take the Method or leave it, but you can't get the benefits without the costs. That's what makes an ultimate totting up so difficult, so personal to the one doing the totting.

One thing we do know about the Method: it enables Rupert to set a tone that makes his executives and staff wake up in the morning eager to get to work, in the case of News to mount still another attack on the establishment and to beat competitors to scoops, stories and creative ideas. Maximising shareholder value is important, but it is best achieved as the by-product of a culture that harnesses the energies and enthusiasms of the executive group. Anyone who visits a News Corp or, now, a 21st Century Fox installation – press room, television studio, movie lot, executive office – will know immediately that Rupert has got it right. The excitement, the sense of urgency, is palpable, and a vivid contrast with what one senses strolling the corridors of the institutions he has chosen to attack. Murdoch knows this. He recognises that his companies' success is based importantly on his personal willingness to take risks and his refusal to be co-opted by the establishment. That is a partial explanation of his desire that his successors be possessed of his outsider's gene.

Although the Murdoch Method has produced the results Rupert intended, it is also fallible – witness the hacking scandal that overtook the company in the UK, the sacrifice of principle in pursuit of the elusive Chinese market, the difficulty Rupert has had in applying the Method to the publishing and entertainment industries. Murdoch ended exclusionary elitism in British broadcasting, causing one critic to complain to me that, with so much sport available from Sky, working-class viewers would never learn to love opera. He made newspapers available to more people by preventing the trade unions from destroying not only his but his competitors' newspapers. He made them accessible by emphasising to his columnists that papers are published for readers, not writers and editors more interested in Pulitzer Prizes, and by using the tabloids to provide a mix of politics, as viewed through an anti-establishment lens, sport and gossip that millions find attractive. He made television news interesting and reflective of an opinion previously unavailable to viewers: turn on Fox News and you are certain to learn of developments not reported by the so-called mainstream media, and be exposed to views different from those on all the more liberal channels and networks.

The story in the field of entertainment is more complicated. The line between ending elitist control of entertainment, and what Gertrude Himmelfarb calls the coarsening and debasement of the culture, is indistinct, and reasonable men may differ sufficiently as to its location to make it difficult to develop policies that shield the public from debasement without entrenching the exclusionary social attitudes of the dominant elite. Murdoch did not initiate the coarsening of the culture with films and television programmes that glorify violence, vulgar language and sexual exhibitionism. An entire industry of filmmakers and programme producers accomplished that long before Rupert came on the scene. It is fair to say that Fox products were stunningly innovative (*The Simpsons*), acceptably raunchy because funny (*Married With Children*), but also in line with the industry's assault on traditional cultural values (*There's Something About Mary* in its day), and Hollywood's almost uniform depiction of priests and businessmen as, well, bad guys, and its reliance on violence to lure audiences. He was and is a collaborator in rather than a *résistant* to the cultural debasement of which he stands accused. The extent to which he is to be condemned for that depends on whether one believes that resistance could have been effective, or if not, whether tilting at windmills – and if you fail, you fail, as Stephen Sondheim puts it – has a value of its own.

The difficulty comes in weighing the failure to resist against the positive effects of increased access to news and entertainment by the formally excluded – the democratisation of the cinema and the television screen, empowering viewers and moviegoers to choose for themselves what suits them. In the highly competitive industries in which Murdoch operates, he has no way of forcing audiences to buy or view his products. Television viewers own remotes and now have access to products available from streamers. Moviegoers can and do pass by any theatres showing films of no interest to them. Newspaper readers in Britain are presented every day with multiple choices on myriad newsstands. Rupert's goal is to expand the range of choices available. He would argue that the net effect of such expansion of choice on the culture is what matters, and that he hasn't done much, if anything, to move the needle in the direction of increased vulgarity. And he has increased choice.

I recognise, of course, that there are circumstances in which recourse to claims of expanding choice is not a complete defence, especially in a world in which impressionable young people are left, unsupervised, in charge of those remotes, and that exposure to some of the entertainment products available to them contributes to their de-moralisation, to borrow again from Himmelfarb, to their inability, as Rupert puts it, to develop standards of 'right and wrong' in an 'era of relativism'.[2] But this is a problem neither of Rupert's creation nor within his, or it seems anyone else's, power to solve.

All it seems reasonable to ask of a man in Murdoch's position is that when it is in his power to draw a line, and insist that his enterprises stay on the side of decency, he does so. I recall one evening shortly before Christmas 1988. We had arranged a dinner at the Connaught for Rupert and a cabinet minister who felt *The Sun* was being more than unkind by printing tales about him from an angry daughter who had problems of her own. Rupert listened carefully. The stories stopped. And then there was a time when a prominent politician asked me to talk to Rupert about the effect on his young children of being watched by reporters so that any false steps might be reported in the press, preferably along with photographs of the misbehaving minors. Rupert called the reporters off – until the children reach the age of eighteen.

In the broader sense, Rupert has to his credit the establishment of a world-class media empire. He has spawned newspapers and television properties in the UK that gave consumers choices they never dreamed they wanted until they became available. He can take credit for breaking the hold of Luddite print unions, and introducing modern technologies that saved not only the Murdoch papers but many of its rivals. In America, the Murdoch Method permitted the company to grow from a few tiny papers, one of them (the *New York Post*) a perennial money loser, into one of the world's largest print conglomerates, a television operation that rivals the major networks, a news organisation that gives voice to views not previously represented on television, and a globe-girdling entertainment and sports operation.

Observers reasonably differ on how to balance the virtues and vices of the Method that has brought James and Lachlan to their positions of power – power not narrowly confined to their companies, but power to affect the politics and cultures of the nations in which their enterprises operate. In my view, the Murdoch Method has conveyed net benefits to society that outweigh the not inconsiderable costs it has imposed, primarily on the culture. Those benefits might not have become available had Rupert not deployed what I have called the Murdoch Method, been more risk-averse in financial matters, less willing to make elites and the establishment uncomfortable and unhappy. Others differ. For the reasonable among them, Rupert's effect on the culture and on the way news is reported are sufficient to make them wish he had not been as effective as he has as what is now called a change agent.

It is perhaps a futile exercise to attempt to judge whether what I have called the Murdoch Method, and he regards merely as his instinct, is capable of drawing the line between the responsible and the irresponsible. I know him well enough to understand that he believes his Method, which relies heavily on what he calls the exercise of 'editorial judgement', does the job as well as it can be done, and is willing to leave a final judgement to the markets for news, books, sport, entertainment and capital. And to Sir Keith and Dame Elisabeth, his parents, should he meet them again, a prospect the occurrence of which he refuses to credit or deny.

ACKNOWLEDGEMENTS

This book could not have been written without the encouragement and help of my wife, Cita. And any such virtues as the reader might decide it has would certainly be absent without her research help, editing, and patience with the disruption in our schedules resulting from the final editing and polishing. I cannot count the many times she has sacrificed her own interests, her own research, her own studies of Winston Churchill, to keep my nose to the keyboard. And how many luncheon breaks and evening conversations we shared, to my benefit and the benefit of this book.

Nor would I have been able to wrestle with the conflicts between the need for a media company to make money and its special responsibility to the national culture had I not had the immense good fortune to meet Gertrude Himmelfarb, the philosopher/historian who, along with her husband, the late Irving Kristol, decided to move me away from the idea that economic efficiency, softened by a bit of equity, should be the guiding light when making public policy. Bea, as she is called by those privileged to call her 'friend', acquainted me with what I should have learned from Adam Smith's *Theory of Moral Sentiments* and her own writings – that unless we retain a decent society, one that has not been de-moralised, had its culture coarsened by the products of media companies, little else much matters. She has made the writing of this book much more difficult than it would have been in my earlier days, for which I am grateful, and disabused me of the idea that there exist 'slippery slopes' beyond the control of policymakers and others actively participating in the economy. Bea and Irving arranged a post in Washington at the American Enterprise Institute, and exposure to them and their friends and colleagues at numerous dinners, brunches and seminars. I am in their debt.

There are others who contributed to making this task easier than it would otherwise have been. Leyre Gonzalez worked as my assistant for more than a decade before returning to London to seek a saner existence than the hectic one we had on offer. That she ended up working for another economist was some relief to us, as it suggests that she did enjoy the life and work while with Cita and myself.

Gayle Damiano, who worked for me for a good part of my consulting career, agreed to come out of retirement to help with the final stages of making certain that the draft we sent to the publisher was well organised, and that readers are pointed in the right direction by the footnotes aimed at helping them to sources they might be tempted to consult. Her assistance at the final stages of manuscript preparartion can only be described as invaluable.

Jeff Raben, our computer consultant and more, enabled me to rise above my technophobia by installing programmes to facilitate editing, revisions, and the like, and taking my calls at all hours when my computer decided to refuse to communicate with me. This is no minor matter as anyone other than a skilled user of the replacement for the fountain pen and yellow pad will know, implements I might still be using had Charles Murray, the distinguished political scientist, not taken time from turning out one policy triumph after another to start me on the path to computerisation. My only regret is that I never did satisfy Jeff Raben's urging to adopt still newer methods. Perhaps now that this book is completed.

Mike Harpley made valuable suggestions throughout the editing process that helped to clarify several of the points I was trying to make, reducing the burden on the reader. I would like to thank Poppy Mostyn-Owen for her meticulous editing and corrections of any errors that crept into the early versions of the manuscript. And Georgina Capel, my agent, encouraged me to believe that this book would see the light of day, and on terms satisfactory to me.

Finally, but not least, I must thank Rupert Murdoch. He did not learn of this book until pre-publication announcements, my way of avoiding a request to review a draft, a process that would make him complicit in any statements with which he will disagree, of which there will be many. The years working with him were exciting, and gave me a front seat on world-changing events and approaches to management problems that cannot be duplicated. I was enabled to witness a revolution in labour relations that probably allowed several British newspapers to survive, and a revolution in UK broadcasting that snatched control of the television industry from the elites and turned it over to consumers, in the process reviving the sports sector. Thanks to Rupert, I also witnessed the end of America's politically monolithic broadcasting industry and was present at the creation of one that in aggregate is more fair and balanced.

Then there are the many personal kindnesses he showed Cita and me, too many to mention.

SELECT BIBLIOGRAPHY

Brandeis, Louis D., *Other People's Money – And How Banker's Use It*, New York: Frederick A. Stokes, 1914.

Curran, James and Jean Seaton, *Power Without Responsibility*, 7th edn, Abingdon, Oxon: Routledge, 2010.

Curtis, Sarah (ed.), *The Journals of Woodrow Wyatt: From Major to Blair*, 3, London: Macmillan, 2000.

d'Ancona, Matthew, *In It Together: The Inside Story of the Coalition Government*, London: Viking, 2013.

Dark, Sidney, *The Life of Sir Arthur Pearson*, London: Hodder & Stoughton, 1922.

Dover, Bruce, *Rupert's Adventures in China*, Edinburgh: Mainstream Publishing, 2008.

Ellison, Sarah, *War at The Wall Street Journal: Inside the Struggle to Control an American Business Empire*, Boston: Houghton Mifflin Harcourt, 2010.

Evans, Harold, *Good Times, Bad Times*, New York: Open Road Integrated Media, 2016 edn.

Folkenflik, David, *Murdoch's World: The Last of the Old Media Empires*, New York: Public Affairs, 2013.

John Gapper, 'The Market Has Written a Requiem for the Tabloids', *Financial Times*, 25 June 2014, https://www.ft.com/content/b6e43e54-f8aG3-11e3-befc-0014feabdc0.

Gilbert, Martin, *Winston S. Churchill*, London: William Heinemann, 1977.

Herken, Greg, 'Friends and Rivals in Cold War Washington', in *The Georgetown Set*, New York: Vintage Press, 2014.

Herzstein, Robert Edwin, *Henry R. Luce, Time, and the American Crusade in Asia*, Cambridge: Cambridge University Press, 2005.

Himmelfarb, Gertrude, *One Nation, Two Cultures: A Searching Examination of American Society in the Aftermath of Our Cultural Revolution*, New York: Alfred A. Knopf, 1999.

Holzer, Harold, *Lincoln and the Power of the Press: The War for Public Opinion*, New York: Simon & Schuster, 2015.

Horsman, S. Mathew, *Sky High: The Inside Story of BSkyB*, London: Orion Business Books, 1997.

Kiernan, Thomas, *Citizen Murdoch*, New York: Dodd Mead, 1986.

Knee, Jonathan A., Bruce C. Greenwald and Ava Seave, *The Curse of the Mogul: What's Wrong with the World's Leading Media Companies*, New York: Penguin Books, 2009.

Kristol, Irving, 'Pornography, Obscenity, and the Case for Censorship', in *Reflections of a Neoconservative*, New York: Basic Books, 1983.

Landes, David S., *Dynasties: Fortune and Misfortune in the World's Great Family Businesses*, London: Penguin Books, 2006.

Langworth, Richard M. (ed.), *Churchill by Himself: The Life, Times and Opinions of Winston Churchill in his Own Words*, London: Ebury Press, 2008.

McGraw, Thomas K., *Prophets of Regulation*, Cambridge, Mass.: Belknap Press of Harvard University Press, 1984.

McKnight, David, *Rupert Murdoch: An Investigation of Political Power*, Sydney: Allen & Unwin, 2012.

Monks, John, *Elisabeth Murdoch: Two Lives*, Sydney: Pan Macmillan, 1994.

Moore, Charles, *Margaret Thatcher: At Her Zenith: In London, Washington and Moscow*, New York: Alfred Knopf, 2016.

Murdoch, Anna, *Family Business*, New York: William Morrow, 1988.

Nasaw, David, *The Chief: The Life of William Randolph Hearst*, Boston: Houghton Mifflin, 2000.

Neil, Andrew, *Full Disclosure*, London: Macmillan, 1996.

Nixon, Richard M., *Six Crises*, New York: Doubleday, 1962.

Norberg, Johan, *Progress: Ten Reasons to Look Forward to the Future*, London: Oneworld, 2016.

Paine, Thomas, *The Crisis*, 1776, reprinted by New York: Anchor Press/Doubleday, 1973.

Rohm, Wendy Goldman, *The Murdoch Mission: The Digital Transformation of a Media Empire*, New York: John Wiley, 2002.

Roman, James, *Love, Light, and a Dream: Television's Past, Present, and Future*, Westport, Conn.: Praeger Publishers, 1998.

Schumpeter, Joseph A., *Capitalism, Socialism, and Democracy*, 2nd edn, New York: Harper & Brothers, 1947.

Shawcross, William, *Murdoch: The Making of a Media Empire*, 2nd edn, New York: Simon & Schuster, 1997.

Shenefield, John H. and Irwin M. Stelzer, *The Antitrust Laws: A Primer*, 4th edn, Washington, DC: AEI Press, 2001.

Stewart, Graham, *The History of The Times: The Murdoch Years*, London: HarperCollins, 2005.

Taylor, S. J., *Shock! Horror! The Tabloids in Action*, London: Bantam Press, 1991.

Thompson, J. Lee, *Northcliffe: Press Baron in Politics: 1865–1922*, London: John Murray, 2000.

Viguerie, Richard A. and David Franke, *America's Right Turn: How Conservatives Used New and Alternative Media to Take Power*, Chicago: Bonus Books, 2004.

Younger, R. M., *Keith Rupert Murdoch: Founder of a Media Empire*, Sydney: HarperCollins, 2003.

NOTES

Epigraphs

1 'Rupert Murdoch Has Potential', Interview, *Esquire*, 11 September 2008, http://www.esquire.com/news-politics/a4971/rupert-murdoch-1008/.
2 John Monks, *Elisabeth Murdoch, Two Lives*, Sydney: Pan Macmillan, 1994, p. 292.
3 'The Leveson Inquiry: The Culture, Practice and Ethics of the Press', testimony of Rupert Murdoch, transcript of hearings, 25 April 2012, p. 39, http://webarchive.nationalarchives.gov.uk/20140122145147T7/http://www.levesoninquiry.org.uk/wp-content/uploads/2012/04/Transcript-of-Morning-Hearing-25-April-2012.pdf.

Introduction

1 Rupert Murdoch, Lecture, 'Technology, Demography and Other Hard Facts Facing the Builders of the Millennium', Builders of the Millennium Series, University College, Oxford, 1 December 1999, https://www.ox.ac.uk/gazette/1999-00/weekly/091299/news/story_4.htm.
2 Andrew Clark, 'Opinions are Split on Murdoch, the Wizard of Oz', *Guardian*, 7 March 2011, https://www.theguardian.com/media/2011/mar/07/rupert-murdoch-australia-opinions.
3 David Folkenflik, 'Five Myths About Rupert Murdoch', *Washington Post*, 8 November 2013, https://www.washingtonpost.com/opinions/five-myths-about-rupert-murdoch/2013/11/08/341837ea-47bf-11e3-b6f8-3782ff6cb769_story.html?utm_term=.077a54cec91e.
4 'Pressmen Strike NY Newspapers', *Chicago Tribune*, 10 August 1978, http://archives.chicagotribune.com/1978/08/10/page/5/article/pressmen-strike-n-y-newspapers.
5 John Friendly, 'Settling the NY Newspaper Strike', *Chicago Tribune*, 9 November 1978, http://archives.chicagotribune.com/1978/11/09/page/45/article/settling-the-n-y-newspaper-strike.
6 BBC Annual Report and Accounts 2015/16, Presented to Parliament by the Secretary of State for Culture, Media and Sport by command of Her Majesty, 12 July 2016, http://bbc.co.uk/annualreport.

7   The Rt Hon. Lord Patten of Barnes CH, 'BBC Must Remain Independent,
     Warns Oxford University Chancellor', Reuter's Institute Lecture at St Anne's
     College, Oxford, 3 May 2016, http://reutersinstitute.politics.ox.ac.uk/news/
     bbc-must-remain-independent-warns-oxford-university-chancellor.

8   Sarah Curtis (ed.), *The Journals of Woodrow Wyatt: From Major to Blair*, 3,
     London: Macmillan, 2000, p. 274.

9   David Smith, 'It's Crazy to Think that I'd Threaten Blair', *Observer*, 17 October
     2004, https://www.theguardian.com/media/2004/oct/17/citynews.politics.

10   Peter Oborne, 'The Man who Calls the Shots', *Spectator*, 24 April 2004, https://
     www.spectator.co.uk/2004/04/the-man-who-calls-the-shots/.

11   'The Leveson Inquiry: The Culture, Practice and Ethics of the Press', testimony of
     Rupert Murdoch, transcript of hearings, 25 April 2012, p. 69, http://webarchive.
     nationalarchives.gov.uk/20140122145147T7/http://levesoninquiry.org.uk/
     up-content/uploads/2012/traanscript-of-hearings-25-april-2012.pdf.

12   Curtis (ed.), *Woodrow Wyatt*, p. 722.

13   https://finance.yahoo.com/quote/fox, and https://finance.yahoo.com/quote/
     nws?ltr+1, accessed 19 September 2017.

14   Press releases, News Corp and 21st Century Fox.

15   Rupert Murdoch, Address by Mr Rupert Murdoch at the News Corporation
     Leadership Meeting, Hayman Island, July 1995, p. 11.

16   Sam Chisholm, Comments made at the News Corporation Leadership Meeting,
     Hayman Island, July 1995.

17   Rupert Murdoch, Address by Mr Rupert Murdoch at the News Corporation
     Leadership Meeting, Hayman Island, July 1995, p. 13.

18   R. M. Younger, *Keith Rupert Murdoch: Founder of a Media Empire*, Sydney:
     HarperCollins, 2003, pp. 30–47.

19   Joseph A. Schumpeter, *Capitalism, Socialism, and Democracy*, 2nd edn, New York:
     Harper & Brothers, 1947, p. 83.

Chapter 1   The Corporate Culture

1   Robert Manne, 'Foreword', in David McKnight, *Rupert Murdoch: An
     Investigation of Political Power*, Sydney: Allen & Unwin, 2012, p. ix.

2   Rupert Murdoch, 'Freedom in Broadcasting', James MacTaggart Memorial
     Lecture, 1989 Edinburgh International Film Festival, 25 August,1989, typescript,
     p. 4, http://www.thetvfestival.com/website/wp-content/uploads/2015/03/
     GEITF_MacTaggart_1989_Rupert_Murdoch.pdf.

3   Sarah Ellison, 'Two Men and a Newsstand', *Vanity Fair*, October 2010, http://
     www.vanityfair.com/magazine/2010/09/contents-201010.

4   For convenience I shall at times refer to the Murdoch enterprises as News Corp.,
     even though it has recently been divided into two companies: News Corp,
     holding the print and some Australian television assets, and 21st Century Fox, an
     entertainment company. Old habits die hard.

5   Monks, *Two Lives*, p. 314.

6   Graham Stewart, *The History of The Times: The Murdoch Years*, London: HarperCollins, 2005, p. 37.

7   Owen Jones, 'The Establishment Uncovered: How Power Works in Britain', *Guardian*, 26 August 2014, https://www.theguardian.com/society/2014/aug/26/the-establishment-uncovered-how-power-works-in-britain-elites-stranglehold.

8   Matthew d'Ancona, *In It Together: The Inside Story of the Coalition Government*, London: Viking, 2013, p. 127.

9   S. J. Taylor, *Shock! Horror! The Tabloids in Action*, London: Bantam Press, 1991, p. 29.

10   David McKnight, *Rupert Murdoch: An Investigation of Political Power*, Sydney: Allen & Unwin, 2012, p. 49.

11   Rupert Murdoch, Address by Mr. Rupert Murdoch at the News Corporation Leadership Meeting, Hayman Island, July 1995, p. 1.

12   Cited by Rupert Murdoch, Remarks, 'Rupert Murdoch on the Role of Australia in Asia', Asia Society, 8 November 1999, http://asiasociety.org/australia/rupert-murdoch-role-australia-asia.

13   Ibid.

14   'Gallipoli letter from Keith Arthur Murdoch to Andrew Fisher, 1915' (manuscript), National Library of Australia, http://nla.gov.au/nla.obj-231555472/view.

15   'Gallipoli Casualties by Country', New Zealand History, https://nzhistory.govt.nz/media/interactive/gallipoli-casualties-country.

16   William Shawcross, *Murdoch: The Making of a Media Empire*, 2nd edn, New York: Simon & Schuster, 1997, p. 32.

17   Ibid., p. 333.

18   Roger Cohen, 'In Defense of Murdoch', *New York Times*, 11 July 2011, http://www.nytimes.com/2011/07/12/opinion/12iht-edcohen12.html.

19   Rupert Murdoch, MacTaggart Lecture, typescript, p. 2.

20   Ibid., p. 5.

21   Bret Stephens, 'Roger Ailes: The Man Who Wrecked Conservatism', *New York Times*, 19 May 2017, https://www.nytimes.com/2017/05/19/opinion/roger-ailes-fox-news-wrecked-conservatism.html?mcubz=1.

22   Gabriel Sherman, 'Fox News is Dropping Its "Fair & Balanced" Slogan', *New York*, 14 June 2017, http://nymag.com/daily/intelligencer/2017/06/fox-news-is-dropping-its-fair-and-balanced-slogan.html.

23   Brian Lowry, 'Does Rupert Murdoch Merit a Spot in the TV Hall of Fame?', *Variety*, 11 March 2014, http://variety.com/2014/voices/columns/does-rupert-murdoch-merit-a-spot-in-the-tv-hall-of-fame-1201128972/.

24   James Roman, *Love, Light, and a Dream: Television's Past, Present, and Future*, Westport, Conn.: Praeger, 1998, p. 66.

25   Ibid., p. 66.

26   '"The Simpsons" "promotes smoking"', *Daily Telegraph*, 1 June 2009, http://www.telegraph.co.uk/news/worldnews/northamerica/usa/5423098/The-Simpsons-promotes-smoking.html.

27 'Last of the Moguls', *The Economist*, 21 July 2011, p. 9, http://www.economist.com/node/18988526.

28 Rupert Murdoch, 'Closing Keynote', 1998 Management Conference, 18 July 1998, Sun Valley, Idaho, p. 35.

29 Jim Rutenberg, 'News Sites Take On Two Digital Giants', *New York Times*, 10 July 2017, https://www.nytimes.com/2017/07/09/business/media/google-facebook-news-media-alliance.html.

30 'Donald Trump Jr. is an Idiot', New York Post Editorial Board, *New York Post*, 12 July 2017, http://nypost.com/2017/07/11/donald-trump-jr-is-an-idiot/.

31 'The Wall Street Journal under Rupert Murdoch', Pew Research Center, Journalism & Media Staff, 20 July 2011, http://www.journalism.org/2011/07/20/wall-street-journal-under-rupert-murdoch/.

32 Jonathan Mahler, 'What Rupert Wrought', *New York*, 11 April 2005, http://nymag.com/nymetro/news/people/features/11673.

33 Peter T. Kilborn, 'Where Page Three Counts', *New York Times*, 20 November 1976, http://www.nytimes.com/1976/11/20/archives/where-page-three-counts.html?mcubz=1.

34 'Presslord Takes City', *Newsweek*, 17 January 1977, p. 56.

35 Paul Harris, 'Murdoch Declares War in the Last Great Battle of the Barons', *Guardian*, 28 September 2008, https://www.theguardian.com/media/2008/sep/28/newscorporation.wallstreetjournal.

36 Cohen, 'In Defense of Murdoch', *New York Times*, 11 July 2011.

37 Joe Flint, 'Fox Sports Dismisses Executive Amid Probe', *Wall Street Journal*, 7 July 2017, http://www.4-traders.com/TWENTY-FIRST-CENTURY-FOX-13440463/news/Twenty-First-Century-Fox-Fox-Sports-Dismisses-Executive-Amid-Probe-WSJ-24699815/.

38 Richard Sandomir, 'Fox's Sports Network Hires an ESPN Veteran for a Reinvention', *New York Times*, 9 May 2016, https://www.nytimes.com/2016/05/09/business/media/jamie-horowitz-tries-again-this-time-to-revive-fs1.html?mcubz=1.

39 'ESPN Ad Sales Fall on "Fewer Impressions and Lower Rates"', *AdAge*, 30 September 2014, adage.com/article/media/Disney-falls-short-earnings-expectations-espn-ad-sales-fall/306717/.

40 Richard Sandomir, 'ESPN Pay Top Dollar for Football but Audience Isn't Buying', *New York Times*, 28 November 2016, https://www.nytimes.com/2016/11/28/sports/football/monday-night-football-tv-ratings-espn.html.

41 Ian Casselberry, 'FS1 Lost More Households in February than ESPN, According to Nielsen Estimates', *AwfulAnnouncing*, http://awfulannouncing.com/ratings/fs1-lost-more-households-february-espn.html.

42 Rob Tornoe, 'Amid Battle with ESPN, Big Lineup Changes at Fox Sports 1', *Philadelphia Inquirer*, 25 February 2017, http://www.philly.com/philly/blogs/pattisonave/Katie-Nolan-big-lineup-changes-at-Fox-Sports-1-ESPN.html.

43 'FS1 Tops All Cable Networks', *Fox Sports Press Pass*, 13 June 2017, http://www.foxsports.com/presspass/latest-news/2017/06/13/fs1-tops-cable-networks.

44 Ty Duffy, 'Is Fox Sports Better Placed for Cable's Future Than ESPN?', *the big*

lead, 10 May 2016, http://thebiglead.com/2016/05/10/is-fox-sports-better-placed-for-cables-future-than-espn/.

45 Peter Doughtery, 'FS1 Leads All Networks with Nine Sports Emmys', *timesunion*, 10 May 2017, http://blog.timesunion.com/sportsmedia/fs1-leads-all-networks-with-nine-sports-emmys/18247/.

46 Shawcross, *Media Empire*, p. 60.

47 Fox Business Network Press Release, 1 May 2017. Note that CNBC announced in 2015 that it would no longer rely on Nielsen ratings since they do not include 'out of home' viewing. Joe Concha, 'Fox Business News Tops CNBC in Total Viewers for Sixth Straight Month', *The Hill*, 28 March 2017, http://thehill.com/homenews/media/326126-fox-business-tops-cnbc-in-total-viewers-for-6th-straight-month.

48 Brian Flood, 'Has Fox Business Dethroned CNBC as New King of Daytime Cable Biz News?', *The Wrap*, 1 March 2017, http://www.thewrap.com/fox-business-network-surpassed-cnbc/.

49 Bob Fernandez, 'Comcast's CNBC Faces a Big Threat from Fox Business Network', *Philadelphia Inquirer*, 30 April 2017, http://www.philly.com/philly/business/Comcast-owned-CNBC-facing-a-big-threat-from-Fox-Business-bill-OReilly-ailes-roger-maria-bartiromo.html.

50 John Gapper, 'The Market Has Written a Requiem For The Tabloids', *Financial Times*, 25 June 2014, https://www.ft.com/contetnt/b6e43e54-f8aG3-11e3-befc-0014feabdc0.

51 Rupert Murdoch, Remarks at St Paul's Cathedral, Melbourne, Australia, 18 December 2012.

52 Murdoch, 'Closing Keynote', pp. 2–3.

53 Ibid., p. 36.

54 Ibid., p. 41.

55 Peter Chernin, 'Opening Keynote', 1998 Management Conference, 13 July 1998, Sun Valley, Idaho, p. 6.

56 Andrew Neil, *Full Disclosure*, London: Macmillan, 1996, p. 183.

57 Stephen Glover, 'Poor Kelvin, Left Carrying the Can', *The Oldie*, July 2017, p. 11, https://www.theoldie.co.uk/article/media-matters-11/.

58 'In the matter of AN ENQUIRY into Standards of Cross Media Promotion before Mr John Sadler CBE and Mr M.D. Boyd', Transcript of evidence of Sir Edward Pickering, Mrs J. Reid, Mr I. Stelzer and Mr J. Shenefield, 2 May 1990.

59 Gertrude Himmelfarb, *One Nation, Two Cultures: A Searching Examination of American Society in the Aftermath of Our Cultural Revolution*, New York: Alfred Knopf, 1999, p. 118.

60 Murdoch, MacTaggart Lecture, typescript, p. 4.

61 Irving Kristol, 'Pornography, Obscenity, and the Case for Censorship', in *Reflections of a Neoconservative*, New York: Basic Books, 1983, pp. 43–54.

62 'Children's Shows Blamed for Fifth of All Television Violence: Power Rangers and Puppets are Most Frequent Offenders', *The Times*, 22 August 1995.

63 Alexandra Frean, 'TV Not to Blame for Violence, Researcher Says', *The Times*, 1

August 1995.

64   Dalson Chen, 'A Tale of Two Cities: Windsor and Detroit Murder Rates Show
     Stark Contrast', *Windsor Star*, 4 December 2012, http://windsorstar.com/news/
     local-news/a-tale-of-two-cities-windsor-and-detroit-murder-rates-show-stark-
     contrast.

65   Elizabeth Kolbert, 'Americans Despair of Popular Culture', *New York Times*, 20
     August 1995, http://www.nytimes.com/1995/08/20/movies/americans-despair-
     of-popular-culture.html?pagewanted=all&mcubz=1.

66   Gene Beresin, 'Research Shows Violent Media Do Not Cause Violent Behavior',
     Mass General News, 26 December 2012, http://www.massgeneral.org/News/
     newsarticle.aspx?id=3929.

67   Angela Neustatter, 'Murdoch Matriarch Reveals a Few Home Truths on Family',
     Sunday Morning Herald, 26 February 2009, http://www.smh.com.au/national/
     murdoch-matriarch-reveals-a-few-home-truths-on-family-20090225-8i23.html.

68   Alan Cowell, 'Murdoch Apologizes for "Grotesque" Netanyahu Cartoon in
     British Paper', *New York Times*, 29 January 2013, http://www.nytimes.com/
     2013/01/30/world/europe/murdoch-apologizes-for-grotesque-netanyahu-
     cartoon.html.

Chapter 2   Power, Politics and the Murdoch Method

1   Stanley Baldwin, Speech, 17 March 1931 (the phrase originated with Rudyard
     Kipling), in James Curran and Jean Seaton, *Power Without Responsibility*, 7th edn,
     Abingdon, Oxon: Routledge, 2010, p. 37.

2   Rupert Murdoch, Lecture, 'Technology, Demography and Other Hard Facts
     Facing the Builders of the Millennium', Builders of the Millennium Series,
     University College, Oxford, 1 December 1999, https://www.ox.ac.uk/gazette/
     1999-00/weekly/091299/news/story_4.htm.

3   John Cassidy, 'Murdoch's Game', *New Yorker*, 16 October 2006, p. 80, https://
     www.newyorker.com/magazine/2006/10/16/murdochs-game.

4   Henry Kissinger, Quoted in, *The New York Times*, 28 October 1971.

5   Rupert Murdoch, Speech given in Singapore, 12 January 1999.

6   Cassidy, 'Murdoch's Game', *New Yorker*, 16 October 2006, p. 69.

7   Neil, *Full Disclosure*, p. 165.

8   Cassidy, 'Murdoch's Game', *New Yorker*, 16 October 2006, p. 74.

9   Duncan Robinson, 'Google Heads Queue to Lobby Brussels', *Financial Times*,
     24 June 2015, https://www.ft.com/content/ea71f74a-19b1-11e5-8201-cbdb03d
     71480.

10   Vicky Carn, 'Google: One of Brussels' Most Active Lobbyists', *LobbyFacts*, 12
     December 2016, https://lobbyfacts.eu/articles/12-12-2016/google-one-brussels
     %E2%80%99-most-active-lobbyists.

11   I have served as a consultant to Google, helping respond to European
     Commission charges of anti-competitive behaviour and market dominance.

12   Johan Norberg, *Progress: Ten Reasons to Look Forward to the Future*, London:
     Oneworld Publications, 2016, p. 207.

13 David Nasaw, *The Chief: The Life of William Randolph Hearst*, Boston: Houghton Mifflin, 2000, p. 102.

14 Curran and Seaton, *Power Without Responsibility*, p. 69.

15 My consulting work for Rupert Murdoch included at least one assignment for FNC.

16 Brian Steinberg, 'A Year After Ailes' Ouster, Fox News Soldiers on Amid Tumult and Stays No. 1', *Variety*, 10 July 2017, http://variety.com/2017/tv/news/fox-news-roger-ailes-tucker-carlson-1202490160/.

17 Thomas Paine, *The Crisis, 1776*, reprinted New York: Anchor Press/Doubleday, 1973, pp. 67–240.

18 Harold Holzer, *Lincoln and the Power of the Press: The War for Public Opinion*, New York: Simon & Schuster, 2015, p. xvi.

19 Ibid., p. xiii.

20 Curran and Seaton, *Power Without Responsibility*, pp. 40, 41.

21 J. Lee Thompson, *Northcliffe: Press Baron in Politics: 1865–1922*, London: John Murray, 2000, pp. 233–43.

22 Nasaw, *The Chief*, p. 132.

23 Ibid., p. 127.

24 Sidney Dark, *The Life of Sir Arthur Pearson*, London: Hodder & Stoughton, 1922, p. 116.

25 Martin Gilbert, *Winston S. Churchill*, 5, London: William Heinemann, 1977, p. 334.

26 Ibid., p. 347.

27 Thompson, *Northcliffe*, p. 22.

28 Robert Edwin Herzstein, *Henry R. Luce, Time, and the American Crusade in Asia*, Cambridge: Cambridge University Press, 2005, p. 1.

29 Curran and Seaton, *Power Without Responsibility*, p. 45.

30 Emphasis in original. Greg Herken, 'Friends and Rivals in Cold War Washington', in *The Georgetown Set*, New York: Vintage Press, 2014, p. 23.

31 Author's notes verified indirectly by *Washington Post* columnist George Will, who knew Alsop and tells me, 'It certainly sounds like Joe.' But Will warns that Alsop typically 'exempted himself from that analysis'. And Alsop biographer Ed Yoder tells me, 'It is the kind of broad-brush comment that Joe could easily have made.'

32 'The Sun and Labour support: How Newspaper Readers Have Voted in UK General elections', *Guardian*, DataBlog, 5 October 2009, www.theguardian.com/news/datablog/2009/0c5/05/sun-labour-newspapers-suport-elections.

33 Curran and Seaton, *Power Without Responsibility*, p. 69.

34 Martin Kettle, 'Actually, It Wasn't the Sun Wot Won It. Sun Readers Did', *Guardian*, 6 June 2008, https://www.theguardian.com/commentisfree/2008/jun/07/media.pressandpublishing.

35 Stephen Glover, 'Why the Fawning? The Sun is Far Less Powerful than Blair Thinks It Is', *Independent*, 6 January 2015, https://www.independent.co.uk/news/media/stephen-glover-on-the-press-409948.html.

36 David R. Davies, 'An Industry in Transition: Major Trends in American Daily Newspapers, 1945–1965, Kennedy and the Press', a doctoral dissertation at

the University of Alabama, of which chapter 8 is 'Kennedy and the Press, 1960–1963', http://ocean.otr.usm.edu/~w304644/ch8.html.

37 John F. Kennedy, Address, 'The President and the Press', before the American Newspaper Publishers Association, New York City, 27 April 1961, https://www. jfklibrary.org/JFK/JFK-in-History/John-F-Kennedy-and-the-Press.aspx.

38 Marisa Guthrie, 'Interview with Roger Ailes', *Hollywood Reporter*, 1 May 2015, p. 48, http://www.hollywoodreporter.com/features/ introspective-roger-ailes-fox-news-789877.

39 David Smith, 'It's Crazy to Think I'd Threaten Blair', *Observer*, 17 October 2004, https://www.theguardian.com/media/2004/oct/17/citynews.politics.

40 'The Leveson Inquiry: Culture, Practice and Ethics of the Press', testimony of Rupert Murdoch, transcript of hearings, 25 April 2012, pp. 53–4, http:// webarchive.nationalarchives.gov.uk/20140122145147/http://www.levesoninquiry. org.uk/about/the-report/.

41 John Gapper, 'Fleet Street's European Bite Remains Sharp', *Financial Times*, 23 June 2016, https://www.ft.com/content/0ea29eac-379e-11e6-a780-b48ed 7b6126f.

42 Louis D. Brandeis, *Other People's Money – And How Banker's Use It*, New York: Frederick A. Stokes, 1914, p. 92.

43 Neil, *Full Disclosure*, p. 170.

44 Curran and Seaton, *Power Without Responsibility*, p. 74.

45 Rupert Murdoch, Statement before House of Commons Culture Committee, 19 July 2011, http://www.parliament.uk/business/committees/committees-a-z/ commons-select/culture-media-and-sport-committee/news/news-international- executives-respond-to-summons.

46 William B. Shew and Irwin M. Stelzer, 'A Policy Framework for the Media Industries', in M. E. Beesley (ed.), *Markets and the Media*, Washington, DC: Institute of Economic Affairs, 1996, p.135. That study is now a bit dated, but the direction of its conclusions is unlikely to have changed.

47 Benjamin Smith, 'Mayor Koch, Self-Proclaimed "Liberal with Sanity" Who Led New York from Fiscal Crisis, Is Dead at 88', *New York Sun*, 1 February 2013 [not a Murdoch paper], http://www.nysun.com/new-york/mayor-koch-self- proclaimed-liberal-with-sanity/88177/.

48 Patrick Brogan, 'Citizen Murdoch', *New Republic*, 10 October 1982, https:// newrepublic.com/article/92429/rupert-murdoch-international-newspaper-empire.

49 Jonathan Mahler, 'For Mario Cuomo, Defeat in 1977 Mayor's Race Cast a Long Shadow', *New York Times*, 5 January 2015, https://www.nytimes. com/2015/01/05/nyregion/for-mario-cuomo-defeat-in-1977-mayors-race-cast-a- long-shadow.html?mcubz=1.

50 Ibid.

51 Robert Scheer, 'Playboy Interview: Jimmy Carter', *Playboy*, 7 March 2016, http:// www.playboy.com/articles/playboy-interview-jimmy-carter.

52 Clyde Haberman, 'Ridiculed Suburbs in Jest, Koch Says', *New York Times*, 25 February 1982, http://www.nytimes.com/1982/02/25/nyregion/ridiculed- suburbs-in-jest-koch-says.html?mcubz=1.

53   William H. Meyers, 'Murdoch's Global Power Play', *New York Times*, 12 June
     1988, http://www.nytimes.com/1988/06/12/magazine/murdoch-s-global-
     power-play.html?pagewanted=all.

54   Bill Carter, 'Murdoch to Sell TV Station to Owners of Boston Celtics', *New York
     Times*, 22 September 1989, http://www.nytimes.com/1989/09/22/business/
     murdoch-to-sell-tv-station-to-owners-of-boston-celtics.html?mcubz=1.

55   'Teaching Mr Murdoch', *New York Times*, 31 March 1993, http://www.nytimes.
     com/1993/03/31/opinion/teaching-mr-murdoch.html.

56   Cassidy, 'Murdoch's Game', *New Yorker*, 16 October 2006, p. 68.

57   Holly Yeager and Caroline Daniel, 'Hillary Clinton Defends Link with Murdoch',
     Financial Times, 10 May 2006.

58   Paul Harris, 'Rupert Murdoch Defiant: I'll Stop Google Taking Our News for
     Nothing', *Guardian*, 7 April 2010, https://www.theguardian.com/media/2010/
     apr/07/rupert-murdoch-google-paywalls-ipad.

59   Dominic Rush, 'News Corp Executive Labels Google "a Platform for Piracy"',
     Guardian, 18 September 2014, with full letter reported at https://www.theguardian.
     com/technology/2014/sep/18/google-news-corp-piracy-platform-european-
     commission.

60   'The Post Endorses Donald Trump', 14 April 2016, Post Editorial Board, *New
     York Post*, http://nypost.com/2016/04/14/the-post-endorses-donald-trump/.

61   Caroline Daniel, 'Murdoch to Host Fundraiser for Hillary Clinton', *Financial
     Times*, 8 May 2006, https://www.ft.com/content/61faabde-deb8-11da-acee-
     0000779e2340.

62   'Row Over Blair's "Murdoch Intervention"', BBC News, 27 March 1998, https://
     news.bbc.co.uk/2/hi/uk/politics/70597.stm.

63   Younger, *Keith Rupert Murdoch*, pp. 31, 352.

64   'The Leveson Inquiry', testimony of Rupert Murdoch, pp. 26–7.

65   Dana A. Scherer, *The FCC's Rules and Policies Regarding Media Ownership,
     Attribution, and Ownership Diversity*, Congressional Research Service,
     16 December 2016, https://fas.org/sgp/crs/misc/R43936.pdf.

66   Meg Jones, 'News Corp. Shareholders Approve of Split into Two Companies', *Los
     Angeles Times*, 12 June 2013, http://articles.latimes.com/2013/jun/12/business/
     la-fi-ct-news-corp-meeting-20130612.

Chapter 3   Deals

1   Rupert Murdoch, 'Closing Keynote', 1998 Management Conference, 18 July
     1998, Sun Valley, Idaho, p. 35.

2   Richard Milne, 'Malone: Murdoch Owes Me a Favour', *Financial Times*, 29 July
     2009, https://www.ft.com/content/b8dfc578-7bd7-11de-9772-00144feabdc0.

3   Dan Sabbagh, 'Rupert Murdoch at 80: Poised to Strike His Biggest Deal Yet',
     Guardian, 7 March 2011, https://www.theguardian.com/media/2011/mar/07/
     rupert-murdoch-80-biggest-deal.

4   Neil, *Full Disclosure*, p. 185.

5   Harold Evans, *Good Times, Bad Times*, New York: Open Road Integrated Media, 2016 edn, pp. 493ff. Evans claims the cause was a policy dispute with Murdoch; Rupert says an employee revolt against Evans forced his hand.

6   Neil, *Full Disclosure*, p. 164.

7   Younger, *Keith Rupert Murdoch*, p. 34.

8   Sarah Ellison and Matthew Karnitsching, 'Murdoch Wins His Bid for Dow Jones', *Wall Street Journal*, 1 August 2007, https://www.wsj.com/articles/SB118589043953483378.

9   Stewart, *The History of The Times*, p. 25.

10 Ibid., p. 23.

11 Stephen Armstrong, 'Meet the Bancrofts, the Media Clans Who Sold Out to Murdoch', *Guardian*, 2 August 2007, https://www.theguardian.com/media/2007/aug/02/pressandpublishing.usnews.

12 Leslie Hill letter to the Dow Jones Corp. board of directors, 31 July 2007, reproduced by the *Wall Street Journal*, 1 August 2007, https://www.wsj.com/articles/SB118598504544284836.

13 'The Future of Times Newspapers. Undertakings by Mr Rupert Murdoch', *New York Times*, 22 January 1981, http://www.nytimes.com/1981/01/23/world/text-opf-statement-on-purchase-issued-by-the-times-of-london.html?mcubz=1.

14 Ciar Byrne, 'Times Goes Tabloid', *Guardian*, 21 November 2003, https://www.theguardian.com/media/2003/nov/21/pressandpublishing.uknews.

15 Ibid.

16 John Morton, 'Bye, Bye Broadsheet?', *American Journalism Review*, June/July 2005, http://ajrarchive.org/article.asp?id=3904.

17 At the time of writing, the members of the independent board were: Rupert Pennant-Rea, chairman of the Economist group and former deputy governor of the Bank of England; Veronica Wadley, London Arts Council chair and former editor of the London *Evening Standard*; Sarah Bagnall, a director of PR agency Pelham Bell Pottinger and once a financial journalist on *The Times*; Lady (Diana) Eccles, a UK delegate to the Council of Europe and a director of Opera North; Lord Marlesford (formerly Mark Schreiber), adviser to financial institutions and one-time *Economist* journalist; Stephen Grabiner, former Telegraph group and Express Newspapers executive (he replaced Sir Robin Mountfield, former cabinet office permanent secretary, who died in November 2011).

18 David Carr, 'Murdoch Gives In, So to Speak', *New York Times*, 6 August 2007, http://www.nytimes.com/2007/08/06/business/media/06carr.html?ref=business&mcubz=1.

19 When fierce competition combined with the fact that Rupert found it unsatisfactory to own newspapers he could not read, including a tabloid he could not edit, he sold the Hungarian papers.

20 'The Wall Street Journal under Rupert Murdoch', Pew Research Journalism Project, 20 July 2011, http://www.journalism.org/2011/07/20/wall-street-journal-under-rupert-murdoch.

21 Sarah Ellison, *War at The Wall Street Journal: Inside the Struggle to Control*

an American Business Empire, Boston: Houghton Mifflin Harcourt, 2010, pp. 236–44.

22 Michael Levin, 'Seven Years Later: What Exactly Did Rupert Murdoch Do to the Wall Street Journal?', *HuffPost*, 31 July 2015, http://www.huffingtonpost.com/michaellevin/seven-years-later-what-ex_b_7912298.html.

23 Ellison and Karnitsching, 'Murdoch Wins His Bid for Dow Jones', *Wall Street Journal*, updated 12 August 2007.

24 Neil, *Full Disclosure*, p. 165.

25 Steve Stecklow, Aaron O. Patrick, Martin Peers and Andrew Higgins, 'In Murdoch's Career, A Hand on the News', *Wall Street Journal*, 5 June 2007, https://www.wsj.com/articles/SB118100557923424501.

26 Ibid.

27 Suzanne Vranica and Jack Marshall, 'Plummeting Ad Revenue Sparks New Wave of Changes', *Wall Street Journal*, 20 October 2016, https://www.wsj.com/articles/plummeting-newspaper-ad-revenue-sparks-new-wave-of-changes-1476955801.

28 Ibid.

29 Daniel Victor, 'New York Times Will Offer Employee Buyouts and Eliminate Public Editor Role', *New York Times*, 1 May 2017, https://www.nytimes.com/2017/05/31/business/media/new-york-times-buyouts.html?mcubz=1.

30 Joseph Weisenthal, 'Murdoch's Bad Bet: How News Corp. Lost Over $6 Billion on Gemstar', GiGAOM, 13 December 2007, https://gigaom.com/2007/12/13/419-murdochs-bad-bet-tallying-the-losses-on-gemstar/.

31 Ibid.

32 'Could Redstone Finally Get His Hands on MySpace?', DealBook, *New York Times*, 24 June 2009, https://dealbook.nytimes.com/2009/06/24/could-redstone-finally-get-his-hands-on-myspace/?mcubz=1.

33 Felix Gillette, 'The Rise and Inglorious Fall of Myspace', *Bloomberg Businessweek*, 22 June 2011, pp. 54–9, https://www.bloomberg.com/news/articles/2011-06-22/the-rise-and-inglorious-fall-of-myspace.

34 Ross Pruden, 'How Facebook Used WhiteSpace to Crush MySpace', Techdirt, 19 January 2011, https://www.techdirt.com/articles/20110114/16303012675/how-facebook-used-white-space-to-crush-myspace.shtml.

35 Scott Anthony, 'MySpace's Disruption, Disrupted', *Harvard Business Review Blog*, 16 December 2009, https://hbr.org/2009/12/lessons-from-myspace.

36 Gillette, 'The Rise and Inglorious Fall of Myspace', *Bloomberg Businessweek*, 22 June 2011.

37 Ibid.

38 'Win Some, Lose Some', Special Report, *Wall Street Journal* D.Live, 3 November 2014, http://www.wsjdlive.wsj.com/wp-content/uploads/2014/11/WSJDLive14_SpecialReport.pdf.

39 Rupert Murdoch, 'Speech to the American Society of Newspaper Editors, Washington, DC', 13 April 2005, https://www.theguardian.com/media/2005/apr/14/citynews.newmedia.

40 Alexander Cockburn, 'The Man Who Bought The New York Post Tells All',

Village Voice, 29 November 1976.

41   William Shawcross, *Murdoch: The Making of a Media Empire*, 2nd edn, New
      York: Simon & Schuster, 1997, p. 191.

42   http://www.afr.com/business/media-and-marketing/publishing/news-corporation-
      flags-big-cuts-to-australian-newspapers-20170811-gxu0q0.

43   http://www.reuters.com/article/newscorp/update-1-dow-jones-costs-news-corp-2-
      8-bln-in-writedown-idINN0646811420090206.

44   Neil, *Full Disclosure*, p. 293.

45   Ibid., p. 297.

46   Mathew Horsman, *Sky High: The Inside Story of* BSkyB, London: Orion Business
      Books, 1997, p. 36.

47   Shawcross, *Media Empire*, p. 306.

48   Horsman, *Sky High*, p. 44.

49   Horsman, *Sky High*, p. 45.

50   Alexander Cockburn, 'The Man Who Bought the New York Post Tells All',
      Village Voice, 29 November 1976.

51   Horsman, *Sky High*, p. 47.

52   Shawcross, *Media Empire*, p. 406.

53   Robert Milliken, 'Sport is Murdoch's "Battering Ram" for Pay TV', *Independent*,
      15 October 1996, http://www.independent.co.uk/sport/sport-is-murdochs-
      battering-ram-for-pay-tv-1358686.html.

54   Murdoch, 'Closing Keynote', p. 33.

55   Thomas Seal, 'Murdoch's Times Bucks Flagging Readership Trend at UK Papers',
      Bloomberg Business, 20 October, https://www.bloomberg.com/news/articles/
      2016-10-20/murdoch-s-times-bucks-flagging-readership-trend-at-u-k-papers2016.

56   Newsline Staff, 'ABCs: The Times up 10% year-on-year', *Mediatel Newsline*,
      16 March 2017, http://mediatel.co.uk/newsline/2017/03/16/abcs-the-times-up-
      10-year-on-year/.

57   Andrew Edgecliffe-Johnson, 'Media Empire Builders are Fighting the Wrong
      Battles', *Financial Times*, 13 August 2014, https://www.ft.com/content/82fcb8fc-
      2254-11e4-9d4a-00144feabdc0.

58   Keach Hagey, 'Fox Mindful of Debt as It Eyes Time Warner', *Wall Street Journal*,
      22 July 2014, https://www.wsj.com/articles/fox-mindful-of-debt-as-it-eyes-time-
      warner-1406072651.

59   Edgecliffe-Johnson, 'Media Empire Builders are Fighting the Wrong Battles',
      Financial Times, 13 August 2014.

60   Hagey, 'Fox Mindful of Debt as It Eyes Time Warner', *Wall Street Journal*, 22 July
      2014.

61   Ed Hammond, 'Fox Lines up Funds for Time Warner siege', *Financial Times*,
      18 July 2014, https://www.ft.com/content/940a5604-0e9a-11e4-as0e-00144.
      feabdc0?mhq5j=el.

62   Hagey, 'Fox Mindful of Debt as It Eyes Time Warner', *Wall Street Journal*, 22
      June 2014.

63   'Win Some, Lose Some', *Wall Street Journal*, 3 November 2014.

64   Sydney Ember and Michael J. de la Merced, 'Sinclair Unveils Tribune Deal, Raising Worries It Will Be Too Powerful', *New York Times*, 9 May 2017, https://www.nytimes.com/2017/05/08/business/media/sinclair-tribune-media-sale.html?mcubz=1.

65   Jonathan A. Knee, Bruce C. Greenwald and Ava Seave, *The Curse of the Mogul: What's Wrong with the World's Leading Media Companies*, New York: Penguin Books, 2009, p. 1.

66   Arash Massoudi and David Bond, 'Sky Acts to Reassure Investor Concerns Over Fox offer', *Financial Times*, 12 December 2016, https://www.ft.com/content/1f4b9bde-bfbe-11e6-81c2-f57d90f6741a.

67   Stephen Wilmot, 'Fox and Sky: The Sequel May Have a Happier Ending', *Wall Street Journal*, Global Ideas Trust, 9 December 2016, http://globalideastrust.com/fox-and-sky-the-sequel-may-have-a-happier-ending-wall-street-journal/.

68   Mark Sweeney, 'James Murdoch's Return as Sky Chair is a Major Concern, Says Investor', *Guardian*, 29 January 2016, https://www.theguardian.com/global/2016/jan/29/james-murdochs-return-as-sky-chair-is-a-major-concern-says-investor.

69   Chad Bray, '21st Century Fox Reaches $14.8 Billion Deal for Remainder of Sky', *New York Times*, 15 December 2016, https://wwwnytimes.com/2016/12/15/business/dealbook/21st-century-fox-reaches-14-8-billion-deal-for-remainder-of-sky.html?r_=0.

70   Matthew Garrahan, 'James Murdoch Says Fox–Sky Deal is Test of Brexit Claims', *Financial Times*, 14 September 2017, https://www.ft.com/content/0208b184-993d-11e7-a652-cde3f882dd7b.

71   Emily Steel, 'Size of O'Reilly Settlement Was "News" to Murdoch', *New York Times*, 10 October 2017, https://www.nytimes.com/2017/10/25/business/james-murdoch-bill-oreilly.html?_r=0.

72   'Behind the bid for Sky is a Less Powerful Murdoch Empire', *The Economist*, 17 December 2016, http://www.economist.com/news/business/21711958-sky-losing-viewers-and-rupert-murdochs-newspapers-have-shed-readers-behind-bid-sky.

73   Michelle Castillo, reporting for CNBC, 31 May 2017, https://www.cnbc.com/2017/05/31/netflix-spending-6-billion-on-content-in-2017-ceo-reed-hastings.html.

74   Nathan McAlone, 'Amazon Will Spend About $4.5 Billion on Its Fight Against Netflix This Year, According to JPMorgan', *Business Insider*, 7 April 2017, http://www.businessinsider.com/amazon-video-budget-in-2017-45-billion-2017-4.

75   John Koblin, 'Tech Firms Make Push Toward TV', *New York Times*, 21 August 2017, https://www.nytimes.com/2017/08/20/business/media/tv-marketplace-apple-facebook-google.html?mcubz=1&_r=0.

76   Andrew Edgecliffe-Johnson, 'Man in the News: James Murdoch', *Financial Times*, 18 June 2010, https://www.ft.com/content/705dfe36-7b19-11df-8935-00144feabdc0.

77   Nicola Clark, 'James Murdoch to Return as Sky Chairman', *New York Times*, 30 January 2016, https://www.nytimes.com/2016/01/30/business/media/james-murdoch-to-return-as-sky-chairman.html?mcubz=1.

78   '21st Century Fox Formalises $US14bn Offer for UK's Sky', *Australian*, 16 December 2016, http://www.theaustralian.com.au/business/media/21st-century-fox-Formalises-us14bn-Offer-for-uks-sky/news-story/3770cb08a958dbc822f1 8c8a6cd3e0bd.

Chapter 4   Economic Regulation

1   Thomas K. McGraw, *Prophets of Regulation*, Cambridge, Mass.: Belknap Press of Harvard University Press, 1984, pp. 301, 302.

2   Gertrude Himmelfarb, *On Looking into the Abyss: Untimely Thoughts On Culture and Society*, New York, Alfred A. Knopf, 1994 p. 96.

3   James Murdoch, 'The Absence of Trust', 2009 Edinburgh International Television Festival, James MacTaggart Memorial Lecture, 28 August 2009, typescript, p. 7, https://www.edinburghguide.com/events/2009/08/28/mactaggartlecturebyjamesmurdoch.

4   John Cassidy, 'Murdoch's Game', *New Yorker*, 16 October 2006, p. 78. https://www.newyorker.com/magazine/2006/10/16/murdochs-game.

5   'Dame Elisabeth Murdoch', *Daily Telegraph*, 5 December 2012, http://www.telegraph.co.uk/news/obituaries/9724323/Dame-Elisabeth-Murdoch.html.

6   Jo Becker, 'An Empire Builder, Murdoch Still Playing Tough', *New York Times*, 25 June 2007, http://www.nytimes.com/2007/06/25/business/worldbusiness/25i-ht-25murdoch.6308907.html.

7   'What is Ofcom?', https://www.ofcom.org.uk/about-ofcom/what-is-ofcom.

8   John H. Shenefield and Irwin M. Stelzer, *The Antitrust Laws: A Primer*, 4th edn, Washington, DC: AEI Press, 2001.

9   'Australia's Real Estate Boom Has Wall Street Wooing a Newspaper Publisher', *New York Times*, 30 May 2017, https://www.nytimes.com/2017/05/30/business/dealbook/fairfax-takeover-property-tpg-hellman-friedman.html?mcubz=1.

10 Office of Fair Trading, 'Newspaper and magazine distribution', Opinions, multiple papers issued October 2008, http://webarchive.nationalarchives.gov.uk/20140525130048/http:/www.oft.gov.uk/OFTwork/publications/publication-categories/reports/competition-policy/oft1025.

11 'In the matter of AN ENQUIRY into Standards of Cross Media Promotion before Mr John Sadler CBE and Mr M.D. Bond', Transcript of Evidence of Sir Edward Pickering, Mrs J. Reed, Mr I. Stelzer and Mr J. Shenefield, 2 May 1990.

12 Rupert Murdoch, Speech given in Singapore, 12 January 1999, typescript, p. 12.

13 In *Jacobellis v. Ohio*, 378 U.S. 184 (1964), https://supreme.justia.com/cases/federal/us/378/184/case.html.

14 'Statement from Rupert Murdoch', Press release, *New York Post*, 24 February 2009, http://nypost.com/2009/02/24/statement-from-rupert-murdoch/.

15 James Murdoch, MacTaggart Lecture, typescript p.7.

16 Mark Sweeney, 'Rupert Murdoch's Sky Takeover Approved by European Regulator', *Guardian*, 7 April 2017, https://www.theguardian.com/business/2017/apr/07/rupert-murdoch-sky-takeover-approved-by-european-commission.

17 Stewart Clarke, 'Fox's Plan for Independent Sky News Failed to Convince Authorities, Tripping Up Takeover', *Variety*, 29 June 2017, http://variety.com/2017/tv/global/fox-plan-for-independent-sky-news-failed-convince-british-authorities-1202482774/.

18 Matthew Garrahan, 'James Murdoch says Fox–Sky deal is test of Brexit Claims', *Financial Times*, 14 September 2017, https://www.ft.com/content/0208b184-993d-11e7-a652-cde3f882dd7b.

19 Ibid.

20 David Lieberman, 'James Murdoch Warns Fox Will Fight Movie Theaters' "Crazy Restrictions"', *Deadline,* 21 September 2016, http://deadline.com/2016/09/fox-ceo-james-murdoch-fight-movie-theaters-crazy-exclusivity-restrictions-1201824103.

Chapter 5   Crisis Management

1 Rupert Murdoch, 'The Dawn of a New Age of Discovery: Media 2006', Speech at the Worshipful Company of Stationers and Newspaper Makers, 13 March 2006.

2 Peter Chernin, 'Opening Keynote', 1998 Management Conference, 14 July 1998, Sun Valley, Idaho, p. 11.

3 'Sailing Through a Scandal', *The Economist*, 20 December 2014, http://www.economist.com/news/business/21636753-why-phone-hacking-affair-has-left-rupert-murdoch-better-sailing-through-scandal.

4 Richard M. Nixon, *Six Crises*, New York: Doubleday, 1962.

5 Steve Stecklow, Aaron O. Patrick, Martin Peers and Andrew Higgins, 'In Murdoch's Career, A Hand on the News', *Wall Street Journal*, 5 June 2007, https://www.wsj.com/articles/SB118100557923424501.

6 Stewart, *The History of The Times*, p. 7.

7 Neil, *Full Disclosure*, p. 90.

8 William Shawcross, *Murdoch: The Making of a Media Empire*, 2nd edn, New York: Simon & Schuster, 1997, p. 224.

9 Ibid., p. 302.

10 Horsman, *Sky High*, p. 72.

11 Ibid., p. 69.

12 Ibid., p. 73.

13 James Fallows, 'The Age of Murdoch', *Atlantic*, September 2003, https://www.theatlantic.com/magazine/archive/2003/09/the-age-of-murdoch/302777/.

14 Neil, *Full Disclosure*, p. 183.

15 Shawcross, *Media Empire*, p. 321.

16 'Win Some, Lose Some', *Wall Street Journal*, 3 November 2014.

17 Sir Harold Evans, 'Murdoch in Good Times and Bad', *Reuters*, Opinion, 29 September 2011, http://www.reuters.com/article/idUS157699227120110919.

18 'Sailing Through a Scandal', *The Economist*, 20 December 2014.

19   Steve Fishman, 'The Boy Who Wouldn't Be King', *New York*, September 2005,
     http://nymag.com/nymetro/news/media/features/14302/.

20   The higher figure is reported by John Gapper, *Financial Times*, 21 July 2016.

21   Brian Stelter, 'Fox News to Earn $1.50 per Subscriber', CNN Media, 16 January
     2015, http://money.cnn.com/2015/01/16/media/fox-news-fee-increase/index.html.

22   Brian Steinberg and Brent Long, 'Roger Ailes Confirms: "My Job Is to Report to
     Rupert and I Expect that to Continue"', *Variety*, 11 June 2015, http://variety.com/
     2015/tv/news/roger-ailes-still-reporting-to-rupert-murdoch-fox-shakeup-120151
     7286/.

23   Brian Stelter, 'Gabriel Sherman: Murdochs Looked the Other Way at Roger Ailes'
     Behavior', CNN Media, 2 September 2016, money.cnn.com/2016/09/02/media/
     roger-ailes-fox-news-gabriel/Sherman.

24   Emily Steel, 'Fox Faces New Lawsuit Claiming Harassment by Roger Ailes', *New
     York Times*, 14 December 2016, https://www.nytimes.com/2016/12/13/business/
     fox-faces-new-lawsuit-claiming-harassment-by-roger-ailes.html.

25   Sarah Ellison, 'Inside the Final Days of Roger Ailes's Reign at Fox News', *Vanity
     Fair*, November 2016, http://www.vanityfair.com/news/2016/09/roger-ailes-fox-
     news-final-days.

26   'Reluctant Heirs', *The Economist*, 5 December 2015, http://www.economist.com/
     news/business/21679451-getting-children-take-over-family-business-can-be-
     hard-reluctant-heirs.

27   Brook Barnes and Emily Steel, 'Murdoch Brothers' Challenge: What Happens
     Next at Fox News?', *New York Times*, 17 July 2016, https://www.nytimes.com/
     2016/07/18/business/media/murdoch-brothers-challenge-what-happens-next-at-
     fox-news.html?mcubz=1.

28   Matthew Belloni, 'The New Age of Murdochs', *Hollywood Reporter*,
     30 October–6 November 2017, p. 63, https://archive.org/stream/
     The_Hollywood_Reporter_October_30_2015#page/n63/mode/2up.

29   Matthew Garrahan, 'Murdoch and Sons: Lachlan, James and Rupert's $62bn
     Empire', *Financial Times*, 25 January 2017, https://www.ft.com/content/
     a530494c-e350-11e6-8405-9e5580d6e5fb.

30   Isaac Chotiner, 'Fox After Ailes', *Slate*, 22 July 2016, http://www.slate.com/
     articles/news_and_politics/interrogation/2016/07/gabriel_sherman_on_roger_
     ailes_trump_and_the_murdochs.html.

31   Jeffrey Gottfried, Michael Barthel and Amy Mitchell, 'Trump, Clinton, Voters
     Divided in Their Main Source for Elections News', Pew Research Center,
     Journalism and Media, 18 January 2017, http://www.journalism.org/2017/01/18/
     trump-clinton-voters-divided-in-their-main-source-for-election-news/.

32   Barnes and Steel, 'Murdoch Brothers' Challenge: What Happens Next at Fox
     News?', *New York Times*, 17 July 2016.

33   Chris Gardner, 'Rose McGowan Calls Out "X-Men" Billboard That Shows
     Mystique Being Strangled', *Hollywood Reporter*, 2 June 2016, http://www.
     hollywoodreporter.com/rambling-reporter/rose-mcgowan-calls-x-men-898538.

34   Ibid.

35 Michael M. Grynbaum, 'Chris Wallace's Debate Role Is a Bright Spot in a Dark Year for Fox', *New York Times*, 18 October 2016, https://www.nytimes.com/2016/10/19/business/media/new-energy-at-fox-as-chris-wallace-prepares-to-moderate-a-presidential-debate.html?mcubz=1.

36 Ellison, 'Inside the Final Days of Roger Ailes's Reign at Fox News', *Vanity Fair*, November 2016.

37 'Roger Ailes Resigns: Rupert Murdoch Becomes Chairman and Acting CEO of Fox News, Fox Business Network, Fox Television Stations', Fox News, 21 July 2016, http://www.foxnews.com/us/2016/07/21/roger-ailes-resigns-rupert-murdoch-becomes-chairman-and-acting-ceo-fox-news-fox-business-network-fox-television-stations.html.

38 'How Fox Got "Done with Roger"', *Daily Mail*, 22 September 2016, http://www.dailymail.co.uk/news/article-3803162/Final-days-Roger-Ailes-reign-Murdoch-sons-turned-former-Fox-News-boss-sex-pest-allegations-save-company-phone-hacking-style-scandal.html.

39 Matthew Garrahan, 'Fox News: Fall of the Cable News Guy', *Financial Times*, 21 July 2016, https://www.ft.com/content/51f9a74a-4fef-11e6-88c5-db83e98a590a.

40 'These Are Bill O'Reilly's Advertisers', Media Matters, 4 April 2017, https://www.mediamatters.org/blog/2017/04/04/these-are-bill-o-reilly-s-advertisers-oreilly-factor/215912.

41 Chris Spargo, 'Silent Partner: How Lachlan Murdoch's Wife Sarah "Convinced Him and Rupert to Fire Bill O'Reilly"', *Daily Mail*, 19 April 2017, http://www.dailymail.co.uk/news/article-4426676/Sarah-Murdoch-convinced-Lachlan-fire-Bill-O-Reilly.html.

42 Michael M. Grynbaum and John Koblin, 'For Fox News, Life After Bill O'Reilly Will Feature Tucker Carlson', *New York Times*, 19 April 2017, https://www.nytimes.com/2017/04/19/business/media/life-after-bill-oreilly-for-fox-news-to-include-tucker-carlson.html?mcubz=1.

43 Daniel Victor, 'Laura Ingraham Will Host 10 O'Clock Show as Part of Fox News Reshuffle', *New York Times*, 18 September 2017, https://www.nytimes.com/2017/09/18/business/media/laura-ingraham-fox-news-sean-hannity.html?_r=0.

44 Joe Flint, 'Fox News Parent Had $10 Million in Harassment Settlement Costs in Quarter', *Wall Street Journal*, 10 May 2017, https://www.wsj.com/articles/fox-news-parent-had-10-million-in-harassment-settlement-costs-in-quarter-1494455894. The company contends that the amounts paid are 'not material' to the company's financial performance.

45 Gabriel Sherman, 'The Rise and Fall of Fox News CEO Roger Ailes', NPR, 26 July 2016, transcript, p. 8, https://www.npr.org/2016/07/26/487483534/the-rise-and-fall-of-fox-news-ceo-roger-ailes.

46 Mark Joyella, 'Lachlan Murdoch: No Changes Planned for "Unique and Important" Voice of Fox News', *TVNewser*, 4 August 2016, http://www.adweek.com/tvnewser/lachlan-murdoch-no-changes-planned-for-unique-and-important-voice-of-fox-news/301351.

Chapter 6   Responsibility

1   'Guys and Dolls dialogue', 1950 Broadway play, 1955 movie, www.script-o-rama. com/movie_scripts/g/guys-and-dolls-script-transcript.html.

2   Younger, *Keith Rupert Murdoch*, p. 110.

3   Rupert Murdoch, 'His Space', Interview with Walt Mossberg and Kara Swisher, *Wall Street Journal*, 9 June 2008, https://www.wsj.com/articles/SB121269889107 049813.

4   Michael Leapman, 'Dame Elisabeth Murdoch: Philanthropist and Key Figure in the Rise of Her Son Rupert', *Independent*, 7 December 2012, http://www. independent.co.uk/news/obituaries/dame-elisabeth-murdoch-philanthropist-and-key-figure-in-the-rise-of-her-son-rupert-8393588.html.

5   Thomas Kiernan, *Citizen Murdoch*, New York: Dodd Mead, 1986, p. 81.

6   Monks, *Two Lives*, p. 228.

7   Stewart, *The History of The Times*, p. 39.

8   Paul Kelly, editor-at-large of the *Australian*, Interview with Rupert Murdoch, 14 July 2014, https://www.youtube.com/watch?v=po6c4RNvnIk.

9   Monks, *Two Lives*, p. 229.

10   David McKnight, *Rupert Murdoch: An Investigation of Political Power*, Sydney: Allen & Unwin, 2012, p. 146.

11   Stewart, *The History of The Times*, p. 22.

12   Lachlan Murdoch, 'We Must Resist Censorship of Every Kind', Sir Keith Murdoch Oration, *Australian*, 24 October 2014, http://www.theaustralian. com.au/opinion/we-must-resist-censorship-of-every-kind-lachlan-murdoch/ news-story/17a5f8290da443b94ff44c3b0401ec07.

13   James Curran and Jean Seaton, *Power Without Responsibility*, 7th edn, Abingdon, Oxon: Routledge, 2010, p. 69.

14   Ken Auletta, 'The Pirate', *New Yorker*, 13 November 1995, http://www.kenauletta. com/pirate.html.

15   'Media Mogul Rupert Murdoch Admits to Controlling Sun's Political Backing', *Daily Mail*, 24 November 2007, http://www.dailymail.co.uk/news/ article-496130/Media-mogul-Rupert-Murdoch-admits-controlling-Suns-political-backing.html.

16   Younger, *Keith Rupert Murdoch*, p. 110.

17   'ABC Evening News', 10 January 1977, News Archive, Vanderbilt Television, https://tvnews.vanderbilt.edu/broadcasts/45651.

18   Neil, *Full Disclosure*, pp. 172–3.

19   Tom Scocca, 'Why Lachlan Flew the Coop: It Was Rupe', *Observer*, 8 August 2005, http://observer.com/2005/08/why-lachlan-flew-the-coop-it-was-rupe-2/.

20   David Folkenflik, *Murdoch's World: The Last of the Old Media Empires*, New York: Public Affairs, 2013, p. 150.

21   Harold Evans, *Good Times, Bad Times*, New York: Open Road Integrated Media, 2016 edn, pp. 493–4.

22   Sarah Curtis (ed.), *The Journals of Woodrow Wyatt: From Major to Blair*, 3, London: Macmillan, 2000, p. 420.

23 Neil, *Full Disclosure*, pp. 162–3.

24 Becket Adams, 'Too Good to Check: Five Times when Journalists Let Stories Get Away from Them', *Washington Examiner*, 10 December 2014, http://www.washington examiner.com/too-good-to-check-five-times-when-journalists-let-stories-get-away-from-them/article/2557203.

25 Jeremy Greenfield, 'Why Amazon Is Going After Publisher Profit Margin', *Forbes*, 16 July 2014, https://www.forbes.com/sites/jeremygreenfield/2014/06/16/why-amazon-is-going-after-publisher-profit-margin/#553c5f9859ad.

26 Constance Grady, 'Amazon made a small change to the way it sells books. Publishers are terrified', *Vox*, 19 May 2017, https://www.vox.com/culture/2017/5/19/15596050/amazon-buy-box-publishing-controversy.

27 Jo Becker, 'An Empire Builder, Murdoch Still Playing Tough', *New York Times*, 25 June 2007, http://www.nytimes.com/2007/06/25/business/worldbusiness/25i-ht-25murdoch.6308907.html.

28 Scott Wong, 'Rubio Lands Deal for Memoir', *Politico*, 5 December 2011, http://www.politico.com/story/2011/12/rubio-lands-deal-for-memoir-069785.

29 Karen Heller, 'Every Candidate an Author: The Ceaseless Boom in Books by Politicians', *Washington Post*, 27 May 2015, https://www.washingtonpost.com/lifestyle/style/every-candidates-an-author-the-ceaseless-boom-in-books-by-politicians/2015/05/27/1d1374ae-fd8c-11e4-8b6c-0dcce21e223d_story.html?utm_term=.5b8718c79da2.

30 Bruce Dover, *Rupert's Adventures in China*, Edinburgh: Mainstream, 2008, p. 3.

31 Ibid., pp.18, 21.

32 Ibid., pp. 21–2.

33 Ibid., p. 22.

34 Curtis (ed.), *Woodrow Wyatt*, p. 273.

35 Wojciech Adamczyk, 'Global Media Corporation Expansion into Asian Markets (China example)', *Media Studies*, 28 January, http://studiamedioznawcze.pl/article.php?date=2007_1_28&content=wadam&lang=pl.

36 John Darnton, 'China Protests BBC Documentary About Mao', *New York Times*, 19 December 1993, http://www.nytimes.com/1993/12/19/world/china-protests-bbc-documentary-about-mao.html.

37 William Tuohy, 'BBC to Air Mao Documentary Over China's Objections', *Los Angeles Times*, 19 December 1993, http://articles.latimes.com/1993-12-19/news/mn-3586_1_chairman-mao.

38 Dover, *Rupert's Adventures*, p. 29.

39 Ibid.

40 Shawcross, *Media Empire*, p. 404.

41 'Murdoch Denies Bowing to China', SBS, 24 May 2007, http://www.sbs.com.au/news/article/2007/05/24/murdoch-denies-bowing-china.

42 Steve Stecklow and others, 'In Murdoch's Career, A Hand on the News', *Wall Street Journal*, 5 June 2007, https://www.wsj.com/articles/SB118100557923424501.

43 Rone Tempest, 'Deng's Daughter Promoting Book That Fills Historical Gap', *Los*

Angeles Times, 11 February 1995, http://articles.latimes.com/1995-02-11/news/mn-30643_1_daughter-deng-rong.

44 Merle Goodman, 'Book Review: *Deng Xiaoping, My Father* by Deng Maomao', *New York Times*, 12 February 1995, https://partners.nytimes.com/library/world/021295deng.html.

45 Michael Kinsley, 'The Talk of the Town', *New Yorker*, 6 February 1995, p. 29, http://www.newyorker.com/magazine/1995/02/06.

46 Dover, *Rupert's Adventures*, p. 32.

47 'Margaret Thatcher: Brought Down by the Sharks in the Water', *Daily Telegraph*, 8 April 2013, http://www.telegraph.co.uk/news/politics/margaret-thatcher/9980358/Margaret-Thatcher-Brought-down-by-the-sharks-in-the-water.html.

48 'HarperCollins Apologises to Patten', *BBC News*, 6 March 1998, http://news.bbc.co.uk/1/hi/uk/62877.stm.

49 Steve Stecklow and Martin Peers, 'Murdoch's Role as Proprietor, Journalist and Plans for Dow Jones', *Wall Street Journal*, 6 June 2007, https://www.wsj.com/articles/SB118115049815626635.

50 'The Leveson Inquiry: Culture, Practice and Ethics of the Press', testimony of Rupert Murdoch, transcript of hearings, 25 April 2012, http://webarchive.nationalarchives.gov.uk/20140122202748/http://www.levesoninquiry.org.uk/wp-content/uploads/2012/04/Transcript-of-Morning-Hearing-25-April-2012.tx.

51 'The Leveson Inquiry', testimony of Rupert Murdoch.

52 Jack F. Matlock Jr, 'Chinese Checkers', *New York Times*, Book Review, 13 September 1998, http://www.nytimes.com/books/98/09/13/reviews/980913.13mattlot.html.

53 *Vanity Fair*, September 1999 (no. 470), p. 321.

54 Bill Carter, 'Media Talk; Murdoch Executive Calls Press Coverage of China Too Harsh', *New York Times*, 26 March 2001, http://www.nytimes.com/2001/03/26/business/mediatalk-murdoch-executive-calls-press-coverage-of-china-too-harsh.html.

55 Lachlan Murdoch, 'We Must Resist Censorship of Every Kind', Sir Keith Murdoch Oration, *Australian*, 24 October 2014.

56 Sarah Lyall, 'Publisher Apologizes to Hong Kong Chief for Canceled Book', *New York Times*, 7 March 1998, http://www.nytimes.com/1998/03/07/world/publisher-apologizes-to-hong-kong-chief-for-canceled-book.html.

57 Yuan Yang, 'Multinationals in China Brace for Online Crackdown', *Financial Times*, 1 August 2017, https://www.ft.com/content/cb4bec0a-75b6-11e7-90c0-90a9d1bc9691.

58 Mike Isaac, 'Facebook Said to Create Censorship Tool to Get Back Into China', *New York Times*, 22 November 2016, https://www.nytimes.com/2016/11/22/technology/facebook-censorship-tool-china.html?mcubz=1&_r=0.

59 Paul Mozer and Vindu Goel, 'To Reach China, LinkedIn Plays by Local Rules', *New York Times*, 5 October 2014, https://www.nytimes.com/2014/10/06/technology/to-reach-china-linkedin-plays-by-local-rules.html?mcubz=1.

60 Katie Benner and Sui-Lee Wee, 'Apple Removes New York Times App From Its Store in China', *New York Times*, 4 January 2017, https://www.nytimes.com/

2017/01/04/business/media/new-york-times-apps-apple-china.html?mcubz=1.

61 Jacob Bernstein, 'Judith Regan is Back. Watch Out', *New York Times*, 8 February 2015, https://www.nytimes.com/2015/02/08/fashion/judith-regan-is-back-watch-out.html?mcubz=1&_r=0.

62 'Raw Data: Judith Regan Statement: "Why I Did It"', Fox News, 17 November 2006, http://www.foxnews.com/story/0,2933,230280,00.html.

63 'Publisher is Fired on the Heels of O.J. Fiasco', *Washington Post*, 16 December 2006, http://www.washingtonpost.com/wp-dyn/content/article/2006/12/15/AR2006121502278_pf.html.

64 'O.J. Deal Leaves Sour Taste in Many Mouths', *Washington Post*, 17 November 2006, http://www.washingtonpost.com/wp-dyn/content/article/2006/11/17/AR2006111700533_pf.html.

65 'News Corp. Cancels O.J. Simpson Book and TV Special', Fox News, 21 November 2006, http://www.foxnews.com/story/0,2933,230838,00.html.

66 Bernstein, 'Judith Regan is Back. Watch Out', *New York Times*, 8 February 2015.

67 Martha Neil, 'OJ Simpson Book, *If I Did It*, a Best-seller', *ABA Journal*, 28 September 2007, http://www.abajournal.com/news/article/oj_simpson_book_if_i_did_it_a_best_seller.

68 Auletta, 'The Pirate', *New Yorker*, 13 November 1995.

69 Rupert Murdoch, Address by Mr Rupert Murdoch at the News Corporation Leadership Meeting, Hayman Island, July 1995, pp. 15–16.

70 Rupert Murdoch, Speech given in Singapore, 12 January 1999.

71 Bob Smithouser, Movie Review, *PluggedIn*, http://www.pluggedin.com/movie-reviews/theressomethingaboutmary/.

72 Ily Goyanes, 'Celloid City: *There's Something About Mary* Filmed at Churchill's Pub and Big Pink', *Miami New Times*, 1 September 2010, http://www.miaminewtimes.com/arts/celluloid-city-theres-something-about-mary-filmed-at-churchills-pub-and-big-pink-6497402.

73 Phelim O'Neill, '*There's Something About Mary*: No. 17 Best Comedy Film of All Time', *Guardian*, 18 October 2010, https://www.theguardian.com/film/2010/oct/18/something-about-mary-comedy.

74 Ibid.

75 Paul Bond, 'TV Executives Admit in Taped Interviews that Hollywood Pushes a Liberal Agenda', *Hollywood Reporter*, 1 June 2011, http://www.hollywoodreporter.com/news/tv-executives-admit-taped-interviews-193116.

76 Matthew Belloni, 'The New Age of Murdochs', *Hollywood Reporter*, 30 October–6 November 2017, p. 66.

77 Matthew Garrahan, 'Lunch with the FT, Barry Diller', *Financial Times*, 7 March 2015, https://www.ft.com/content/ab6ec72c-c1d1-11e4-bd24-00144feab7de.

78 Keach Hagey, 'How Chase Carey Helped Build Fox into a Major Player', *Wall Street Journal*, 16 June 2015, https://www.wsj.com/articles/how-chase-carey-helped-build-fox-into-a-major-player-1434509031.

79 Ted Johnson, 'Clinton vs. Trump in Hollywood: Who's Giving', Center for Responsive Politics, *Variety*, 7 October 2016, http://variety.com/2016/biz/news/hillary-clinton-donald-trump-hollywood-1201878938/.

80 Tate Williams, 'An Heir to a Media Empire. And Now an Environmental Funder, Too', *Inside Philanthropy*, 20 January 2015, https://www.insidephilanthropy.com/marine-rivers/2015/1/17/an-heir-to-a-media-empire-and-now-an-environmental-funder-to.html.

81 Jonathan Glancey, 'James Murdoch's Sky Scraper', *Guardian*, 26 September 2010, https://www.theguardian.com/artanddesign/2010/sep/26/james-murdoch-bskyb-harlequin-architecture.

82 Joe Coscarelli, 'Stephen Chao, Fired Fox President, Takes Questions on Reddit, Calls Murdoch a "Journalist Through and Through"', *Village Voice*, 11 December 2010, https://www.villagevoice.com/2010/12/11/stephen-chao-fired-fox-president-takes-questions-on-reddit-calls-murdoch-a-journalist-through-and-through/.

83 Othello, of course, had been misled by the scheming Iago into firing a blameless Cassio. This situation was somewhat different, but the quote, and Rupert's obvious sadness, had a startling impact, nonetheless.

84 Coscarelli, 'Stephen Chao, Fired Fox President, Takes Questions on Reddit, Calls Murdoch a "Journalist Through and Through"', *Village Voice*, 11 December 2010.

85 Gertrude Himmelfarb, *One Nation, Two Cultures: A Searching Examination of American Society in the Aftermath of Our Cultural Revolution*, New York: Alfred A. Knopf, 1999, p. 127.

Chapter 7 Protecting His Assets

1 Barry Diller on Rupert Murdoch when parting company, in William Shawcross, *Murdoch: The Making of a Media Empire*, 2nd edn, New York: Simon & Schuster, 1997, p. 390.

2 'Last of the Moguls', *The Economist*, 21 July 2011, p. 9, http://www.economist.com/node/18988526.

3 Rupert Murdoch, Lecture, Yale University, 1999.

4 Ken Auletta, 'The Pirate', *New Yorker*, 13 November 1995, http://www.kenauletta.com/pirate.html.

5 Richard A. Viguerie and David Franke, *America's Right Turn: How Conservatives Used New and Alternative Media to Take Power*, Chicago: Bonus Books, 2004, p. 220.

6 Rupert Murdoch, 'Closing Keynote', 1998 Management Conference, 18 July 1998, Sun Valley, Idaho, p. 3.

7 Robert J. Shapiro and Kevin A. Hassett, *The Economic Value of Intellectual Property*, Washington, DC: American Enterprise Institute, 2006, p. 2.

8 John P. Ogler, 'Intellectual Property, Finance and Economic Development', *WIPO Magazine*, February 2016, http://www.wipo.int/wipo_magazine/en/2016/01/article_0002.html.

9 Joint Project Team, 'Intellectual Property and the U.S. Economy: 2016 Update', p. ii, https://www.uspto.gov/sites/default/files/documents/IPandtheUSEconomySept2016.pdf.

10 'Creative Capitalism', *The Economist*, 1 November 2014, https://www.economist.com/news/business/21629377-other-industries-have-lot-learn-hollywood-creative-capitalism.

11   Karl Taro Greenfeld, 'Let The Games Begin', *Bloomberg Businessweek*, 18 July 2013.

12   Bernard Weintraub, 'Who's Lining Up at Box Office? Lots and Lots of Girls; Studios Aim at Teen-Agers, a Vast, Growing Audience', *New York Times*, 23 February 1998, http://www.nytimes.com/1998/02/23/movies/who-s-lining-up-box-office-lots-lots-girls-studios-aim-teen-agers-vast-growing.html?mcubz=1.

13   '21 Amazing Facts About Sinking of Titanic', *Technology Trends*, 21 February 2015, http://techrosoft.com/21-amazing-facts-about-sinking-of-titanic/.

14   Neil, *Full Disclosure*, p. 175.

15   Shawcross, *Media Empire*, p. 390.

16   Ibid., p. 391.

17   John Cassidy, 'Murdoch's Game', *New Yorker*, 16 October 2006, p. 85, https://www.newyorker.com/magazine/2006/10/16/murdochs-game.

18   Simon Briggs, 'How Sky Sports Became One of the Most Influential Sports Broadcasters Over the Last 20 Years', *Daily Telegraph*, 18 April 2011, http://www.telegraph.co.uk/sport/8459452/How-Sky-Sports-became-one-of-the-most-influential-sports-broadcasters-over-the-last-20-years.html.

19   Meg James, 'Veteran Fox Executive David Hill Departing Company', *Los Angeles Times*, 23 June 2015, http://www.latimes.com/entertainment/envelope/cotown/la-et-ct-david-hill-fox-sports-murdoch-american-idol-20150623-story.html.

20   Cynthia Littleton, 'David Hill Ends Long Run at 21st Century Fox, Sets Production Banner (Exclusive)', *Variety*, 23 June 2015, http://variety.com/2015/tv/news/david-hill-21st-century-fox-sports-hilly-production-1201525758/.

21   Ibid.

22   James, 'Veteran Fox Executive David Hill Departing Company', *Los Angeles Times*, 23 June 2015.

23   Shawcross, *Media Empire*, p. 390.

24   James Roman, *Love, Light, and a Dream: Television's Past, Present, and Future*, Westport, Conn.: Praeger, 1998, p. 89.

25   'Profile: Barry Diller', *Forbes*, 10 July 2017, https://www.forbes.com/profile/barry-diller/.

26   'Peter Chernin Net Worth', *Celebrity Net Worth*, https://www.celebritynetworth.com/richest-businessmen/producers/peter-chernin-net-worth.

27   Alan Citron and John Lippman, 'Diller Stuns Hollywood, Quits Fox, Inc.', *Los Angeles Times*, 25 February 1992, http://articles.latimes.com/1992-02-25/news/mn-2629_1_killer-diller.

28   Eriq Gardner, 'Supreme Court Hands Broadcasters Huge Win in Aereo Battle', *Hollywood Reporter*, 25 June 2014, http://www.hollywoodreporter.com/thr-esq/aereo-ruling-supreme-court-hands-711333.

29   Charles Moore, *Margaret Thatcher: At Her Zenith: In London, Washington and Moscow*, New York: Alfred Knopf, 2016, p. 523.

30   Sarah Curtis (ed.), *The Journals of Woodrow Wyatt: From Major to Blair*, 3, London: Macmillan, 2000, p. 582.

31   Ibid., p. 583.

Chapter 8   The Succession and the Pivot

1   'Rupert Murdoch Has Potential', *Esquire*, 11 September 2008, http://www.esquire.com/news-politics/a4971/rupert-murdoch-1008/.

2   Monks, *Two Lives*, pp. 287, 292–3.

3   David S. Landes, *Dynasties: Fortune and Misfortune in the World's Great Family Businesses*, London: Penguin Books, 2006, pp. xiv, 290.

4   Sarah Rabil and Joe Flint, 'Rupert Murdoch Says Disney Deal Is a Pivot, Not a Retreat', *Wall Street Journal*, 14 December 2017, https://www.wsj.com/articles/rupert-murdoch-says-disney-deal-is-a-pivot-not-a-retreat-1513280513.

5   William Langley, 'The Truth about Rupert Murdoch and Jerry Hall', *Australian Women's Weekly*, 12 May 2016, http://www.nowtolove.com.au/celebrity/celeb-news/the-truth-about-rupert-murdoch-and-jerry-hall-9978.

6   Wendy Goldman Rohm, *The Murdoch Mission: The Digital Transformation of a Media Empire*, New York: John Wiley, 2002, p. 41.

7   'Sir Edward Pickering Memorial Service', *The Times*, 2 December 2003, https://www.thetimes.co.uk/article/sir-edward-pickering-memorial-service-fjj0gh7xwxs.

8   John Gapper, 'Rupert Murdoch and Masayoshi Son Are Back in Charge', *Financial Times*, 21 July 2016, https://www.ft.com/content/8061632c-4e5d-11e6-88c5-db83e98a590a.

9   Lara O'Reilly, 'The 30 Biggest Media Companies in the World', *Business Insider*, 31 May 2016, http://www.businessinsider.com/the-30-biggest-media-owners-inthe-world-2016-5.

10 'Sky: First Half Results 2017', https://corporate.sky.com/documents/results_26_jan_17/sky-q2-2017-investor-presentation.pdf.

11 'News Corp Has Always Been Rebellious', *Der Spiegel*, 29 October 2009, http://www.spiegel.de/international/business/spiegel-interview-with-james-murdoch-news-corp-has-always-been-rebellious-a-657628.html.

12 Hugh Muir and Jane Martinson, 'James Murdoch at the Independent: "Like Something out of Dodge City"', *Guardian*, 22 April 2010, https://www.theguardian.com/media/2010/apr/22/james-murdoch-independent-dodge-city.

13 Andrew Emery, 'When James Murdoch was a Hip-Hop Mogul', *Guardian*, 11 July 2011, https://www.theguardian.com/media/2011/jul/11/james-murdoch-hip-hop.

14 Joe Leahy and Kenneth Li, 'James Murdoch Plans Shakeup of Star TV operations in Asia', *Financial Times*, 24 July 2009, https://www.ft.com/content/3dcc9818-77c5-11de-9713-00144feabdc0.

15 Amy Willis, 'James Murdoch Profile: The Tattooed Hip-Hop Rebel who Became Heir Apparent', *Daily Telegraph*, 22 July 2011, http://www.telegraph.co.uk/news/uknews/phone-hacking/8640700/James-Murdoch-pro_le-the-tattooed-hip-hoprebel-who-became-heir-apparent.html.

16 Nicola Clark, 'James Murdoch Returns to Sky as Chairman', *New York Times*, 29 January 2016, https://www.nytimes.com/2016/01/30/business/media/james-murdoch-to-return-as-sky-chairman.html?mcubz=1&_r=0.

17   James Murdoch, 'The Absence of Trust', 2009 Edinburgh International Television Festival, James MacTaggart Memorial Lecture, 28 August 2009, https://www.edinburghguide.com/events/2009/08/28/mactaggartlecturebyjamesmurdoch.

18   Rupert Murdoch, 'Freedom in Broadcasting', 1989 Edinburgh International Television Festival, James MacTaggart Memorial Lecture, 25 August 1989, transcript, p. 6, http://www.thetvfestival.com/website/wp-content/uploads/2015/03/GEITF_MacTaggart_1989_Rupert_Murdoch.pdf.

19   Elisabeth Murdoch, no title, 2012 Edinburgh International Television Festival, James MacTaggart Memorial Lecture, 23 August 2012, typescript, pp. 4 and 6, https://www.edinburghguide.com/video/11381-videotranscriptelisabethmurdochsmactaggartlecture.

20   'News Corp. Has Always Been Rebellious', *Der Spiegel*, 29 October 2009.

21   Jamie Doward and Lisa O'Carroll, 'Murdochs "in Family Fallout" Over Crisis', *Guardian*, 16 July 2011, https://www.theguardian.com/media/2011/jul/16/elisabeth-james-murdoch-family-crisis.

22   Kevin Draper, 'The Rise and Sudden Fall of a TV Sports Mastermind', *New York Times*, 7 July 2017, https://www.nytimes.com/2017/07/06/sports/jamiehorowitz-fox-sports-_red-sexual-harassment.html?_r=0.

23   Ashley Cullins, 'Fox Business Host Suspended Amid Sexual Harassment Investigation', *Hollywood Reporter*, 6 July 2017, http://www.hollywood reporter.com/thr-esq/fox-business-host-suspended-sexual-harassmentinvestigation-1019161.

24   'Last of the Moguls', *The Economist*, 21 July 2011, p. 9.

25   Tim Arango, 'The Murdoch in Waiting', *New York Times*, 19 February 2011, http://www.nytimes.com/2011/02/20/business/media/20james.html.

26   Belloni, 'The New Age of Murdochs', *Hollywood Reporter*, 30 October–6 November 2015, p. 66.

27   Landes, *Dynasties*, p. 290.

28   News Corp press release, 26 March 2014, http://investors.newscorp.com/secfiling.cfm?filingID=1181431-14-13993&CIK=1564708.

29   Mark David, 'Lachlan Murdoch Drops $29 Million on 45-Acre Equestrian Spread in Aspen', *Variety*, 21 September 2017, http://variety.com/2017/dirt/real-estalker/lachlan-murdoch-aspen-buttermilk-mountain-1202565785/.

30   Ross Kelly, 'Murdoch Son Notched Hits, Misses in Australia', *Wall Street Journal*, 2 April 2014, https://www.wsj.com/articles/for-lachlan-murdoch-some-hits-andsome-misses-in-australia-1396373821.

31   'How Lachlan Murdoch Turned $10 Million into More Than $3 Billion', *Big News Network*, 5 February 2014, https://archive.is/20130213021215/http://www.bignewsnetwork.com/index/php/sid220002499/scat/5c99d63b6637bd7/ht/how-lachlan-Murdoch-turned-10-billion-into-more-than-$3-billion.

32   Sarah Rabil and Joe Flint, 'Rupert Murdoch Says Disney Deal Is a Pivot, Not a Retreat', *Wall Street Journal*, 14 December 2017, https://www.wsj.com/articles/rupert-murdoch-says-disney-deal-is-a-pivot-not-a-retreat-1513280513.

33 'An Investor Calls', *The Economist*, 7 February 2015, https://www.economist.com/news/brie_ng/21642175-sometimes-ill-mannered-speculative-and-wrongac-tivists-are-rampant-they-will-change-american.

34 Darren Davidson, 'US Firm Southeastern Asset Management Selling Stake in News Corp', *Australian*, 21 November 2014, http://www.theaustralian.com.au/business/media/us-firm-southeast-ern-asset-management-selling-stake-in-news-corp/news-story/f20c4ae28d8b5819b19aa5fa074cbb4c.

35 *Financial Times*, 18 November 2014.

36 Matthew Garrahan, 'Cable Cowboy John Malone Views a New Landscape', *Financial Times*, 10 May 2017, https://www.ft.com/content/4531665e-349d-11e7-bce4-9023f8c0fd2e.

37 'Murdoch and Malone End Battle over Liberty Media's Stake in News Corp.', *New York Times*, 22 December 2006, http://www.nytimes.com/2006/12/22/business/worldbusiness/22iht-murdoch.3991109.html?mcubz=1.

38 Ibid.

39 Garrahan, 'Cable cowboy John Malone views a new landscape', *Financial Times*, 10 May 2017.

40 Ken Auletta, 'The Pirate', *New Yorker*, 13 November 1995, http://www.kenauletta.com/pirate.html.

41 Matthew Garrahan, 'Lunch with the FT: Barry Diller', *Financial Times*, 6 March 2015, https://www.ft.com/content/ab6ec72c-c1d1-11e4-bd24-00144feab7de?mhq5j=e1.

42 Meaghan Kilroy, 'Institutional Investor Coalition Announces Corporate Governance Framework', *Pensions & Investments*, 31 January 2017, http://www.pionline.com/article/20170131/ONLINE/170139957/institutional-investor-coalition-announces-corporate-governance-framework.

43 *Wall Street Journal*, 18 August 2015.

44 'Valuation of Shares of Companies with a Dual Class Structure', American Society of Appraisers, Advanced Business Valuation Conference, 14 September 2016, http://www.appraisers.org/docs/default-source/event_doc/2016_bv_presentation_matthews.pdf?sfvrsn=2.

45 David Streitfeld, 'Behind Amazon's Success Is a Prodigious Tolerance for Failure', *New York Times*, 18 June 2017, https://www.nytimes.com/2017/06/17/technology/whole-foods-amazon.html?_r=0.

46 'Business in the Blood', *The Economist*, 1 November 2014, https://www.economist.com/news/business/21629385-companies-controlled-founding-fami-lies-remain-surprisingly-important-and-look-set-stay.

47 Ronald C. Anderson and David M. Reeb, 'Founding-Family Ownership and Firm Performance: Evidence from the S&P 500', *Journal of Finance*, 2003, vol. 58, issue 3, pp. 1301–27, http://econpapers.repec.org/article/blaj_nan/v_3a58_3ay_3a2003_3ai_3a3_3ap_3a1301-1327.htm.

48 Christian Casper, Ana Karina Dias, and Heinz-Peter Elstrodt, 'The Five Attributes of Enduring Family Businesses', *McKinsey Journal*, January 2010,

http://www.mckinsey.com/business-functions/organization/our-insights/
the-five-attributes-of-enduring-family-businesses.

49   Cristina Cruz Serrano and Laura Nuñez Letamendia, 'Value Creation in Listed
     European Family Firms (2001–2010)', Banca March and IE Business School,
     undated, http://foreigners.textovirtual.com/empresas-familiares/62/53818/
     ex_summary_english.pdf.

50   David B. Audretsch, Marcel Hülsbeck and Erik E Lehmann, 'The Benefits of
     Family Ownership, Control and Management of Financial Performance of
     Firms', Research Paper No. 2010-1-03, School of Public and Environmental
     Affairs, Indiana University (2010), https://papers.ssrn.com/sol3/JELJOUR_
     Results.cfm?form_name=journalBrowse&journal_id=1859708.

51   Chase Peterson-Withorn, 'New Report Reveals the 500 Largest Family-Owned-
     Companies in the World', *Forbes*, 20 April 2014, http://www.cii.org/files/
     publications/misc/05_10_17_dual-class_value_summary.pdf.

52   Dorothy Shapiro Lund, 'The Case for Nonvoting Stock', *Wall
     Street Journal*, 5 September 2017, https://www.wsj.com/articles/
     the-case-for-nonvoting-stock-1504653033.

53   Gabriel Morey, 'Does Multi-Class Stock Enhance Firm Performance? A
     Regression Analysis', Council of Institutional Investors, 10 May 2017, p. 7,
     http://www.cii.org/files/publications/misc/05_10_17_dual-class_value_summary.
     pdf.

54   Ronald Anderson, Augustine Duru and David Reeb, 'Investment policy
     in family controlled firms', *Journal of Banking & Finance*, vol. 36, issue
     6, June 2012, pp.1744–58, http://www.sciencedirect.com/science/
     journal/03784266/36/6?sdc=1.

55   'Putting Politics before Family', *The Economist*, 18 April 2015, https://www.
     economist.com/news/americas/21648696-michelle-bachelet-keiko-fujimori-and-
     sins-relatives-putting-politics-family.

56   Mark J. Perry, 'Fortune 500 Firms in 1955 vs. 2014', American
     Enterprise Institute,18 August 2014, http://www.aei.org/publication/
     fortune-500-firms-in-1955-vs-2014-89-are-gone-and-were-all-better-off-because-
     of-that-dynamic-creativedestruction/.

57   Joseph A. Schumpeter, *Capitalism, Socialism, and Democracy*, 2nd edn, New York:
     Harper & Brothers, 1947.

58   Peter Preston, 'Rupert Murdoch Is Now an Old Man on a Lonely Throne at
     News Corp', *Guardian*, 2 June 2013, https://www.theguardian.com/media/2013/
     jun/02/rupert-murdoch-news-corp-lonely-throne 2013.

59   Peter Preston, 'It's the Post-Rupert Era at 21st Century Fox – But Don't
     Cheer too Loudly, *Guardian*, 27 August 2017, https://www.theguardian.com/
     media/2017/aug/27/post-rupert-era-at-21st-century-fox-but-dont-cheer.

60   Doward and O'Carroll, 'Murdochs "in Family Fallout" Over Crisis', *Guardian*,
     16 July 2011.

61   Brooks Barnes and Sydney Ember, 'In House of Murdoch, Sons Set About an

Elaborate Overhaul', *New York Times*, 22 April 2017, https://www.nytimes.com/2017/04/22/business/media/murdoch-family-21st-century-fox.html.

Epilogue

1 Rupert Murdoch, Speech given in Singapore, 12 January 1999, typescript, pp. 11–12.
2 Rupert Murdoch, Address by Mr Rupert Murdoch at the News Corporation Leadership Meeting, Hayman Island, July 1995, p. 17.

INDEX